Financial Modelling
in Practice

For other titles in the Wiley Finance series
please see www.wiley.com/finance

Financial Modelling in Practice

A Concise Guide for Intermediate and Advanced Level

Michael Rees

A John Wiley and Sons, Ltd., Publication

Other Wiley Editorial Offices

John Wiley & Sons Inc., 111 River Street, Hoboken, NJ 07030, USA

Jossey-Bass, 989 Market Street, San Francisco, CA 94103-1741, USA

Wiley-VCH Verlag GmbH, Boschstr. 12, D-69469 Weinheim, Germany

John Wiley & Sons Australia Ltd, 42 McDougall Street, Milton, Queensland 4064, Australia

John Wiley & Sons (Asia) Pte Ltd, 2 Clementi Loop #02-01, Jin Xing Distripark, Singapore 129809

John Wiley & Sons Canada Ltd, 6045 Freemont Blvd, Mississauga, ONT, L5R 4J3, Canada

Wiley also publishes its books in a variety of electronic formats. Some content that appears
in print may not be available in electronic books.

Library of Congress Cataloging-in-Publication Data

Rees, Michael, 1964-
  Financial modelling in practice : a concise guide for intermediate and advanced level /
Michael Rees.
    p. cm. – (Wiley finance series)
  Includes bibliographical references and index.
  ISBN 978-0-470-99744-4 (cloth/cd)
  1. Finance–Mathematical models. 2. Corporations–Finance–Mathematical models. 3.
Options (Finance)–Mathematical models. 4. Microsoft Excel (Computer file) I. Title.
  HG106.R44 2008
  332.01′51–dc22

                                                            2008038607

British Library Cataloguing in Publication Data

A catalogue record for this book is available from the British Library

ISBN 978-0-470-99744-4 (H/B)

Typeset in 11/12 Times by Laserwords Private Limited, Chennai, India
Printed and bound in Great Britain by CPI Antony Rowe, Chippenham, Wiltshire

To My Family

Contents

Background, Objectives and Approach

The decision to write this book was driven by several beliefs about the current needs of the modelling community:

- Many modellers have a reasonable knowledge of core Excel functionality, but desire to increase and consolidate their knowledge in a way that is prioritised, focused, practical and application-driven. In this text we cover those aspects of Excel that are most frequently needed in many intermediate and advanced situations. Such functionality is demonstrated with practical examples, which in most cases have been drawn from real-life situations in which the author has been involved.
- There is a need for a text that helps modellers to design, structure and build models that are relevant, accurate and readily understandable. Many texts and training courses in the modelling area put their emphasis either on Excel functionality, or on financial theory, or on mathematical models, but seldom address the modelling process. This text aims to cover the modelling issues that are relevant to facilitate the construction of robust and readily understandable models.
- There is an increasing need to conduct uncertainty analysis as part of the modelling process. Not only are the benefits of such analysis becoming better understood, but also the tools required in practice to do so are becoming more intuitive and easier to implement. The willingness of decision-makers to accept single-point forecasts is likely to continue to reduce. Currently, most modelling texts either do not adequately treat the topic of risk analysis, or treat it from a mathematical perspective that is both inaccessible to many modellers and lacking in practical tools. This text aims to address this need in a way that is accessible and practical to the general reader.

The contents of this book are based on many years' experience of building models in business and finance, and of training others how to do so. The aim has been to write a guide that is not only as comprehensive as possible within the space available, but is also concise, disciplined and focused in its selection of topics. The book is structured into six chapters:

- Chapter 1 reviews a selection of Excel functions that are generally most relevant for building intermediate and advanced level models. It presents many practical examples of the application of these functions.

- Chapter 2 discusses the principles involved in designing, structuring and building relevant, accurate and readily understandable models. Topics covered include the use of sensitivity analysis, best practice modelling principles and related issues, and model auditing tools.
- Chapter 3 covers the modelling of financial statements and of cash flow valuation. We discuss a variety of ways to deal with each of the core modelling issues that arise in these applications.
- Chapter 4 covers risk and uncertainty modelling. Many practical applications and example models are presented in an intuitive and accessible way. We use an add-in to Excel to implement simulation models; such an approach also allows readers to rapidly build their own models.
- Chapter 5 covers options and real options modelling, treating these as a natural extension of risk modelling. The approach to real options modelling is less theoretical than in some other texts, and does not specifically require knowledge of financial market derivatives. Models are implemented using Excel as well as add-ins for simulation and decision trees, and readers should be able to build their own models after reading this chapter.
- Chapter 6 covers VBA for financial modelling applications. The topics selected for inclusion have been established by consideration of the core types of financial models that frequently require the use of VBA. The chapter should provide beginners in this area with a focused and practical guide to the topic, and a base on which to discover the richer possibilities available to modellers by using VBA.

There are of course many topics that either cannot be covered in this text, or can be dealt with only in a cursory fashion. For example, it is assumed that the reader is familiar with basic Excel operations and functions, so that the Excel functionality covered is that which is most relevant at the intermediate and advanced level. It is also assumed that the reader is comfortable with the core principles of finance, corporate finance, accounting and financial market products. Although some aspects of these topics are presented as contextual reminders, the focus is on the modelling issues. It is believed that the readers will be able to complement the tools of this text with an adequate knowledge of their own application to build models appropriate to their situation. The Further Reading lists a small selection of works that may be referred to by readers wishing to enhance their knowledge and to explore some topic areas that may not have been covered in detail in this text.

The model examples are included in an attached CD-ROM. This text is designed to be read in conjunction with these models; readers relying purely on the text and the screenshots are unlikely to obtain the maximum benefit. The examples are generally built and presented in Excel 2007. Users of Excel 2003 should nevertheless find this text of equal value: first, menu sequences for Excel 2003 are also provided; second, the text may facilitate Excel 2003 users who wish to convert to Excel 2007. A few of the example files (in Chapter 1 and Chapter 2 only) use functions that are new in Excel 2007; in such cases opening them in Excel 2003 will give a warning message and result in a read-only file, but the essence of such examples should generally still be relevant. Excel functions and menu icons are generally presented in **bold**, and menu sequences with a (the VBA code and menu items in Chapter 6 are presented in `Courier New`). For conciseness, the Excel menu group generally is not displayed unless it is required for the purposes of clarity (e.g. **Formulas/Trace Dependents** is used rather than **Formulas/Formula Auditing/Trace Dependents**).

The model examples in Chapter 4 use the Excel add-in @RISK from Palisade Corporation, and those in Chapter 5 use both @RISK and PrecisionTree (also from Palisade Corporation). A free time-limited trial version of these products can be downloaded from the Palisade website (see Chapter 4). The models using these software are built in Excel 2003 (but still presented in the screenshots in Excel 2007); this is due to some backward compatibility issues with the Palisade software that were present at the time of writing.

About the Author

Michael Rees gained a B.A. with First Class Honours and a Doctorate in Mathematics from Oxford University in 1985 and 1988 respectively. In 1992 he gained an MBA with Distinction from INSEAD, and in 2003 graduated in first position on the Certificate in Quantitative Finance program, also winning the Wilmott award.

Michael started his career as a strategy consultant with Braxton Associates and Mercer Management Consulting, and later worked as an analyst at J.P. Morgan. Since 2002 he has worked independently. He provides services in topics related to financial modelling, such as training, transaction support and valuation, general financial and business planning, model review, validation and rebuilding, and portfolio optimisation modelling.

Michael lives in Richmond, UK. He was born in Canada, has lived in several countries, and is fluent in French and German.

He can be contacted at michaelreesfmp@gmail.com.

Acknowledgements

I would like to thank those people who were most influential either directly or indirectly in the existence of this book. My parents created an environment which encouraged and supported learning during my early years. During my academic studies, Graham Hoare, Dr Martin Powell, Prof. William Morton and Dr Paul Wilmott were especially influential. Many former colleagues from Braxton Associates were instrumental in laying the foundations of my business modelling knowledge and in supporting my career development at that time. In particular, Jim Bacos, Faisal Rahmatallah and Michael Schwarz deserve special mention. Palisade Corporation was also helpful in preparing this book, by allowing me the flexibility to draw on the materials developed by me for their training courses.

Michael Rees

May 2008

1
Building Blocks: Selected Excel Functions and Tools

This chapter provides examples of the use of a selection of Excel functions. It is not possible within the scope of this text to provide complete coverage of all Excel functions; rather the focus is on those that are generally important in financial modelling at the intermediate and advanced level. Readers may naturally refer to other texts on Excel or to the **Help** menu within Excel (**F1** short-cut) to learn more about the full range of functions.

CORE FUNCTIONS FOR FINANCIAL MODELLING

This section summarises the basic functions required for many financial modelling applications. While many of these are essentially self-explanatory and are likely to be well known to many readers, certain aspects of their use and features are worth highlighting.

Arithmetic Operations

The basic functions for arithmetical operations (classified in Excel within either the **Math & Trig** or **Statistical** categories) include:

- **AVERAGE** calculates the average of a set of numbers.
- **COUNT** counts the number of cells that contain numbers (**COUNTA** counts the number of non-empty cells, and so includes the counting of text fields).
- **MIN** and **MAX** calculate the minimum and maximum of a set of values.
- **PRODUCT** multiplies its arguments.
- **SUBTOTAL** calculates the sum (or other values) of a range of cells, ignoring other **SUBTOTAL** functions, so avoiding potential double-counting of values.
- **SUM** adds up a set of numbers.
- **SUMPRODUCT** multiplies the corresponding elements of two ranges and forms their sum.

Example: PRODUCT

Where the values in a contiguous range of cells are to be multiplied, the **PRODUCT** function provides a smaller formula with easier updating than the alternative approach (in which individual cell references are multiplied).

The file Ch1.Core.xlsx (PRODUCT worksheet) (Figure 1.1) shows an example in which a range of cells containing probabilities is multiplied. It shows that there is a probability of just less than 50% that a group of 23 people have birthdays on different days to each other. That is, in a group of 23 people, it is more likely than not that at least two people share a birthday.

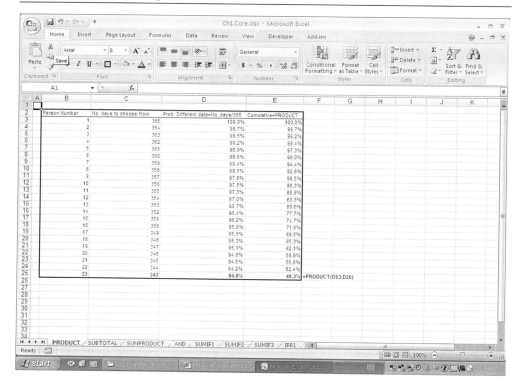

Figure 1.1

Example: SUBTOTAL

The **SUBTOTAL** function ignores other **SUBTOTAL** functions, and so avoids double-counting when applied to a range that contains this function (unlike the **SUM** function, which would lead either to double-counting or to a large set of cumbersome, inflexible and error-prone formulae).

The function has an argument that allows different calculations to be performed on the data set. For example, the sum of the range requires the use of the argument 9, whereas the average and count require the value of 1 and 2 respectively (see the **Help** menu for the full description).

Frequent uses of the function include:

- The creation of subtotals in a large list of data that is sorted into categories.
- In financial statement modelling, where a company's total assets may be calculated from the (subtotal) of its fixed and current assets, which may themselves each be calculated as the subtotal of a more detailed breakdown (such as equipment, working capital, etc.).
- The analysis of sets of filtered data (see later), where the function ignores any hidden rows that result from a list having been filtered (unlike **SUM**, **COUNT**).

The **SUBTOTAL** function can be entered either by direct insertion into a cell (by explicit typing or insertion from the **Math & Trig** category), or by use of **Data/Subtotal (Data/**

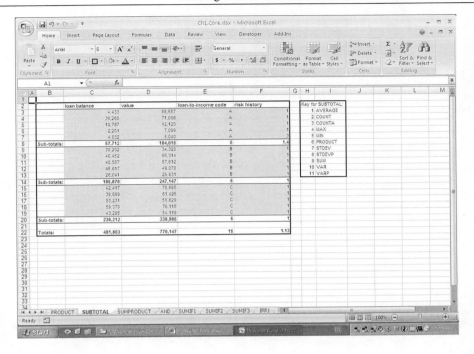

Figure 1.2

Subtotals in Excel 2003) when applied to a list or table of data. In the latter case the data will usually have first been ordered or sorted in some way (perhaps through use of the **Data/Sort** menu), so that the inserted subtotals are at the relevant break-points in the list. This latter route will result in grouped data appearing.

The file Ch1.Core.xlsx (SUBTOTAL worksheet) (Figure 1.2) shows an example where the function was entered by direct insertion (the arguments for the different types are also shown for convenience).

Example: SUMPRODUCT

The file Ch1.Core.xlsx (SUMPRODUCT worksheet) (Figure 1.3) shows an example of the **SUMPRODUCT** function in a simple portfolio analysis situation. It is used in order to calculate the weighted average (i.e. expected) return of a portfolio that consists of assets with given weights and expected returns.

Logical Operations

The basic logical functions include:

- **AND** checks if two conditions both hold, and returns **TRUE** or **FALSE** accordingly. Similarly **OR** and **NOT** functions exist. These can be useful to avoid writing embedded **IF** statements when checking multiple conditions.

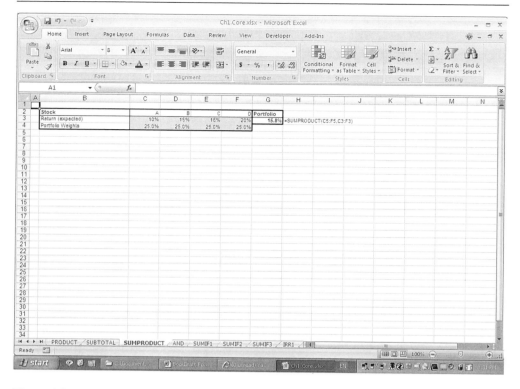

Figure 1.3

- **IF** checks whether a condition is true or not and returns a specified value in each case. Its use is implicit in a direct comparison expression such as =**F7**>**F6**, which would evaluate to either **TRUE** or **FALSE** (these are not text strings, but when used in any subsequent formulae, are interpreted by Excel as 1 or 0 respectively). Therefore =**50*(F7**>**F6)** would return either 50 or 0. Similarly, while one may write =**IF(F7**>**F6,1,0)**, this would not be the same as =**IF(F7**>**F6,"TRUE","FALSE")**, which returns text strings (and is therefore generally inconvenient when the results of such expressions are to be used in further numerical calculations).

Related functions include:

- **SUMIF** (classified in the **Math & Trig** category) adds the values of cells in a given range according to whether a criterion is met in another range. Excel 2007 also has a **SUMIFS** function in which a range is summed according to multiple criteria being met; an example is shown later in this chapter. In addition, in some cases the use of **Database** functions, **PivotTables**, or the **Conditional Sum Wizard** can provide more appropriate alternatives (see later).
- **COUNTIF** (classified in the **Statistical** category) counts the number of cells that meet a specified criterion. In Excel 2007, the **AVERAGEIF** function exists, as do **AVER-AGEIFS** and **COUNTIFS** when multiple criteria are to be met.

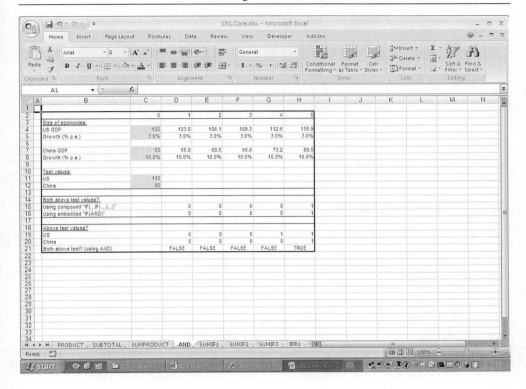

Figure 1.4

Example: AND

The file Ch1.Core.xlsx (AND worksheet) (Figure 1.4) shows the hypothesised development of the gross domestic product (GDP) of the US and Chinese economies (indexed so that the starting value of the US is 100), and demonstrates the use of **AND** to check whether two conditions hold simultaneously. Various possibilities are shown, including a compound **IF** statement, the **AND** function embedded within the **IF** statement, and the **AND** statement applied to the result of checking individually whether each of the conditions is met. Note that in the previous example, the **AND** function returns either **TRUE** or **FALSE**.

Example: SUMIF

The **SUMIF** function adds the values of the cells in a range according to whether a criterion is met in another range.

The file Ch1.Core.xlsx (SUMIF1 worksheet) (Figure 1.5) shows its use to calculate the total capital expenditure from Year 7 onwards in a 10-year forecast, as well as to lookup the capital expenditure in Year 9 (this could also be achieved with a **Lookup** function, described later).

The **SUMIF** function can be particularly useful in modelling applications where the values of some model inputs are themselves derived from data sets.

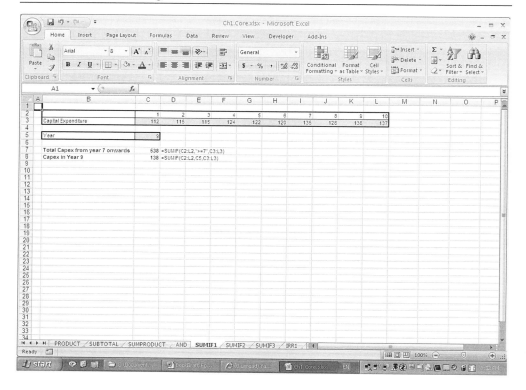

Figure 1.5

The file Ch1.Core.xlsx (SUMIF2 worksheet) (Figure 1.6) shows the use of the function to perform simple database queries. It also shows how the concatenation of multiple database fields (using **&** or the **CONCATENATE** function) can often be used to create a sum according to the multiple criteria being met. This approach can sometimes be easier and more flexible than the alternatives (which are discussed later, including the **SUMIFS** function, the **Conditional Sum Wizard**, **Database** functions (which would require setting up many criteria ranges with field headings for each), or **PivotTables** (where there would be no live-link to the data set).

The file Ch1.Core.xlsx (SUMIF3 worksheet) (Figure 1.7) shows how the function may be used to determine the number of unique records in a list.

Financial Calculations

Certain functions are frequently used in financial calculations (and are classified in either the **Financial** or **Math & Trig** categories) including:

- **IRR** calculates the internal rate-of-return of equally spaced cash flows, and has a number of applications, such as in project evaluation and yield analysis. (The **XIRR** function can be used where the cash flows are not equally spaced, and the **YIELD** function for

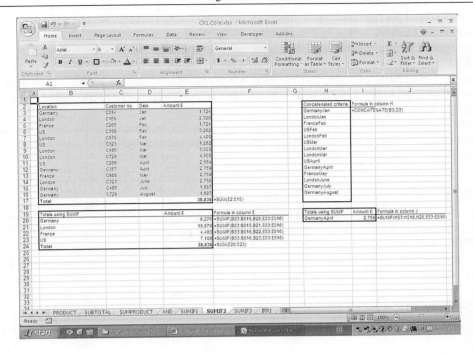

Figure 1.6

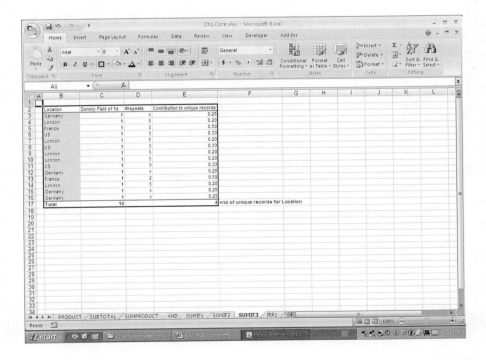

Figure 1.7

bond-related applications; these functions are included in Excel 2007, but are part of the **Analysis ToolPak** add-in in Excel 2003; see later.)

- **LN** calculates the natural logarithm of a number (and **EXP** the exponential).
- **NPV** calculates the net present value of equally spaced cash flows at a given discount rate. (The **XNPV** function can be used when cash flows are not equally spaced; this function is included in Excel 2007, but is part of the **Analysis ToolPak** add-in in Excel 2003; see later.)
- **PMT** calculates the constant level of repayment required on a loan (interest and principal) with a fixed interest rate (similarly **PPMT** calculates the principal repayment component only).

Example: IRR

The file Ch1.Core.xlsx (IRR1 worksheet) (Figure 1.8) uses the **IRR** function to calculate the yield on a bond with an assumed current purchase price and a repayment schedule. The **YIELD** function could also be used for such a calculation, and this is also shown. Of course the **IRR** function can be used for any profile of periodic cash flows, whereas the **YIELD** function is only applicable in the specific application of bond yields (as the periodic cash flows are implicit from the face value, maturity and coupon frequency, and do not need to be explicitly calculated).

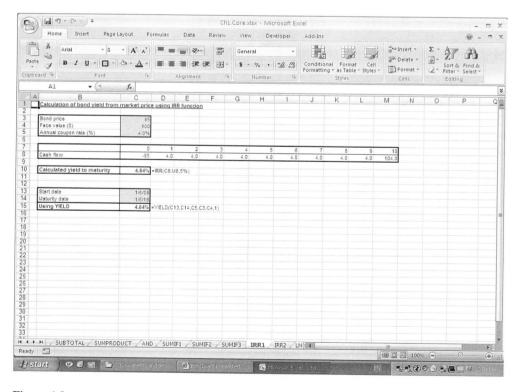

Figure 1.8

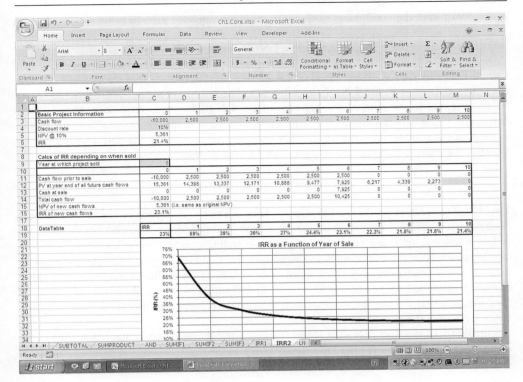

Figure 1.9

The internal rate-of-return is the discount rate that would result in the net present value of the cash flows being equal to zero. It is well-known that its use as a measure of project performance is inadequate. For example, when the cash flows of a project change sign over time, there will be several values possible values for the internal rate-of-return. More subtly, if a project may at any point be sold for its future net present value, then the internal rate-of-return of the project depends on the date at which the project is sold. This means that its use as a measure of performance or of project selection can be misleading.

The file Ch1.Core.xlsx (IRR2 worksheet) (Figure 1.9) demonstrates this (it also uses the **Data Table** functionality described in Chapter 2 to test the sensitivity of the internal rate-of-return to the date at which the project is sold).

Example: LN

The **LN** function is useful in many contexts, including the calculation of the growth rates of asset values and the calculation of half-lives in maintenance modelling. If the value of a process halves every T years, its value at the end of each year is equal to **EXP(LN(0.5)/T)** of the value at the beginning of the year. Similarly, if an asset's value grows continously in time, then its future value will grow exponentially. When calculating asset returns, the use of the **LN** function applied to the ratio of the ending to beginning values over a period of time will give the continuous time (constant compounding) growth rate:

$$\text{Growth rate} = \mathbf{LN}(\text{Ending/Starting})$$

One of the properties of this method of calculating growth rates is that the periodic growth rates are additive, e.g. the **LN** of the ratio calculated from year end and beginning asset values is equal to the sum of the changes of the **LN** of the ratio on a daily basis. When considering very short periods (such as daily changes) it makes little difference to the individual measurements whether the **LN** function is applied to the ratios of values or whether the change is measured using the alternative formula:

$$\text{Growth rate} = \text{Ending/Starting} - 1$$

This latter formula is used in applications where the passage of time is considered to be a discrete process, rather than a continuous one. Note that the additive property of the changes is lost when this approach is used. However, the ending period asset value when using the two approaches in a forecasting sense would be the same as long as each methodology is used in a self-consistent way. That is, the calculation of an ending value when the input change is assumed to be measured by the first formula would require use of the **EXP** function, whereas for the second approach it would involve a multiplication of the starting value by 1 plus the growth rate.

The file Ch1.Core.xlsx (LN worksheet) (Figure 1.10) shows the two calculation approaches using a set of daily data for the Dow Jones index in 2007.

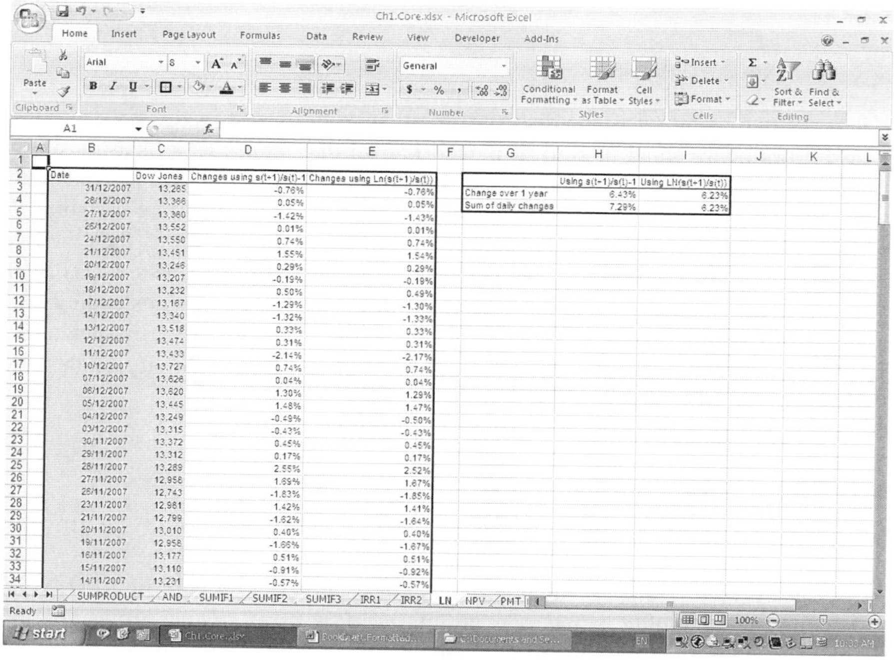

Figure 1.10

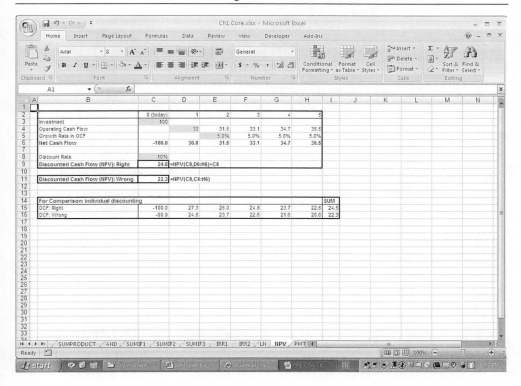

Figure 1.11

Example: NPV

The use of the **NPV** function to calculate the discounted value of a set of cash flows is essentially straightforward providing one is familiar with the concept of discounting. The main area where mistakes are often made is to overlook that the function implicitly assumes that the value in the first cell of the range is discounted for one period, the second value for two periods, and so on.

The file Ch1.Core.xlsx (NPV worksheet) (Figure 1.11) shows an example in which the cash outflow associated with an investment that is being made immediately would not require discounting, and should be excluded as an argument of the **NPV** function (otherwise all cash flows will be discounted by one period too many).

Example: PMT and PPMT

The **PMT** and **PPMT** functions can be useful to calculate respectively the total and the principal component of the periodic repayments required on a loan (the interest payment being the difference, but which can more easily be calculated directly from the interest rate and loan balance).

The file Ch1.Core.xlsx (PMT worksheet) (Figure 1.12) shows the explicit calculations of the repayments (split between interest and principal), where the required total repayment level must be found by trial and error (or by using Excel's **GoalSeek** or **Solver** described

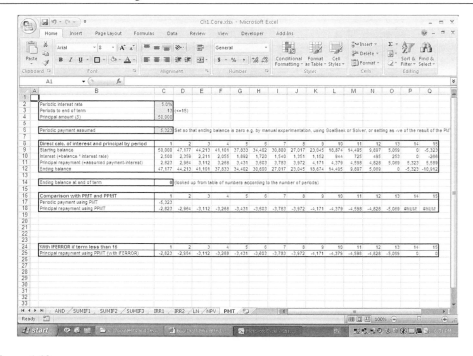

Figure 1.12

later). The results are compared with those that would result if the **PMT** and **PPMT** functions were used directly. (In the example shown, the term of the loan is set to be equal to 13, and hence a **#NUM** error is returned for periods beyond that. In this case, such an error has no real consequence for the situation at hand. Nevertheless, the example also shows how Excel 2007's **IFERROR** function (see later for more details) can be used to reset the error value to zero in such cases.)

When using these functions, frequent mistakes include having an interest rate that is inconsistent with the periods used (e.g. monthly/annual), or overlooking that the sign of the cash flows is negative (when repayments are required). Errors can be particularly hard to spot if the functions are used in embedded formulae in non-annual models.

DATABASE FUNCTIONS, FEATURES AND PIVOT TABLES

The analysis of data sets is important in a number of modelling applications, such as the calibration of model inputs, the assessment of important factors or drivers of behaviour in a situation, as well as being generally important as a stand-alone application. This section discusses a number of Excel's tools in this area, including:

- **Database** functions, which return calculations of the values in a database that meet certain criteria without explicitly extracting the relevant data points.
- **Filter** and **Advanced Filter** options, which present or extract a filtered data set whose elements meet specific criteria.

- **PivotTables**, which create summary reports by category and cross-tabulations.

Note that in some cases the **SUMIF** or **SUMIFS** functions (see earlier) or the **Conditional Sum Wizard** (see later) can provide appropriate alternatives to the use of **Database** functions. In addition, Excel has other tools to analyse data sets, including **Statistical** functions and simple regression analysis, some of which are discussed in the next section.

Example: Database Queries using DSUM and other Database Functions

The **Database** functions (such as **DAVERAGE, DCOUNT DCOUNTA DMIN, DMAX, DSUM**) calculate the relevant figure (average, count, etc.) of the numbers in a range that meet specified criteria. Statistical quantities, such as the standard deviation of the data points meeting the criteria, can also be calculated with **DSTDEV** (or **DSTDEVP**, when the sample is intended to represent the whole population) and functions such as **DVAR** and **DVARP** exist for calculating the variance.

When using **Database** functions, the field headings must be included in the definition of the database and criteria ranges. The criteria range can consist of multiple contiguous rows, where each row is equivalent to an **OR** condition (so that the presence of any blank row within the criteria range would select all records); multiple criteria within a row are equivalent to an **AND** condition, i.e. that all criteria within the row need to be met.

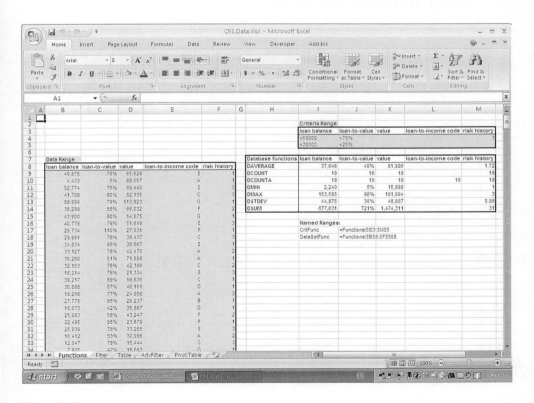

Figure 1.13

The file Ch1.Data.xlsx (Functions worksheet) (Figure 1.13) shows an example of the use of these functions (named ranges have been used for the database and criteria ranges; see Chapter 2 for more information on their use).

Example: Filtering

A range of data can be filtered by selecting the range including field headers (the short-cut **CTRL+SHIFT+DOWN** can be used), and applying the **Data/Filter** command (**Data/ Filter/AutoFilter** in Excel 2003). A drop-down list of potential filter criteria for each field appears (in Excel 2007 these include the application of numerical or text filters); the drop-down arrows can be removed by repeating this procedure. Statistical analysis of a filtered list can be done with the **SUBTOTAL** function (see earlier). The use of **SUM, COUNT,** etc., will pick up those hidden points that do not meet the criteria.

The file Ch1.Data.xlsx (Filter worksheet) (Figure 1.14) shows an example.

Example: Tables in Excel 2007

In Excel 2007, a range can also be turned into a **Table** by selecting it (including field headers) and using **Home/Format as Table** (or **Insert/Table**); a **Table** can be converted back to a range by clicking on the **Table** and using **Table Tools/Convert to Range**.

The file Ch1.Data.xlsx (Table worksheet) (Figure 1.15) shows an example, once again using the **SUBTOTAL** function on the filtered data.

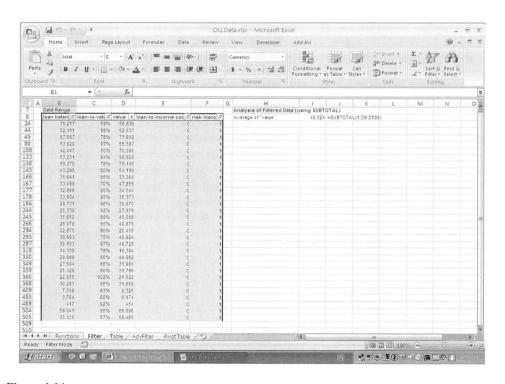

Figure 1.14

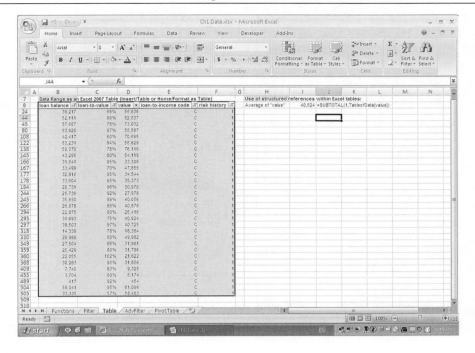

Figure 1.15

Example: Advanced Filtering

Potential disadvantages of the standard **Filter** approach include that the criteria used to filter the data set are embedded within the drop-down menus and are not explicit. Also, more complex criteria can be difficult or impossible to set up. The **Advanced Filter** (**Data/AdvancedFilter** or **Data/Filter/AdvancedFilter** in Excel 2003) can overcome these limitations, as there is an explicit criteria range, and it also allows those records that meet the criteria to be extracted to a separate area. Any named ranges that may have been set up can be accessed (for example, when completing the **List range** box) by pressing **F3**.

The file Ch1.Data.xlsx (AdvFilter worksheet) (Figure 1.16) shows an example.

Example: PivotTables

PivotTables can be used to produce cross-tabulation reports which summarise aspects of a database by category. The data range should be selected (including the field names) before using **Insert/PivotTables** (**Data/PivotTables** in Excel 2003), and then following the step-through menu ("**wizard**"), which is essentially self-explanatory. Row and column labels (including multiple labels to create subcategories) can be placed on the **PivotTable** by dragging from the field list, or right-clicking on the fields. The **PivotTable Tools** (displayed when clicking on the table) can be used to change aspects of the table, such as the **Field Settings** (which determine whether, for example, the sum or the average of the relevant entry is to be displayed), as well as using the **Refresh** button if the values in the data set change. Labels can be removed by clicking on them in the **Field List** or dragging them

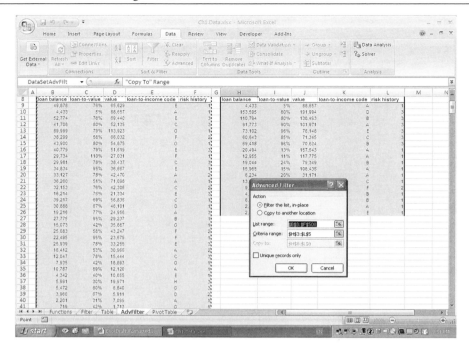

Figure 1.16

back from the labels area of the **Field List** window. A **PivotTable** can be deleted using the **PivotTable Tools** by choosing **Select/Entire PivotTable** and then clearing the contents. **PivotCharts** can also be produced and are essentially self-explanatory once one is familiar with **PivotTables**.

The file Ch1.Data.xlsx (PivotTable worksheet) (Figure 1.17) shows an example.

STATISTICAL FUNCTIONS

Statistical functions are often required to conduct analysis of historic data (for example, to calibrate model inputs) and to analyse the results of models (such as simulation models, where the output is typically a large data set). Basic arithmetic operations can be conducted with functions such as **AVERAGE**, **COUNT**, **MIN** and **MAX** described earlier.

Certain statistical functions relate to the variability found in data sets, such as:

- **CORREL** calculates the correlation coefficient between two data sets.
- **COVAR** calculates the covariance of two data sets (the extent to which the data sets co-vary, such as large values in one set occurring generally when large values in the other occur).
- **SLOPE** calculates the slope of the linear regression line of two data sets.
- **STDEV** calculates the standard deviation of a population based on a sample. Similarly, **VAR** calculates the variance (i.e. the square of the standard deviation). **STDEVP** and

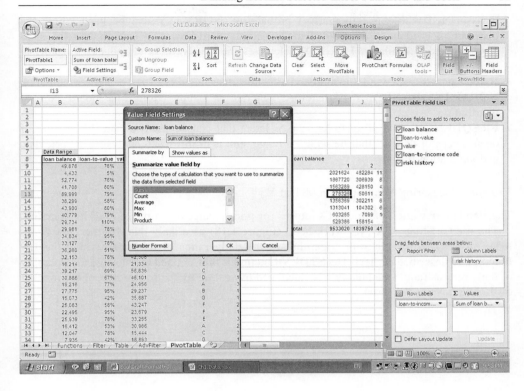

Figure 1.17

VARP calculate the same figures assuming that the data provided is the whole population rather than a sample, hence requiring no correction for biases introduced by samples.

Functions that provide further statistical measures about a data set include:

- **KURT** calculates the coefficient of excess kurtosis (i.e. the figure is adjusted by subtracting 3, so that a Normal distribution would have a **KURT** of zero). The meaning of this is discussed in Chapter 4.
- **SKEW** calculates the coefficient of skewness; its meaning is also discussed in Chapter 4.

Functions that provide measures of the order of points within the data set include:

- **LARGE** and **SMALL** show the value of a point with a certain rank in the data set (e.g. the kth largest or smallest value).
- **RANK** calculates the rank (i.e. ordered position) of a data point within its data set.

When implementing simulation techniques (see Chapter 6), other frequently required functions include:

- **NORMSINV** calculates the inverse cumulative Normal distribution, i.e. requires a probability as an input and calculates the value from a standard Normal distribution that is associated with this (cumulative) probability. **NORMINV** can be used where the distribution is to have a specified mean and standard deviation (rather than the standard 0 and 1). Similarly, **LOGINV** calculates the inverse of a cumulative Lognormal distribution.

- **RAND** generates a random number uniformly distributed on [0, 1]. The combination **NORMSINV(RAND())** will therefore generate a sample from a standard Normal distribution.
- **FREQUENCY** is an array function (see later) that can be used to find the number of occurrences of data set that lie within a range, and is useful when analysing historic data and simulation results.

Example: Measuring Volatility using STDEV

The standard deviation of an asset's returns (or price changes) is a measure of its volatility.

The file Ch1.Stats.xlsx (Vol worksheet) (Figure 1.18) uses daily data for the Dow Jones index in 2007 to calculate the logarithm of the daily ratios of the index (using the **LN** function, as described earlier). The **STDEV** function is then applied to calculate the volatility of daily returns (and an annual rate is calculated by scaling by the square root of the number of trading days in the year).

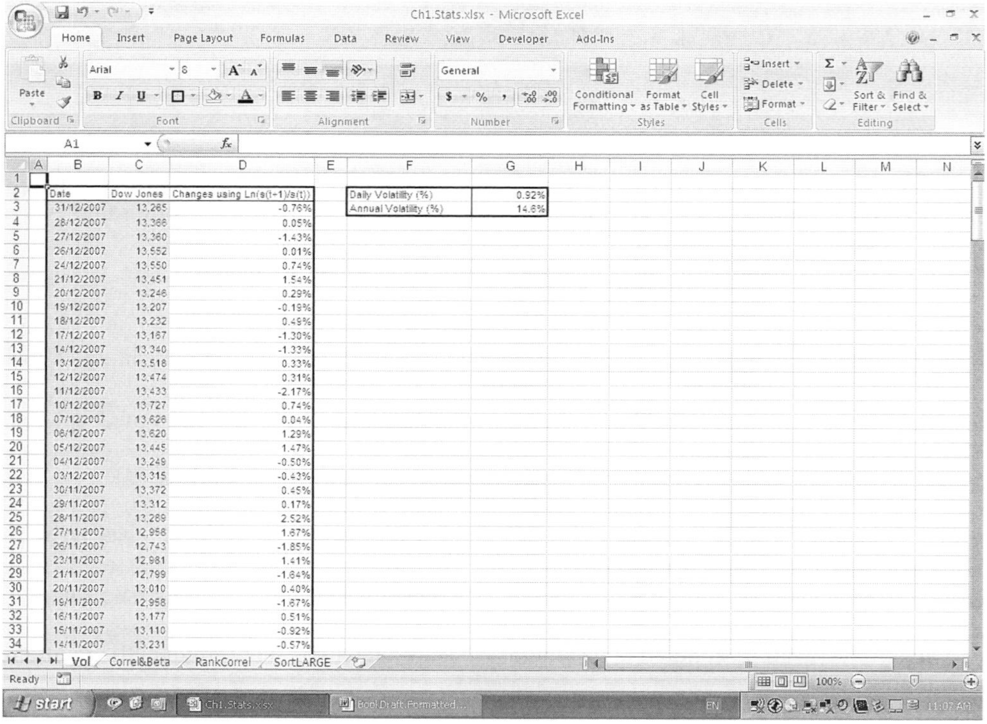

Figure 1.18

Example: Correlation, Covariance, and β using CORREL, COVAR, SLOPE

The measurement and use of the correlation coefficient between the returns of assets arises in many contexts, for example:

- The construction of an optimal portfolio of assets generally requires that the correlation coefficient between them be estimated.
- The estimation of the cost-of-capital for a project using the Capital Asset Pricing Model (see Chapter 3) involves the correlation coefficient either explicitly or implicitly.
- The use of correlated sampling is an important way to capture dependency relationships between variables in simulation models (see Chapter 4).

In the context of cost-of-capital calculations, the beta (β) of a project (or of a particular asset, such as a stock) can be expressed in several ways, including the covariance of the stock's returns with those of the market, or the correlation coefficient of the stock's returns with the market's, scaled by the ratio of the standard deviation of returns:

$$\beta_s = \frac{\text{cov}(r_s, r_m)}{\text{cov}(r_m, r_m)} = \frac{\rho_{sm}\sigma_s\sigma_m}{\sigma_m\sigma_m} = \frac{\rho_{sm}\sigma_s}{\sigma_m}$$

Here, r_s and r_m denote the return on the asset and market respectively, ρ_{sm} the correlation coefficient between the returns, and σ_s and σ_m the standard deviation of the returns.

It is known from statistical theory that these expressions correspond to the slope of the regression line (where the stock's return is on the y-axis and the market's return is on the x-axis). The slope of such a line can be shown by creating a **Scatter** (or **XY**) **chart**, right-clicking on one of the data points to **Add Trendline**, and under **Options** selecting **Display Equation on chart**.

The file Ch1.Stats.xlsx (Correl&Beta worksheet) (Figure 1.19) shows an example. It contains the monthly (logarithmic) returns for a five-year period of the S&P500 and a NYSE-quoted company, Kennametal. The functions **CORREL**, **COVAR**, **STDEVP** and **SLOPE** are used to calculate the statistics on correlation and volatility, and the β is calculated by use of these methods, as well as being shown as the slope of the regression line.

Example: Rank Correlation using RANK and CORREL

The classical measure of correlation discussed above is known as the Pearson Product Moment (or linear) correlation. When using correlation in simulation techniques (and in some other applications), the creation of correlation between random variables usually requires a less stringent definition of correlation, and for this a rank correlation (Spearman Rank correlation) is often used. Rank correlations are based on calculating the correlation coefficient using a modified data set in which each data point is replaced by its position (or rank) within its own set (i.e. the smallest value is given a rank of 1, and so on). Variables that are 100% rank correlated will not necessarily form a linear relationship (i.e. will not in general be 100% linearly correlated), but rather form a monotonic set. In this sense the use of rank correlation allows for more flexibility in the creation and sampling of multivariate distributions.

The file Ch1.Stats.xlsx (RankCorrel worksheet) (Figure 1.20) shows the use of the **RANK** function to calculate a new data set derived from the position of each point within its own set

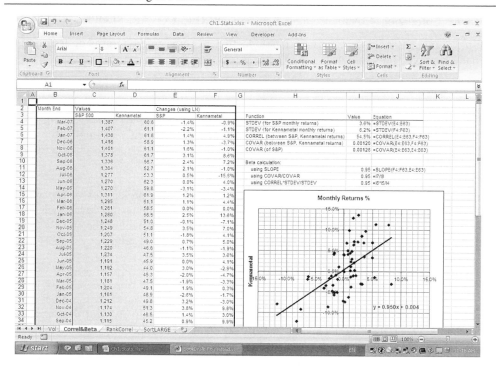

Figure 1.19

(when ordered in ascending order). The **CORREL** function is applied to both sets of data. There is a slight difference in the correlation coefficients calculated by the two methods. (Note that Excel also has a function **PEARSON**, which is equivalent to **CORREL**.)

Example: Automatic Sorting of Data using LARGE

The **LARGE** function can be used to automate the sorting of a data set into ascending or descending order. An advantage over the use of **Data/Sort** is that the sorted list is lived-linked to the data set and so will update automatically if it changes (e.g. as new daily data comes in).

The file Ch1.Stats.xlsx (SortLARGE worksheet) (Figure 1.21) shows an example in which a data set is sorted by applying **LARGE**, where a set of integers from 1 upwards is used in order to place the points in descending order. As covered in the next section, to find the date on which any of these specific returns occurred, **Lookup** functions (such as the combination of **INDEX** with **MATCH** or **VLOOKUP** if the data set were re-ordered appropriately) can be used.

LOOKUP AND REFERENCE FUNCTIONS

Many Excel users have only a cursory awareness of **Lookup** and **Reference** functions. However a good knowledge of them is arguably one of the single most important capabilities required to construct intermediate and advanced models.

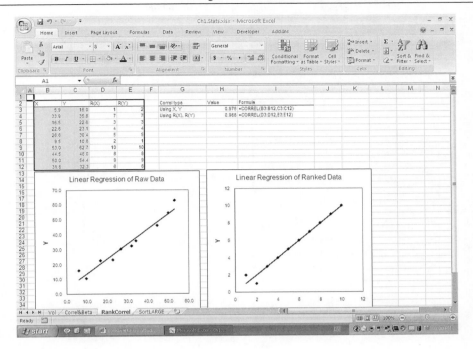

Figure 1.20

Some frequently used examples are:

- **MATCH** finds the relative position of a specified value in an array.
- **HLOOKUP (VLOOKUP)** searches the top row (left column) of a table for a specified value and finds the column in that row (row in that column) that contains that value. It then provides the value that is at a specified row (column) within the table.
- **INDEX** looks up the value in a specified row and column of a matrix. The function also exists in a reference form, where it returns a reference to specified cells rather than to the value of a cell.
- **OFFSET** provides the value in a cell that is a specified number of rows and columns from a specified reference cell or range. It can also be used to return the values in a range of cells (rather than an individual cell) that is a specified number of rows and columns from a certain reference cell or range.
- **CHOOSE** uses one of a set of values according to some key, and can be used where the arguments are in a non-contiguous range. In some cases, the function can provide more flexibility than the other **Lookup** functions.
- **INDIRECT** returns the reference specified by a text string.

There are other functions that may on occasion be useful, such as **COLUMN** (or **ROW**) to find the column (row) number of the given reference, and **COLUMNS** or (**ROWS**) to find the number of columns (rows) of a reference range.

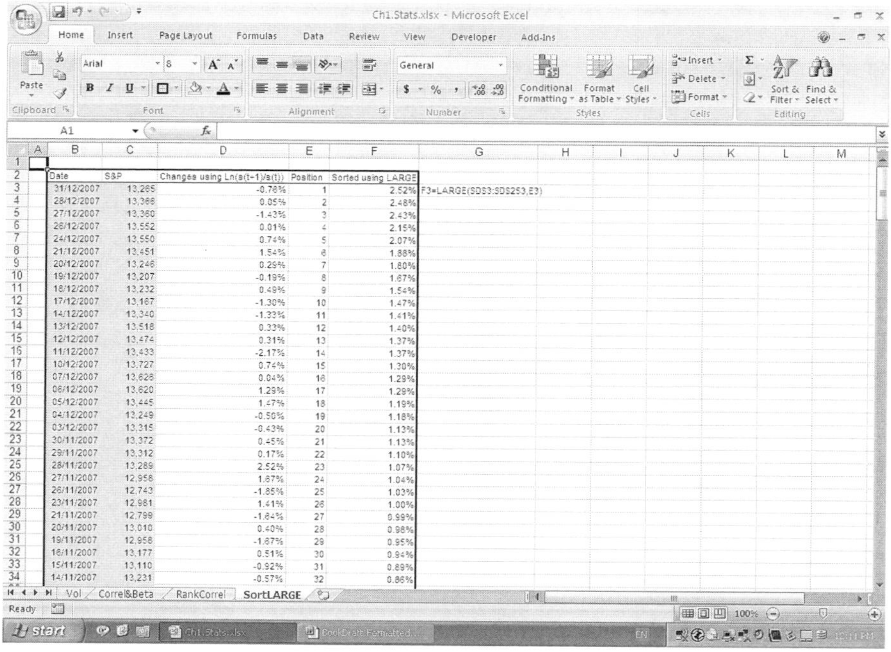

Date	S&P	Changes using Ln(s(t-1)/s(t))	Position	Sorted using LARGE
31/12/2007	13,265	-0.76%	1	2.52%
28/12/2007	13,366	0.05%	2	2.48%
27/12/2007	13,360	-1.43%	3	2.43%
26/12/2007	13,552	0.01%	4	2.15%
24/12/2007	13,550	0.74%	5	2.07%
21/12/2007	13,451	1.54%	6	1.88%
20/12/2007	13,246	0.29%	7	1.80%
19/12/2007	13,207	-0.19%	8	1.67%
18/12/2007	13,232	0.49%	9	1.54%
17/12/2007	13,167	-1.30%	10	1.47%
14/12/2007	13,340	-1.33%	11	1.41%
13/12/2007	13,518	0.33%	12	1.40%
12/12/2007	13,474	0.31%	13	1.37%
11/12/2007	13,433	-2.17%	14	1.37%
10/12/2007	13,727	0.74%	15	1.30%
07/12/2007	13,626	0.04%	16	1.29%
06/12/2007	13,620	1.29%	17	1.29%
05/12/2007	13,445	1.47%	18	1.19%
04/12/2007	13,249	-0.50%	19	1.18%
03/12/2007	13,315	-0.43%	20	1.13%
30/11/2007	13,372	0.45%	21	1.13%
29/11/2007	13,312	0.17%	22	1.10%
28/11/2007	13,289	2.52%	23	1.07%
27/11/2007	12,958	1.67%	24	1.04%
26/11/2007	12,743	-1.85%	25	1.03%
23/11/2007	12,981	1.41%	26	1.00%
21/11/2007	12,799	-1.64%	27	0.99%
20/11/2007	13,010	0.40%	28	0.98%
19/11/2007	12,958	-1.67%	29	0.95%
16/11/2007	13,177	0.51%	30	0.94%
15/11/2007	13,110	-0.92%	31	0.89%
14/11/2007	13,231	-0.57%	32	0.86%

Figure 1.21

The following provides some simple examples of uses of these functions. In many cases, there is not a unique way to achieve a particular purpose, so that alternative formulations with different functions may exist.

Example: Finding Equivalent Values using MATCH

The file Ch1.Lookup.xlsx (Match worksheet) (Figure 1.22) uses the earlier hypothesised development of the US and Chinese economies, and aims to find the first year in which the GDP of China will be larger than that of the US. (For ease of presentation the example uses conditional formatting as discussed in Chapter 2 to colour the cells when this is the case.)

The **MATCH** function is applied to the range containing the results of the GDP comparison, to find the relevant position in the range. (Depending on whether the logical test is set to return **TRUE/FALSE** or 1/0, the argument used in the **MATCH** function would need to be changed appropriately.) In this example, the GDP of China would be larger than that of the US for the first time in Year 11. Note that the **MATCH** function has an optional argument, which is the type of match required, with zero representing an exact match (see Excel **Help** or **F1** on the function for more details).

Example: Volume Discounts using HLOOKUP

The file Ch1.Lookup.xlsx (HLOOKUP worksheet) (Figure 1.23) uses the **HLOOKUP** function to find, for a specified quantity of a product purchased, the discount that applies according to some schedule. Note that the last parameter of the function is set to **TRUE**

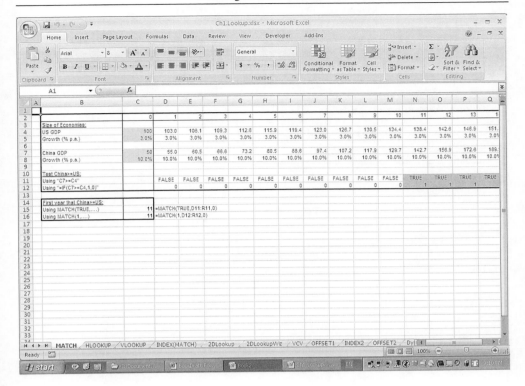

Figure 1.22

(or 1), so that the closest match in ascending order is found (rather than an exact match); this is necessary here, as the volume discounts must apply to all intermediate points in the table, i.e. the discount that applies to a quantity of 7 should be the same as that which applies to any number from 5 to (just less than) 10.

Example: Currency Conversion I–using VLOOKUP

The items in a multi-currency database can be converted into a common currency by looking up the appropriate exchange-rate for each item.

The file Ch1.Lookup.xlsx (VLOOKUP worksheet) (Figure 1.24) shows how the **VLOOKUP** can be used to find the appropriate row for each currency, and then to pick out the value of the exchange rate, which is then used as an input to a regular Excel formula to convert the local currency amount to the sterling equivalent. The application of this function assumes that the data is arranged vertically, and that the left column contains the currency names.

Example: Currency Conversion II–using INDEX(MATCH)

One of the constraints on using the **H-** and **VLOOKUP** functions is that the contiguous range in which the data is to be looked up must be arranged so that the top row (or left column) contains the items to be searched. On occasion this can be inconvenient, and a

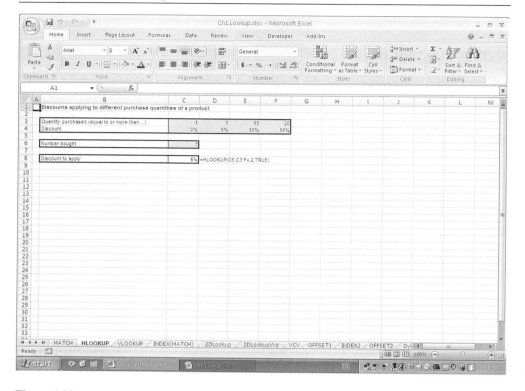

Figure 1.23

more flexible approach to the same problem can be implemented using a combination of the **INDEX** and **MATCH** functions.

The file Ch1.Lookup.xlsx (INDEX(MATCH) worksheet) (Figure 1.25) shows the currency conversion example used above, but as the lookup field is in the right-hand column, the **VLOOKUP** function cannot be used. Instead, the **MATCH** function is used to determine the correct row to lookup the value and the **INDEX** function used to lookup the exchange rate. (The example shows this procedure performed step-by-step and also using a compound formula. As described in Chapter 2, a robust way to build the compound formulae (where desired) is to create the step-by-step process and paste a copy of the **MATCH** function from within the **Formula Bar** in place of the reference to that cell within the **INDEX** formula.)

Example: Two-Dimensional Look-Up using INDEX(MATCH)

The **INDEX(MATCH)** combination can also be used to perform a two-dimensional lookup. For example, a volume discount may also be product-specific.

The file Ch1.Lookup.xlsx (2DLookup worksheet) (Figure 1.26) shows the use of the **MATCH** function to lookup the relevant row and column number, which are then used as arguments of the **INDEX** function to calculate the discount that applies according both to the product and volume purchased. In this case an exact **MATCH** is required when determining the row number (match type $= 0$), but a less-than-or-equal match is necessary for the column number (match type $= 1$).

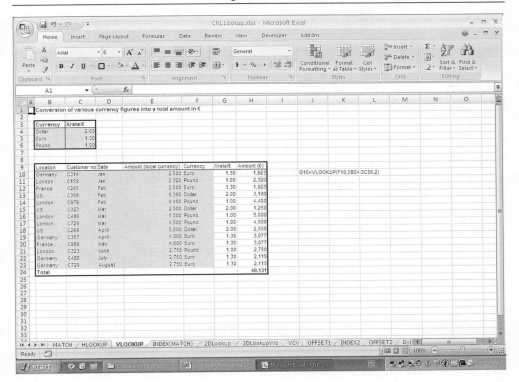

Figure 1.24

In the (2DLookupWiz worksheet) a similar result can be generated in an essentially automated way by the use of the **Lookup** wizard. This is an add-in that can be loaded under **Office/Excel Options/Add-ins** (or **Tools/Add-ins** in Excel 2003), with the menu then appearing under **Formulas/Solutions** (or **Tools** in Excel 2003). The use of the wizard is essentially self-explanatory once it is loaded, and is also similar to the use of the **Conditional Sum Wizard** that is discussed later in this chapter.

Example: Variance–Covariance Matrices using H- and VLOOKUP

When considering a portfolio of assets with given weights and assumed expected returns, volatilities (standard deviations) and correlations of returns, the portfolio's expected return can be calculated using the **SUMPRODUCT** function (as shown earlier). However, the calculation of the portfolio's standard deviation (as the square root of its variance) requires matrix multiplication involving the vector of portfolio weights (w) and the variance–covariance matrix (VCV):

$$\text{Variance of portfolio} = w\,VCV\,w^t$$

The implementation of such matrix multiplication is discussed later in this chapter (using the **MMULT** function). Here we assume that a correlation matrix has been calculated (either using the earlier method using **CORREL**, or–as shown later–using the **OFFSET** or other

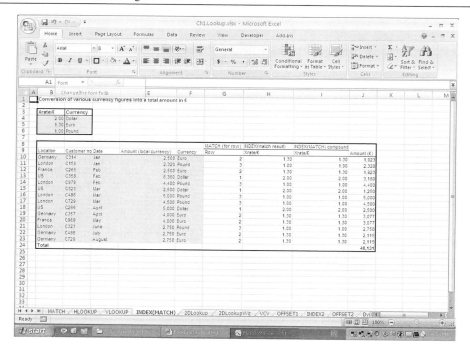

Figure 1.25

Lookup functions to create a formula that can be copied to all cells of the correlation matrix), and are concerned with the calculation of the *VCV* matrix.

The elements of the *VCV* matrix are given by:

$$VCV_{ij} = \rho_{ij}\sigma_i\sigma_j$$

where ρ_{ij} represents the correlation coefficient between the return of assets i and j, and σ_i the standard deviation of asset i.

The file Ch1.Lookup.xlsx (VCV worksheet) (Figure 1.27) shows the use of **HLOOKUP** (**VLOOKUP** could be used if the standard deviation data were arranged in a column) to create a formula in one cell of the variance–covariance matrix that can be copied to all other cells in the matrix. Especially for large matrices such an approach would be much less time-consuming than one using standard cell references, as such formulae would need to be set up individually for each cell in the matrix in accordance with the required data sets that need to be referenced.

Example: Time Axis as a Variable using OFFSET or INDEX

Lookup functions can also be used to create situations in which the time-axis of a model is variable, at least in a discrete sense (for example, that each column represents a year, but precisely which year it represents is flexible or can be determined by the user). For example, if the time-line of part of a project is altered (e.g. due to a delay) then it would generally be very cumbersome to change the formula links in the model, especially where different

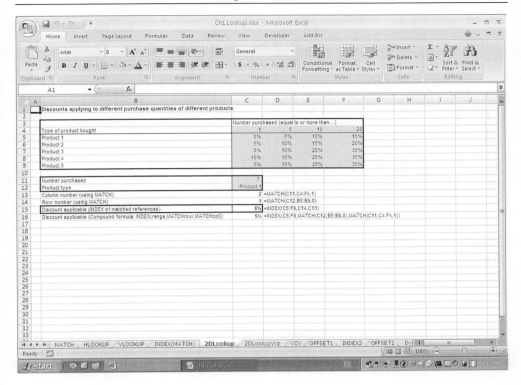

Figure 1.26

variables or parts of a model may have their own separate time-lines. Example applications include:

- The modelling of revenues (or profit or cash flow) that may arise from a portfolio of projects (e.g. in drug development) when the expected launch date of each project may need to be updated as more information becomes available.
- The base case cost for a project where parts of the project could be delayed by different amounts.
- The calculation of a depreciation schedule for a book of assets purchased at different times, where the depreciation profile of each asset may be different.
- The cash repayment profile for a portfolio of bonds or other commitments where one initially set up such a portfolio (in terms of the timing of the repayment of individual elements) so that it is optimised in some way (e.g. the maximum repayment is held below some level or is matched as closely as possible with cash inflow profile of the business). In this case one would wish to create a model in which the repayment timing on each element of the portfolio can be varied.

The file Ch1.Lookup.xlsx (OFFSET1 worksheet) (Figure 1.28) shows the use of the **OFFSET** function to translate a generic schedule of bond repayments after the year of issue of each into a specific schedule once the issue date is decided. One can then experiment

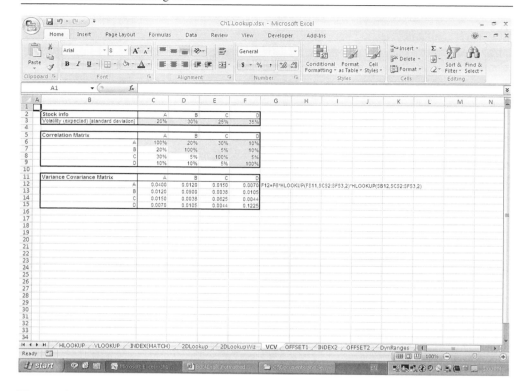

Figure 1.27

with the issue date (and the other input variables) to select a suitable repayment profile. Note that this could also be implemented using the **INDEX** function. The screen shot for the INDEX2 worksheet should be indentical to that for the OFFSET1 worksheet.

Example: Transposing References using OFFSET

The file Ch1.Lookup.xlsx (OFFSET2 worksheet) (Figure 1.29) shows an example of the use of the **OFFSET** function to transpose data or formula references.

Example: Flexible Ranges using INDEX, OFFSET and INDIRECT

The **OFFSET**, **INDEX** and **INDIRECT** functions can each be used to create formulae that refer to ranges that are flexible (i.e. whose size varies and automatically adjusts).

The **OFFSET** function can be used to return the values in a range (rather than just the contents of an individual cell). The optional height and width arguments of the function can be used to specify the size of the output range (where these optional arguments are omitted, the size of the output range is assumed to be the same as that of the reference range, which in the examples above was only a single cell, but in general need not be).

The **INDEX** function exists in a reference form, in other words it returns a reference to specified cells rather than the value of a cell. When used in this form, the range referred to by the function will generally be directly used as a range argument in another function.

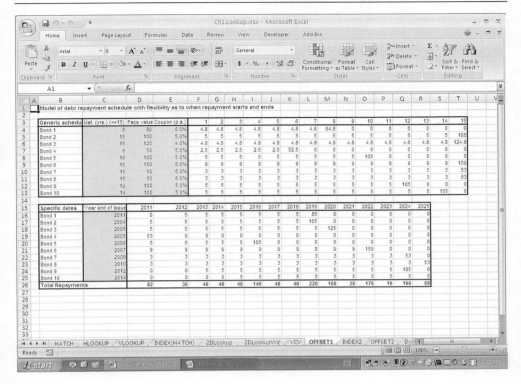

Figure 1.28

The **INDIRECT** function has a cell reference as its argument and returns the value that is in that cell.

The file Ch1.Lookup.xlsx (DynRanges worksheet) (Figure 1.30) shows the use of each of these to create a formula that calculates the moving average of points in a data set, where the look-back period for the calculation can be varied by the user (i.e. the number of points used in the calculations is flexible).

Example: Flexible Correlation Matrix using OFFSET

Another example of the use of **OFFSET** in a form where it returns an array (directly as an argument of a formula) is for the calculation of correlation matrices. For anything but a small number of assets, this would be a much quicker way of calculating the correlation matrix than using individual entries of the **CORREL** function, as the range arguments would need to be changed from cell to cell within the matrix.

The file Ch1.Lookup.xlsx (OFFSET3Correl worksheet) (Figure 1.31) shows an example.

TEXT FUNCTIONS

Excel's **TEXT** functions can be useful not only in their own right but also to allow manipulation of numerical fields by first turning them into text, operating on the text fields and

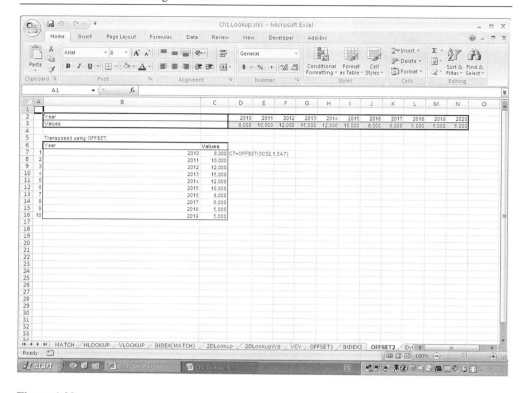

Figure 1.29

turning the text back into a numerical field. A selected list of some of these functions includes:

- **LEN** counts the length of a string.
- **MID** refers to text in the middle of a text string.
- **REPLACE** replaces a portion of text, starting at a specified place.
- **SEARCH** determines the starting position of a text fragment within a string; similarly, **FIND** finds the position of one text string within another.
- **TEXT** formats a numerical value and converts it to text.
- **VALUE** converts a text string that "looks like" a value to an actual value.

Example: Manipulating Data I using TEXT, MID and VALUE

Occasionally one may need to take a set of multi-digit numbers and split each one into individual digits. For example, a sequence of digits such as 100100001 may represent whether an individual borrower was up-to-date or not with repayments of a loan or mortgage, where every digit represents the position at the end of a given month. It may be required to analyse the aggregate monthly position of a portfolio of borrowers, requiring each individual digit to be present in a separate cell.

The file Ch1.Text.xlsx (SplitNo worksheet) (Figure 1.32) shows the use of the **TEXT** function to convert each number into text, from which each relevant digit can be extracted

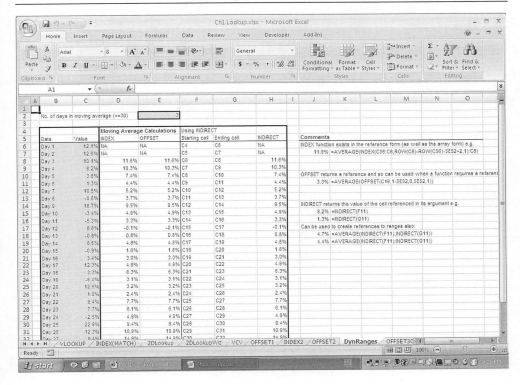

Figure 1.30

as a text field (using the **MID** function), before converting this text field into a value (using the **VALUE** function).

Example: Manipulating Data II using SEARCH, MID and VALUE

Sometimes one may be required to extract a value that is embedded within a text field.

The file Ch1.Text.xlsx (DataSet1 worksheet) (Figure 1.33) shows an example where it is desired to know the total time spent on a set of customer projects for various customers, where this data is contained within the corresponding text field. The key part of solving such a problem is to identify a commonality that defines the position of the relevant field; in this case it is that the field is directly after the first bracket. The **SEARCH** function is used to find the position of the bracket (**FIND** could also be used), following which the **MID** function extracts the text field that immediately follows the bracket. The **VALUE** function is used to convert this text field to data, allowing the total number of days to be calculated.

Example: Updating Text Labels and Graph Titles using TEXT

When producing charts whose titles or legends contain numbers (perhaps themselves calculated from a data set in the model), it can be useful if these fields update automatically if the numbers or data set change. This is especially true if several graphs of different cases

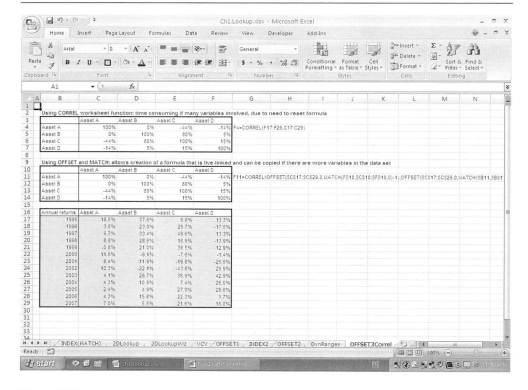

Figure 1.31

or sensitivities are required, as it will help to avoid confusion about which graph shows which scenario. This is a two-step process. The first step involves creating the desired title and labels as Excel formulae which update as the data changes (using the **TEXT** function). The second step involves linking these formulae to the chart labels and title.

The file Ch1.Text.xlsx (GraphLabels worksheet) (Figure 1.34) shows an example. The creation of the updating labels is achieved with the use of the **TEXT** function, such as:

=**"USA ("&TEXT(C5,"0.0%")&" p.a. growth)"**

As a formula, the expression must of course begin with an equals (=) sign, with the first part of the expression being made into a text label by enclosing it in inverted commas, which is then joined to the rest of the formula using &. The **TEXT** function has a first argument which refers to the cell containing the number to be updated, and a second argument which defines the format to be used (another frequent format is to use **"0.0"** to show a numerical field with one decimal point, or **"0"** to show no decimal places, as used for the chart title). Some spaces may need to be added at appropriate places within the text fields, e.g. immediately after an opening inverted comma or before a closing one.

The linking of the series names from a chart to the updating cells can be done when editing the data source of the chart. For chart titles, one must edit the title field typing = within

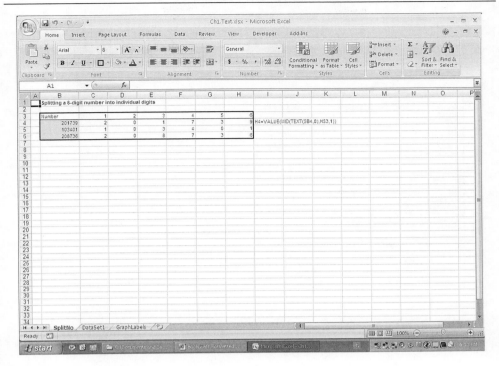

Figure 1.32

the Excel **Formula Bar**, point to the cell containing the required title, and press **RETURN**.

INFORMATION FUNCTIONS

Excel has a number of **Information** functions, many of which return **TRUE** (1 if used within a formula) or **FALSE** (0 if used within a formula) according to whether some condition holds. These can be used in many ways, including:

- Writing comments within numerical formulae. A formula can be multiplied by **ISTEXT** with a comment as its argument (e.g. =**105*ISTEXT("data from 2007")**) will evaluate to 105). **ISNUMBER** could also be used in this context, where the corresponding formula is added rather than multiplied, as the presence of the text comment would result in this formula evaluating to zero.
- General error checking (including in VBA code). **ISERROR** can be used to check for any error value (#**N/A**, #**VALUE!**, #**REF!**, #**DIV/0!**, #**NUM!**, #**NAME?**, or #**NULL!**). The function **IFERROR** (in Excel 2007) returns the value of an expression or an alternative value when the base value returns an error. **ISERR** checks for any error value except #**N/A** (value not available), and **ISNA** checks specifically for the #**N/A** error.
- Providing other information about the content, position or format of a cell, using functions such as **CELL** and **TYPE**.

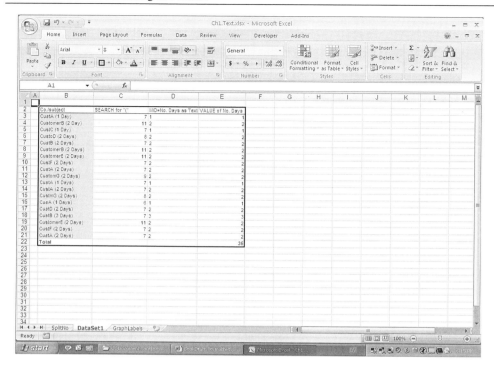

Figure 1.33

Example: Summing a Range using IFERROR

IFERROR is a **Logical** function in Excel 2007. It can be used to check for errors, returning a base value when the value of an expression is not an error, and an alternative value in the case of an error. An example is where one wishes to sum a range, but where some elements in the range result from a **Lookup** function, which in some cases may return an error, and where in such cases a value of zero is desired to be used for that value in the range. (In Excel 2003, similar functionality can be achieved by using **ISERROR** embedded within an **IF** statement, but this required a more complex and cumbersome format.)

The file Ch1.Info.xlxs (IFERROR worksheet) (Figure 1.35) shows an example where it is desired to form the sum of a subset of the values in the data set, where the subset is defined according to the labels (country names) that the user will define. The **INDEX(MATCH)** combination (see earlier) is used to search for the relevant values. In the first part of the example no error-check is made, whereas in the second part, **IFERROR** is used to perform an error-check (so that if no country label is defined in the cells of the range, a zero value is returned and the sum can still be formed).

Example: Updating Labels using CELL

The **CELL** function provides information about the position, content or format of a cell. Its arguments include the information type that is sought (such as the address, column or row

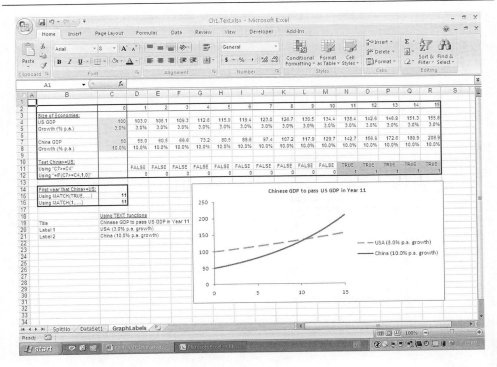

Figure 1.34

number of a cell or its values) and a reference that specifies the cell for which information is desired. It can be used in a variety of ways, such as:

- To provide an updating label for a variable (so that, for example, its description refers to the data range that is being used in the formula for that variable).
- To show the cell in a workbook that was most recently changed, by using it in the form **CELL("address")**, i.e. without a reference argument.

The file Ch1.Info.xlxs (CELL worksheet) (Figure 1.36) shows an example.

ARRAY FUNCTIONS, FORMULAE AND MATRIX CALCULATIONS

The use of array formulae is in some circumstances both powerful and unavoidable. Examples include matrix multiplication and transposition, and formulae to count the frequency of the occurrence of a set of points within a set of values.

Array formulae return arrays as their output, and must be entered in Excel using **CTRL+SHIFT+ENTER** (rather than the usual **ENTER**). Some array functions extend over multiple cells, in which case the entire range must first be highlighted and the formula entered in the **Formula Bar** or by selecting the function using the **Formulas** menu before entering with **CTRL+SHIFT+ENTER**.

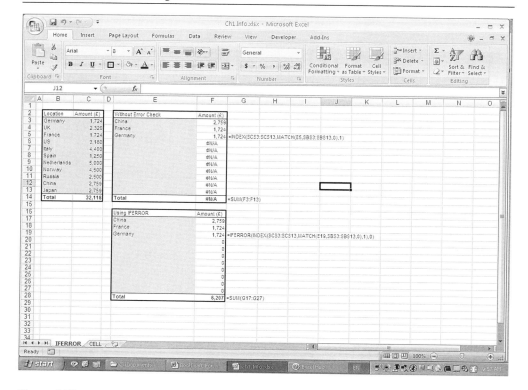

Figure 1.35

Despite their potential power, there are several disadvantages with using array functions and formulae. First, their use can slow down the calculation of a workbook. Second, a failure to enter the formula correctly (e.g. by using just **ENTER**) could result in a value appearing in the cell, but one that is incorrect, so that inadvertent errors may arise (in contrast to when a **#VALUE** error message appears). Third, many users are not familiar with them, which may result in the model being harder for others to understand or interpret, or where the user may accidentally edit a formula and return **ENTER**, leading to an error message or an incorrect value (if the ranges with array formula are not protected).

Example: SUMPRODUCT using SUM as an Array Formula

The file Ch1.Array.xlsx (SUMPasArray worksheet) (Figure 1.37) shows a basic example for illustrative purposes in which the **SUM** function is used to create an array function which produces a result that is the same as the **SUMPRODUCT** function. In this case the function is created by selecting the first range, using the times symbol, selecting the second range and entering using **CTRL+SHIFT+ENTER.**

Example: Histogram of Returns using FREQUENCY

FREQUENCY is a **Statistical** function that counts the number of times that points within a data set lie within each of a set of predefined ranges (or bins). It can be used to create

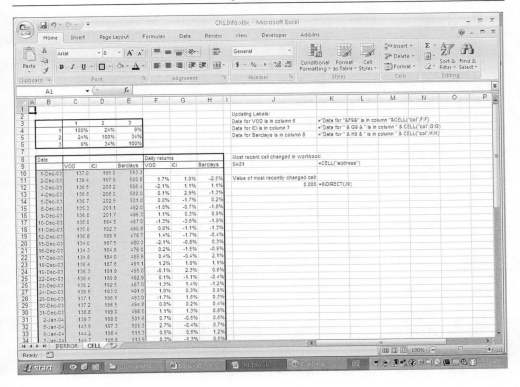

Figure 1.36

the data to produce a histogram of the data set. In practice, the choice of the definition of the width of the bins will be important; if the bin size is too wide the histogram will not be sufficiently detailed, whereas for narrow bin widths the histogram will look fragmented and multi-moded.

When using the **FREQUENCY** function, the entire range that is to contain the function must be selected (this range must be one cell larger than the bin range because there could be data points larger than the upper value of the largest bin), and the function must be typed within the **Formula Bar** or by selecting the function using the **Formulas** menu (rather than by direct typing in the first cell of the range, for example). On pressing **CTRL+SHIFT+ENTER** the function will show the number of data points in the set that lie between the lower bin value and the upper bin value. Once this function is entered the relative frequency of each bin can be calculated.

The file Ch1.Array.xlsx (FREQ worksheet) (Figure 1.38) shows an example where the average daily movement of the Dow Jones index for the period under consideration (2007) is 0.02% with a standard deviation of 0.92%. The bin size is set to 0.25%, starting at -3.00%. As mentioned above, the range in which the function is entered is one cell larger than the range containing the bins, to account for the data points that are larger than the maximum bin value.

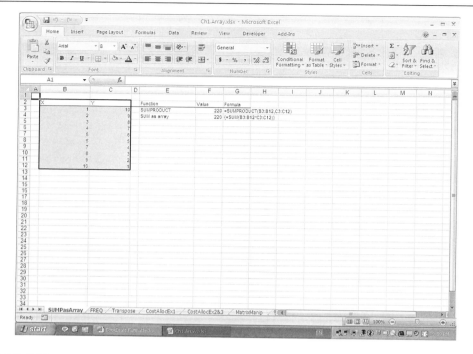

Figure 1.37

Example: Capex and Depreciation Schedules using TRANSPOSE

The **TRANSPOSE** function can be used to turn a row of entries into column format. For example, if a capital expenditure (capex) profile has been defined or determined over time, and a depreciation policy has been set, then one may wish to calculate the depreciation charge by year.

The file Ch1.Array.xlsx (Transpose worksheet) (Figure 1.39) shows an example. The year numbers and the capex amounts in the rows are transposed to columns (cells B12 through B21 and C12 through C21). A depreciation policy has then been applied, in this case using the **VDB (Financial)** function.

Example: Cost Allocation using TRANSPOSE

The file Ch1.Array.xlsx (CostAllocEx1 worksheet) (Figure 1.40) shows the use of array formulae to allocate the projected costs of a set of central overhead departments to business units, based on an allocation matrix and the **TRANSPOSE** formula. That is, each year the costs allocated to each business unit is the sum of the product of the range containing the indirect costs with the percentages from the allocation matrix. The layout of the allocation matrix requires that the percentages are transposed using **TRANSPOSE** in order for the **SUMPRODUCT** function to be used.

The file Ch1.Array.xlsx (CostAllocEx2&3 worksheet) (Figure 1.41) shows that if the allocation matrix had been initially set up in a way that was structurally transposed, then the use of **TRANSPOSE** and the array formula would not be necessary. The section of

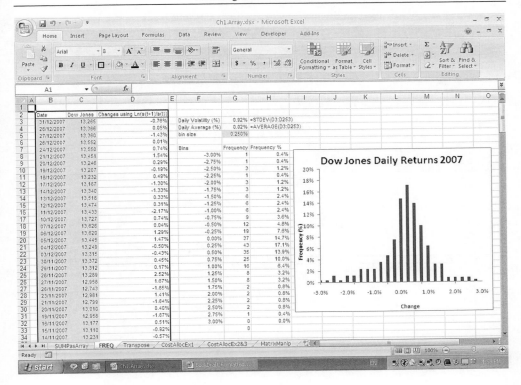

Figure 1.38

the worksheet titled Example 2 uses a formula that can be copied to all relevant cells within a row but needs to be edited separately when copying downwards. The section titled Example 3 uses the **INDEX/MATCH** combination (using the reference form of the **INDEX** function) to create a single formula that can be copied from one cell to the entire range.

Each of the three approaches has its advantages and disadvantages. The third avoids the use of array functions and presents the general formula that can be copied. On the other hand, the second example is generally the easiest to understand and may be preferable in situations where there are only a few business units or allocation objects (as in this example), so that the number of individual edits of the formulae is manageable. (Of course, in situations where the allocation matrix is predefined in the format of Example 1, the **TRANSPOSE** function could be applied as an array function to the whole matrix in order to turn it into the format of Examples 2 and 3.)

Example: Matrix Multiplication using MMULT and TRANSPOSE

Matrix multiplication can be achieved with the array function **MMULT**. Other matrix functions include **MDETERM** and **MINVERSE**, which calculate the determinant and inverse of a matrix respectively. As mentioned earlier, the calculation of the portfolio's variance

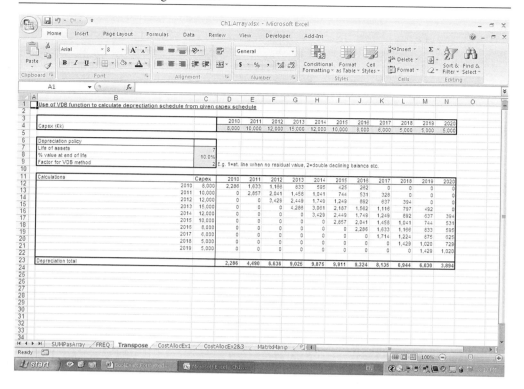

Figure 1.39

requires matrix multiplication involving the vector of portfolio weights (w) and the variance-covariance matrix (VCV):

$$\text{Variance of portfolio} = w\,\text{VCV}\,w^t$$

The file Ch1.Array.xlsx (MatrixManip worksheet) (Figure 1.42) shows an example. The variance–covariance matrix is calculated using the **HLOOKUP** function from the volatility of each asset and the matrix of correlations (as described earlier in the section on **Lookup** functions). The variance of the portfolio is calculated using the **TRANSPOSE** function and the **MMULT** function, with the standard deviation being the square root of the variance.

GOALSEEK AND SOLVER

Example: Required Growth Rate using GoalSeek

GoalSeek (under **Data/What If Analysis** or under **Tools** in Excel 2003) can be used to find the value of a single input cell that will result in a single model output having a desired value. This can be used to calibrate a model or reset the input in some way.

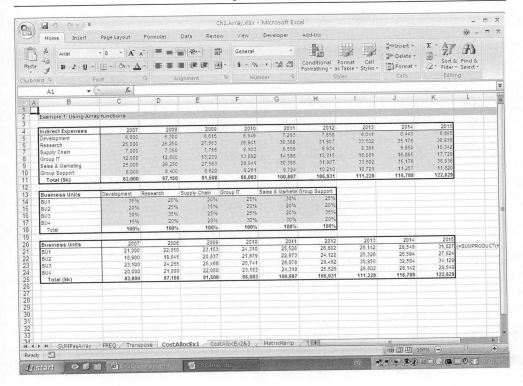

Figure 1.40

When using **GoalSeek** (and **Solver**) it is often more transparent and flexible to set up an output calculation with the objective of setting this equal to zero. For example:

- Where it is desired to find the input value so that a calculated quantity is equal to a fixed number, then the difference between this calculation and the fixed number can be set as an output that should be zero.
- Where it is desired that two calculated quantities be equal, then the difference between them can be calculated as an output, with the aim making this equal to zero.

The file Ch1.GS&Solver.xlsx (GS1 worksheet) (Figure 1.43) of shows an example using the earlier US and Chinese GDP forecast, where it is desired to find the growth rate required so that Chinese GDP would exceed that of the US for the first time in Year 8. The **GoalSeek** menu is essentially self-explanatory, and results in a periodic growth rate of about 13.6%.

Example: Implied Volatility using GoalSeek

GoalSeek can also be used to find the implied volatility of a European option, i.e. the volatility required in the Black–Scholes (BS) formula so that the observed market price is equal to the option value according to the formula.

The file Ch1.GS&Solver.xlsx (GS2 worksheet) (Figure 1.44) calculates the BS value of a European option under assumptions about the key parameters and variables (the formula

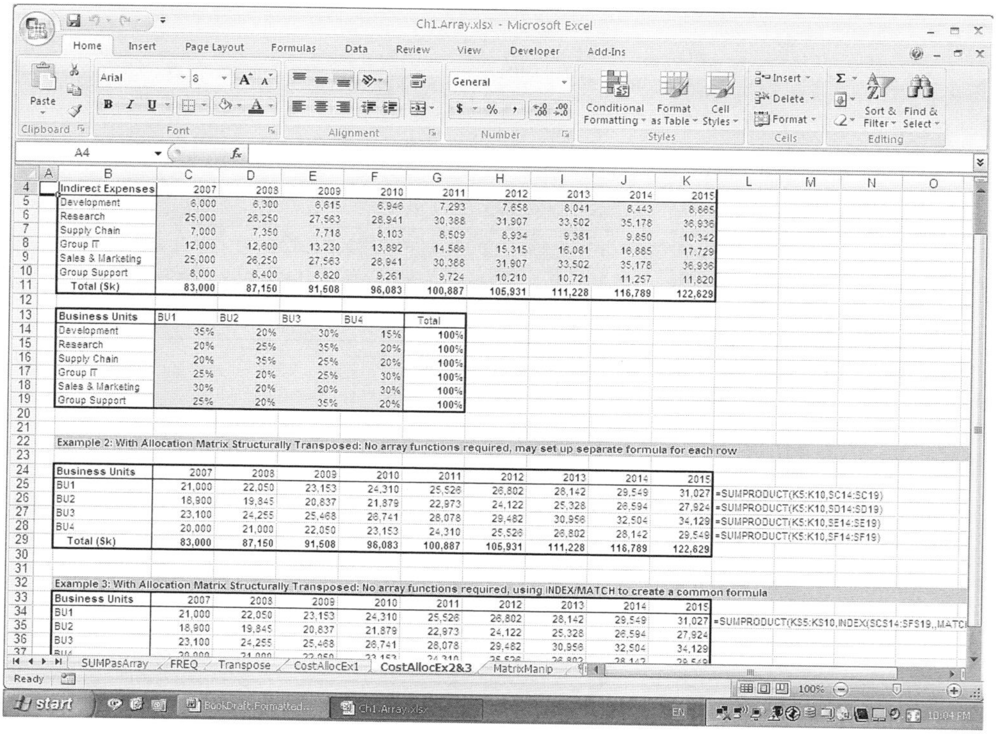

Figure 1.41

is described in more detail in Chapters 2 and 5). **GoalSeek** is used to find the volatility so that the calculated option value is equal to the observed market price of 5; this gives an implied volatility of around 22% p.a.

Example: Portfolio Optimisation using Solver

The **Solver** add-in provides more extensive capability than **GoalSeek,** in that multiple inputs may be varied in order to achieve some result for the output, and constraints may be imposed. **Solver** is found under the **Analysis** group on the **Data** tab (under **Tools** in Excel 2003). If **Solver** (or the **Analysis** group) is not displayed it can be installed (and uninstalled) using the **Manage** tool for add-ins under **Office/Excel Options/Add-ins** (or **Tools/Add-ins** in Excel 2003).

The file Ch1.GS&Solver.xlsx (Solver worksheet) (Figure 1.45) shows an example whose objective is to find the mix of assets that maximise the return on the portfolio for a given level of the risk. The Excel array formulae covered earlier are used to implement the required matrix multiplications. **Solver** has been run several times, using a range of target values for the standard deviation (in Chapter 6, a similar example is used where the process of running **Solver** several times is automated using VBA). Two separate runs of **Solver** were used, one where the weights for each asset were constrained to be non-negative and another where the weights were not constrained. The constraints for the weights were set up by creating a cell that calculates the minimum of the weights and constraining that value to

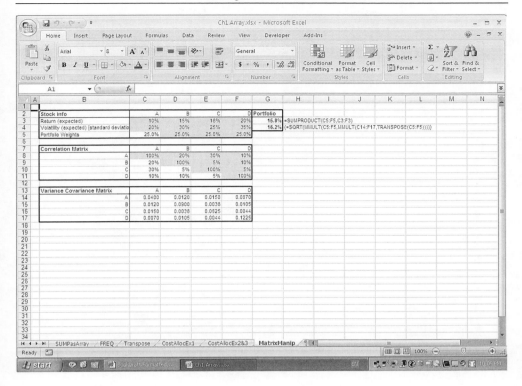

Figure 1.42

be non-zero. (An explicit individual constraint for each weight could also have been set up. The **Solver/Options** menu could have been invoked, as this allows the limiting of the solution search to non-negative values; in this case some further adaptation of the model or the constraint would be necessary to ensure that the weight of asset A was also considered and did not become negative.) The results show that an unconstrained situation allows for larger returns in some cases, corresponding to short-selling of the respective assets.

THE ANALYSIS TOOLPAK AND OTHER ADD-INS

The following gives an introduction to key aspects of some of the add-ins that are included with Excel 2007, including the **Analysis ToolPak** (which provides statistical tools, and which in Excel 2003 also provides some additional worksheet functions that are directly included in Excel 2007), the **Conditional Sum Wizard** (which helps to create formulae that adds values based on a condition or set of conditions) and **Solver** (which finds a combination of inputs that lead to the output having some value, with constraints). Other add-ins included with Excel 2007 that are not covered further here are the **Lookup Wizard** (an example was provided earlier in the section on **Lookup** functions), **Euro Currency Tools** (which allows conversions between legacy currencies in the Euro-area and related topics), and tools for VBA programmers (the **Analysis ToolPak-VBA** and the **Internet Assistant VBA**).

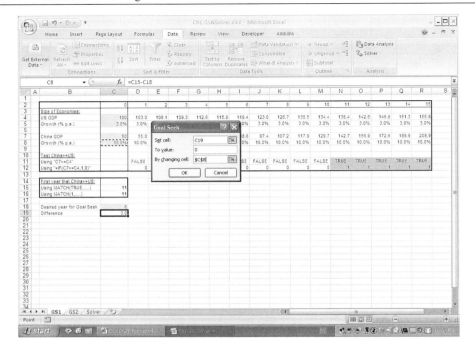

Figure 1.43

As mentioned earlier, add-ins can be installed (and uninstalled) using the **Manage** tool for add-ins under **Office/Excel Options/Add-ins** (or **Tools/Add-ins** in Excel 2003). Once loaded the add-ins may appear in several places in Excel (**Solver** and the **Analysis Tool-Pak** appear under **Data/Analysis**, the **Conditional Sum Wizard** appears under **Formulas/Solutions** and so on. In Excel 2003, they appear under **Tools**).

The Analysis ToolPak

The **Analysis ToolPak** provides statistical tools to enhance the capabilities of Excel. In Excel 2003, the add-in contains some functions that are directly included as worksheet functions in Excel 2007 (and are accessible without the add-in being loaded). Some of the most relevant for financial modelling include:

- **XNPV** calculates the net present value of non-equally spaced cash flows.
- **XIRR** calculates the internal rate-of-return of non-equally spaced cash flows.
- **YEARFRAC** calculates the fraction of the year corresponding to the number of days between two dates.
- **YIELD** calculates the yield on a bond or security that pays constant periodic interest.

The add-in is relatively straightforward to use providing one is familiar with the underlying statistical procedures. Most of these (e.g. analysis of variance, F-tests, t-tests, Fourier analysis, and so on) are beyond the scope of this text. For the purposes here, the most

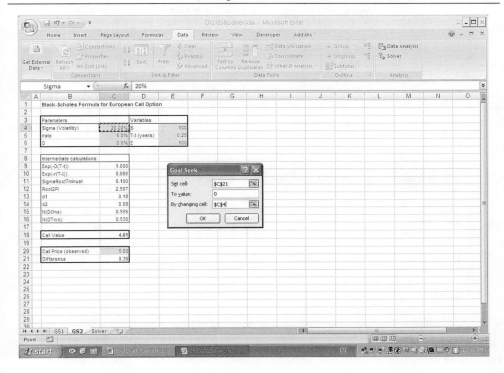

Figure 1.44

directly relevant include the calculation of correlation coefficients (or covariances) and the calculation of multiple regression coefficients and related statistics. An example of the use of the **Correlation** option is provided below.

Example: Correlation Matrices Revisited

The **Correlation** tool within the **Analysis ToolPak** is especially useful to create correlation matrices for large sets of data, and provides an alternative to the earlier methods shown (which consisted of either manually setting up the formula for each element of the matrix or using **Lookup** functions to create a general formula that can be copied to all matrix elements.) One advantage of the use of the **Data Analysis** tool is to avoid the potential complexities of using the **Lookup** functions. On the other hand a disadvantage of this approach is that the correlation matrix is not live-linked and so needs to be updated if the data changes.

The file Ch1.OtherTools.xlsx (DataAnalysisCorr worksheet) (Figure 1.46) shows an example.

Example: Complex Conditional Sums using the Conditional Sum Wizard

The **Conditional Sum Wizard** can in some circumstances provide a more appropriate alternative to the use of **Database** functions, **PivotTables**, or the **SUMIF** function. (As mentioned earlier Excel 2007 also has a **SUMIFS** function in which a range is summed

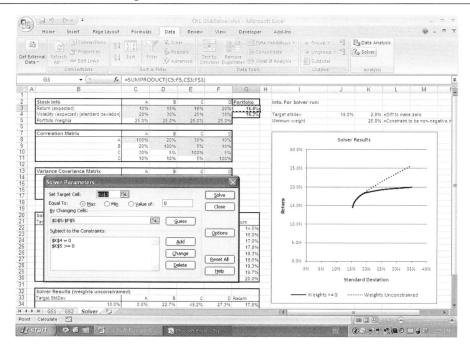

Figure 1.45

according to multiple criteria being met, and this can also be used in this context; an example
is also shown.)

The wizard can be used to generate formulae with multiple embedded conditions in an
automated way. The formula generated is an array function, therefore if it is edited or
modified it will need to be entered using **CTRL+SHIFT+ENTER** (see earlier).

The step-by-step wizard is essentially self-explanatory. When on step three, the option
copy the formula and conditional values can be chosen to ensure that the formula generated during step four refers to the value of particular conditions (which will be placed
in separate individual cells); in this way, the formula is easier to adapt, copy and modify
so that different conditional values can be tested, i.e. that multiple database queries can be
set up. Note that if a different query is required (such as requiring three conditions to be
satisfied instead of two), then it is generally easier to re-run the wizard than to try to adapt
the formula directly. However, where the number of conditions to be satisfied is unchanged,
then often a direct adaptation of the formula is easy to achieve (e.g. adapting a base formula
which tests for two conditions so that two different conditions are satisfied).

The file Ch1.OtherTools.xlsx (CondSum worksheet) (Figure 1.47) shows an example
of the result of applying the wizard in this way. The results are compared with the use of
the **DSUM** formula shown earlier and with the use of the **SUMIFS** function. Note that the
formula can be copied to different cells so that different criteria can be created, whereas
the use of the **DSUM** function would require a new criteria range for each application of
the function.

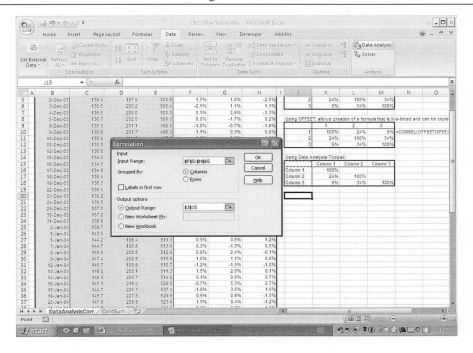

Figure 1.46

SELECTED EXCEL SHORT-CUTS

Many Excel operations can be performed quickly using keyboard short-cuts. On occasion, an excessive use of short-cuts may lead to a lack of robustness in the modelling process, with too much focus placed on the rapid building of the model, rather than on the modelling itself. It is perhaps to be recommended that the individual modeller should therefore develop a good familiarity with those short-cuts that will be most relevant, but not to be unduly concerned with knowledge of the full range of possible short-cuts.

Some core short-cuts and related tools that the author uses regularly include:

- **CTRL+C** to copy a cell, **CTRL+V** to paste, **CTRL+X** to cut, and **CTRL+Z** to undo.
- **CTRL+1** to display the **Format Cells** menu.
- **Format Painter** (on the **Home** tab) to format one cell as another. Double-clicking on the icon will ensure that it remains active so that it can be applied to multiple ranges in sequence (and clicking the icon again will deactivate it).
- **F4** to implement absolute cell references when editing a formula in the **Formula bar** (e.g. place a $ before a row reference); repeated pressing of the key will cycle through all possible row and column combinations.
- **CTRL+SHIFT+ARROW** to select the range from the current cell to end of range in the direction of the arrow (**CTRL+ARROW** to move to the end of current region in the direction of the arrow without selecting the intermediate cells).
- **CTRL+ENTER** to enter the same value in all cells of an already selected range.
- **F1** (help); **F2** (editing formulae); **F7** (check spelling); **Ctrl+F** (find).

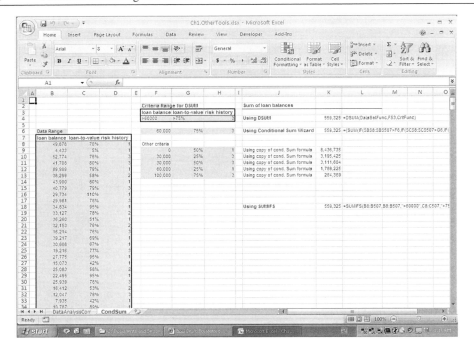

Figure 1.47

- **F3** to paste a list of all named ranges (includes those whose scope is the workbook and the particular worksheet, but not those whose scope is only another worksheet; see Chapter 2 for more information).
- **F5** to go to a cell or range; particularly useful if there are named ranges in the worksheet, and also using the **Special** option to find formulae, constants, etc.; see Chapter 2 for more information.
- **Home** to move to column A; **CTRL+Home** to move to cell A1.
- Use of the **AutoSum** icon (on status toolbar) to check sums, averages, count, etc., and hence readily perform extra cross-checks to the model.
- In Excel 2007, the **KeyTips (ToolTips)** can be displayed by pressing **ALT**. This shows the letters that may be typed to directly access the menu. For example, **ALT** followed by **M** (for **Formulas**) and then **H** (**Show Formulas**) will display the formulae (equivalent to **CTRL+'**).

Principles of Modelling

In this chapter we discuss the key factors that distinguish good models from poor ones, and present a variety of thought-processes and tools to facilitate the development of good models. We aim to highlight a few key principles that can be considered when designing and building models; the objective is to be effective and practical, but not overly prescriptive. This approach should allow modellers to make their own (informed) judgements in their particular circumstances and perhaps even to break the rules in a conscious manner when there is believed to be good reason to do so. Much emphasis is placed on the use of sensitivity analysis as the glue that holds a robust modelling process together, with each stage of the modelling process having a different form of the appropriate sensitivity analysis. We also discuss a number of other issues that need to be considered in creating good models, such as their logical flow and structural compactness, the use of named ranges, of circular references, of formatting, the creation of robust formulae, as well as the presentation of results, and model auditing tools.

WHAT IS A GOOD MODEL?

It is probably fair to say that the majority of models built in practice are of mediocre quality. It is often very time-consuming for someone other than the author to understand such models, which are generally complex to audit or validate. They are hard to share with others, and require an over-dependence on the original model-builder to maintain or use. They may also require significant rework if it is desired to implement fairly minor changes in logic. Frequently such models also suffer from a lack of clarity of objectives, which can lead to an inability to address essential questions. Invariably, such models contain errors, or assumptions which are implicit and may have unintended consequences or be invalid in certain circumstances.

As a general rule, a good model typically has a number of characteristics:

- **It requires minimal time to understand**. A model that is easy to understand will have a clear logical flow (usually left-to-right, top-to-bottom). It will have a simple and non-fragmented structure, keeping related items close together. It is likely to be broken into manageable components, with each logical step shown explicitly. It will be clear which variables are the inputs, and will use formatting and comments to enhance a user's understanding and draw attention to key aspects. Such models do not use the more complex functionality of Excel (e.g. macros, complex user interfaces and perhaps circular references) except where truly necessary.
- **It is objectives-driven**. A good model will, of course, meet the decision-support needs of its clients, providing insight into a range of questions related to the situation. It will use a set of input variables and outputs that are appropriate to the situation, and be built at a level of detail that is appropriate, excluding unimportant variables.

- **It is free from errors.** As well as being free from errors in calculations or formulae, there should be no unintended consequences, nor unacceptable implicit assumptions. Often the logic of a model results in a behaviour of the output that does not correspond to the modeller's intentions, for example as to how the output should behave when certain input values are changed. A good model will need to correctly capture the dependency relationships between all variables and be designed so that it can be calibrated with relative ease, i.e. so that key inputs and outputs can be compared with historic data, expert opinion, judgement or common sense.

The above criteria are often appropriate to judge a model once it has been built, but do not provide a toolset to actually design and build good models. A main thesis of this chapter is that sensitivity analysis is the glue that holds a robust modelling process together. This is different to the traditional approach to sensitivity analysis (i.e. to use it as a tool only once the model is built). Its precise form is different at each stage of the process:

- At the model design stage, it is of a conceptual nature (which we call sensitivity analysis thinking). It is used as a thought process which demands an answer to the question: What sensitivity analysis will be required once the model is built? This helps to clarify the objectives, and to create a focus on those variables that should be inputs versus those that are calculated. Very often this question is considered at only a superficial level (if at all), resulting in a model that is inappropriate or excessively detailed for the purposes at hand.
- As the model is being built, sensitivity analysis can be used to test it for the absence of logical errors, to ensure that more complex formulae are implemented correctly, and that the relationships between the variables are correctly captured.
- Once the model is built, sensitivity analysis can be used in the traditional sense, i.e. to better understand the range of possible variation around a point forecast.

MODEL DESIGN

At the model design stage there are a number of important issues to consider, including:

- What are the key objectives and outputs of the model?
- What types of variables should be included?
- Should some variable types be used at a detailed or aggregated level?
- What should be the logical flow, in terms of variables that are inputs, calculations and outputs?
- What dependency relationships between the variables must be captured?

In many cases, the answer to some of these questions is straightforward. However, in others, the apparently straightforward choices may not be the most appropriate ones; in such cases, sensitivity analysis thinking is generally a powerful tool to address these questions.

Selection of Model Variables and their Dependencies

The selection of the appropriate variables is of course an important point. A model with an inappropriate choice of variables could suffer from a number of drawbacks, including an inability to generate the required insight into the situation, or to answer key questions that one may wish to pose. It may also be difficult to calibrate correctly.

For example, a sales forecasting model could be based on a number of possible formulae, such as:

- Sales = Volume multiplied by price
- Sales = Market size multiplied by market share
- Sales = Sum of the sales per customer
- Sales = Sum of sales per product
- Sales = Sum of sales per product group.

Similarly, an energy company building a model of the construction cost of a gas pipeline might consider various possibilities, such as:

- Cost = Sum of cost for each section of the pipeline
- Cost = Sum of cost categories (materials, labour, etc.)
- Cost = Sum of construction cost per month.

In the above formulae it is generally intended to imply that the variables on the left are calculated quantities (model outputs or intermediate quantities), and that the quantities on the right are the inputs. However, such formulae are of course simply a statement of logic. It is equally true, for example, that:

- Volume = Sales divided by price
- Price = Sales divided by volume,

and so on.

Therefore the decision about model variables needs to include not only the selection of the types of variables but also the logic flow of the model, and the relationships between the variables. It is perhaps surprising how often this fundamental decision is made poorly, resulting in a model that is ineffective at addressing the key questions, or is excessively cumbersome to work with. Frequent but fundamental errors involve the inclusion of variables as calculated quantities, which are more appropriate to be considered as inputs and *vice versa*.

Example: Variable Selection I

The file Ch2.VarSel.xlsx (VarSel1 worksheet) (Figure 2.1) shows a simple calculation of the sales of a product, derived by multiplying the price and volume. On the one hand, a model might at first sight appear to be reasonable (for example, the calculation is correct, and the inputs are shown separately to the output). On the other hand, by asking what would happen in reality if the price were to differ from the base case (e.g. being $9 or $11, resulting in sales of $900 or $1100 respectively), one could be drawn to further relevant questions, in particular:

- Is the volume really independent of the price or is there a relationship between price and volume?

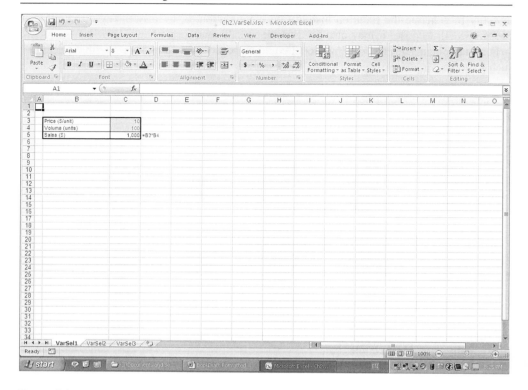

Figure 2.1

- If volume and price are related in some way, then is it the case that the volume is determined from the price level set (so that price is the independent variable and volume calculated), or rather that the price is a result of the decision of what volume to sell (so that volume is the independent variable and price calculated)?

In other words, even this simple model could not correctly be built without considering (before the model is implemented) the nature of the required sensitivity analysis that will be required once the model is complete. Such a use of sensitivity analysis thinking forces one to decide which variable is independent (the model input) and which is dependent (which would then of course have to be specified through Excel formulae).

This example also illustrates several other features and potential pitfalls of Excel modelling:

- The assumption (almost always implicit) that variables are independent of each other is the default position, resulting from the absence of the modeller explicitly defining the relationship between them in any other way (i.e. through Excel formulae).
- It can be useful to make a conceptual distinction between a model and a database. Many Excel workbooks are in fact little more than stores of data with a few supplementary calculations, rather than truly dynamic models. The flexibility of the Excel environment to deal with many very different applications, as well as its powerful tools to manage

and manipulate data sets, often result in this distinction being lost. The result is that applications that are closer to databases are thought of, and presented, as models, even though they have not been built in a way that is sufficiently flexible for the questions that may be asked of them, or for the inputs to be changed validly.

- A distinction between variables or parameters can sometimes be useful. Input variables are those for which the model is designed to remain valid when they are changed (perhaps within a specified range), whereas input parameters are fixed numbers. Typical parameters could be conversion factors (such as converting days to months, ounces to grams and so on, as well as any other numerical quantities that must remain fixed in terms of the validity of the model). Similarly, the price of a product could be considered to have the role of a parameter within a model whenever the model is not explicitly designed to be valid when the price is varied.

Example: Variable Selection II

Sensitivity analysis thinking can also help in the design of time-series models.

The file Ch2.VarSel.xlsx (VarSel2 worksheet) (Figure 2.2) shows an example of two possible implementations (Model 1 and Model 2) for a situation in which the revenues of a business start at $100 m p.a. and are then expected to grow by 5% p.a. The models of course produce the same calculated values in this base case, but there is clearly a significant

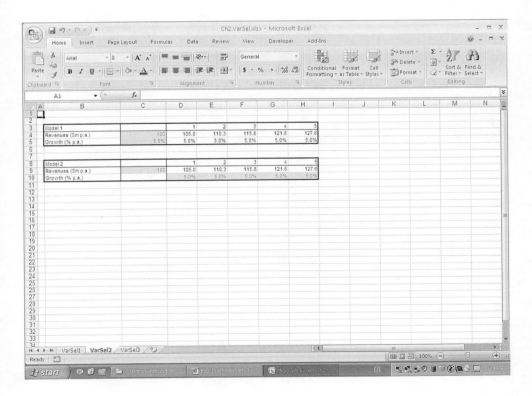

Figure 2.2

difference between them in terms of the ease in which sensitivity analysis can be conducted and in the nature of the implied assumptions behind such analysis. For Model 1, a change in the growth assumption would apply equally to every year, whereas for Model 2 the growth assumptions are independent of each other.

Model 1 will clearly more readily allow a simple sensitivity analysis. This is not to say that it is superior to Model 2; it may indeed be fairer to believe that the growth rates from year to year are independent of each other. The issue is that the appropriate model can only be selected by careful consideration of the sensitivities that one may need to conduct on the completed model, and the appropriateness of the scenarios generated.

In many practical situations a mixed approach can be used, i.e. where the growth rates in the early years are independent of each other, with the growth rate in later years assumed to be a single number. Such approaches may be suitable, for example, in financial statement and cash flow valuation models, where it may be desired not only to reflect some known information about the development of a business in the early years of a forecast, but also to be able to readily conduct a sensitivity analysis on the valuation as the long-term growth rate is varied.

Example: Variable Selection III

The file Ch2.VarSel.xlsx (VarSel3 worksheet) (Figure 2.3) shows a forecast of the volume of minerals extracted from a mine for a 10-year period. The first three years have

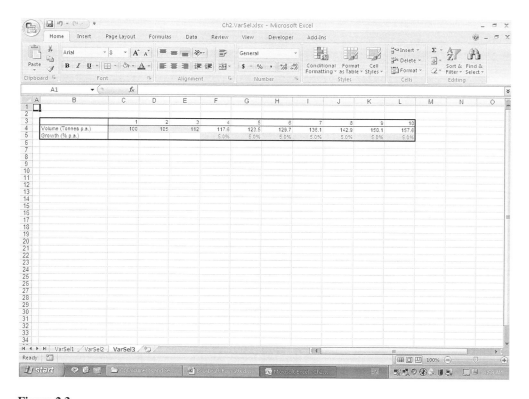

Figure 2.3

hard-coded volumes (corresponding to a base case expectation), and thereafter a growth rate assumption is used. The model may appear to be reasonable until one considers some of the sensitivities that may need to be conducted, and whether in these cases the model would reflect the reality of the real-world situation. For example, one could ask how an increase in year 1 volume would affect the volumes in subsequent years, some possibilities being:

- *The future volumes would remain unchanged.* This is the assumption implicit in the original model, corresponding to volumes from year to year being independent of each other.
- *The future volumes would increase.* If the increase in Year 1's volume is to reflect that the total volume of mineral resources is initially unknown, but the change in Year 1's volume reflects a resolution of that uncertainty, then presumably this would also increase the volume in future years.
- *The future volumes would decrease.* If the total amount of available mineral resources is known and fixed, then an increase in Year 1's volume would lead to a decrease in future volume (perhaps spread over several years).

The formulae within the model would of course need to reflect the reality of the actual situation, and would be very different in each case.

Hyper Sensitivity to a Variable

On occasion a model may be hypersensitive to an input variable. Examples include some models which use market share to predict sales (e.g. an assumption of 11% versus 10% market share will make a large difference to the result in absolute terms, although it may at first sight appear to be a small change), and in situations with high fixed costs with assumptions on capacity utilisation rates (e.g. for hotels or certain factories). Models which include the occurrence of rare events are also typically hypersensitive to input variables, as well as to the logical accuracy of the model.

As a general rule it is of course better to try to build models where there is no such hypersensitivity, but this is not always easy to achieve. In the case where hypersensitivity is present, in order to achieve an accurate model for decision-making purposes, one will need to invest more effort in several areas:

- Establishing accurate values for the base case assumptions.
- Ensuring that any sensitivity analysis is only considered and presented within the true range of variability that could apply to these inputs (and not over a larger range).

Level of Detail or Aggregation

It is a frequent belief that a good way to improve the accuracy of a model is to make it more detailed; that is, to add more variables (in particular by replacing some of the original variables by calculated quantities determined from a larger set of new inputs). This thought process often results from the idea that, generally, a static base case forecast (e.g. a budget) can indeed often be made more accurate by breaking down individual line items into detail, as this can help to ensure that relevant factors are considered explicitly.

On the other hand, from the perspective of a (dynamic) model (rather than what is essentially a database) there are potential (interrelated) drawbacks that arise as a model becomes more detailed:

- The model may be too detailed to address the questions that a user or decision-maker may wish to ask. For example, if a sales forecast were made by adding the individual forecasts for many products or regions, but the decision-maker wishes to know only the aggregate effect of the sales growth being different to the base value (but may not be particularly interested in the change in product mix that caused this), then the detailed model may not be able to address this question.
- The model may incorrectly reflect the relationships between the variables. The number of possible relationships grows as the number of variables increases. If the relationships are not captured correctly, then the detailed model is likely to be no more accurate than the aggregate model, especially when uncertainty of the output is to be considered.
- There is a greater chance of errors or unforeseen implicit assumptions in a more detailed model.
- The model may be hard to calibrate. If variables are chosen without regard to the availability of historic data (or to the ability to make sound judgements about the values of the variables), then the model may be less accurate. Particularly when uncertainty is considered, the lack of data may create a situation where the true possible range of values that a variable could take is hard to estimate, and so the potential variability in the model's output will be incorrectly assessed.

One may therefore consider that there is an optimum level of detail for every modelling situation, and the process of sensitivity analysis thinking can help to clarify this.

Example: Choices in Model Detail 1

The file Ch2.ModelDetail.xlsx (Detail1-Models1&2 worksheet) (Figure 2.4) shows two modelling possibilities for the cost of renovation for a set of 10 similar houses. It is believed that each house will cost $100 000 to renovate, resulting in a total budget of $1 000 000. Such a model could of course be implemented in various ways and with different levels of detail, such as:

- Model 1: Based on the costs of each house separately, e.g. 10 rows of an Excel worksheet.
- Model 2: Splitting the line item for each house into a line item for each of the (assumed) two floors in the house, where the costs of each are independently set. (Other ways in which a more detailed model could be built include breaking down the costs of each house into building costs, electrical costs, plastering costs, decorating costs, materials costs, etc.).

Of course, *a priori* neither of these models is better than the other; it is conceivable that there are situations where either of these would be the more appropriate. However, the decision between them could be facilitated by consideration of sensitivity and calibration issues. For example, let us assume that historic data suggests a cost of $100 000 per house, with a possible range from $80 000 to $120 000. Since the historic data contains no information about the range of cost for each floor, one may be tempted to consider that the appropriate range would be $40 000 to $60 000. However, if the model is built (as Model 2

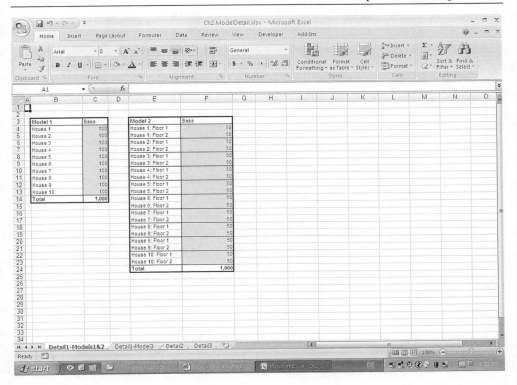

Figure 2.4

above) with independence between the costs of the floors, then this assumption on the range per floor would underestimate the true uncertainty. For example, although the worst case cost for each house is the same ($120 000), the likelihood of this outcome is implicitly less for the second model, e.g. the worst case for each input could crudely be considered to happen in one-third of cases, so that the worst case for each house in Model 2 would happen only in one-ninth of cases, compared to one-third for Model 1.

The file Ch2.ModelDetail.xlsx (Detail1-Model3 worksheet) (Figure 2.5) shows how a third model could be created, in which the cost of the second floor of each house is set to be equal to the costs of the first floor. The objective here is not to state that one or other of these models is preferable *per se*, but rather to highlight that the issues of calibration and sensitivity need to be considered when selecting between them.

Example: Choices in Model Detail 2

Another frequent modelling approach is to split large items into more detail, so that the inputs are of approximately equal magnitude. While there may be some general validity to this approach, the question of materiality of a variable can really only be answered by consideration of sensitivity analysis. Specifically, the absolute range of variability of any uncertain inputs, and the impact of such variability on the model's output must be considered.

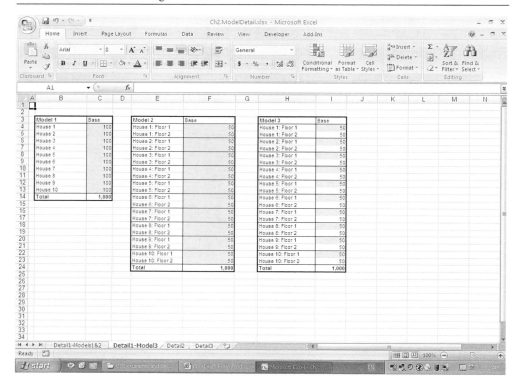

The spreadsheet shows the following tables:

Model 1	Base
House 1	100
House 2	100
House 3	100
House 4	100
House 5	100
House 6	100
House 7	100
House 8	100
House 9	100
House 10	100
Total	1,000

Model 2	Base
House 1: Floor 1	50
House 1: Floor 2	50
House 2: Floor 1	50
House 2: Floor 2	50
House 3: Floor 1	50
House 3: Floor 2	50
House 4: Floor 1	50
House 4: Floor 2	50
House 5: Floor 1	50
House 5: Floor 2	50
House 6: Floor 1	50
House 6: Floor 2	50
House 7: Floor 1	50
House 7: Floor 2	50
House 8: Floor 1	50
House 8: Floor 2	50
House 9: Floor 1	50
House 9: Floor 2	50
House 10: Floor 1	50
House 10: Floor 2	50
Total	1,000

Model 3	Base
House 1: Floor 1	50
House 1: Floor 2	50
House 2: Floor 1	50
House 2: Floor 2	50
House 3: Floor 1	50
House 3: Floor 2	50
House 4: Floor 1	50
House 4: Floor 2	50
House 5: Floor 1	50
House 5: Floor 2	50
House 6: Floor 1	50
House 6: Floor 2	50
House 7: Floor 1	50
House 7: Floor 2	50
House 8: Floor 1	50
House 8: Floor 2	50
House 9: Floor 1	50
House 9: Floor 2	50
House 10: Floor 1	50
House 10: Floor 2	50
Total	1,000

Figure 2.5

The file Ch2.ModelDetail.xlsx (Detail2 worksheet) (Figure 2.6) shows an example of the cost budget for two projects. The total cost in Model 1 would appear to be equally sensitive to all inputs, whereas in Model 2 it would appear to be most sensitive to cost item 1. Of course, such an analysis rests on the implicit assumption that the possible percentage change in each variable is of equal magnitude, and therefore larger variables would be more important. On the other hand, if, for Model 2, cost item 1 represents the cost of an outsourced service to be supplied at a guaranteed fixed price (but where there is still some uncertainty as to the costs for the other items), then cost item 1 would be the variable to which the model is least sensitive. In order words, the level of materiality of a variable (and hence the potential benefit of breaking it down into smaller subvariables) can only be defined and judged with reference to the range of values that the variable may take, in other words by consideration of sensitivity analysis issues.

Example: Choices in Model Detail 3

The file Ch2.ModelDetail.xlsx (Detail3 worksheet) (Figure 2.7) shows a revenue forecast conducted at two possible levels of detail (Model 1 at the aggregate level, and Model 2 at the level of individual products). Once again, the nature of the required sensitivity analysis can play a core role in the selection of the appropriate model. The two models will be very different in terms of the sensitivities that can readily be conducted, and each form of such

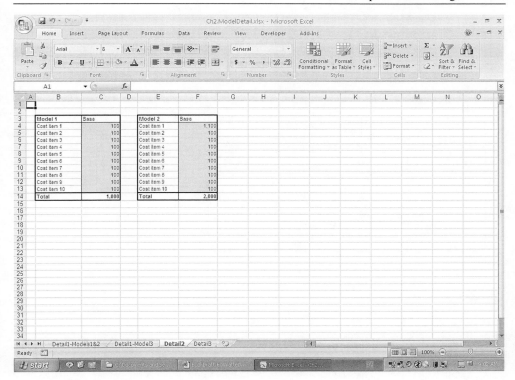

Figure 2.6

analysis may have different levels of relevance to the decision-maker. Model 1 will allow the user to test what-if? scenarios at the aggregate business level (e.g. what is the value of the business if sales growth is 3% p.a. rather than the forecast 5% p.a.?), whereas addressing such questions with Model 2 would be cumbersome. In other words, it could be that Model 2 is not only too detailed for the purposes at hand but may also hinder a simple analysis of the situation. Once again, this is not to say that one of the models is better *per se*, but rather that the choice between them can be facilitated by a consideration of the type of sensitivity analysis that will be conducted on the completed model.

Granularity of the Time Axis

Where models have a time component, it is important to consider the granularity of the time axis; for example, whether a model should be based on annual or quarterly periods. As a general rule, it is usually better to build the model at the most detailed level of time granularity for which results will be required. It is usually very cumbersome to take a model built in annual periods and attempt to derive quarterly or semi-annual quantities from it; not only will any growth over time mean that there is no simple and practical way to allocate figures across smaller time periods (e.g. dividing an annual figure by four to give quarterly figures will not capture the growth), but the results of a more granular model can be slightly

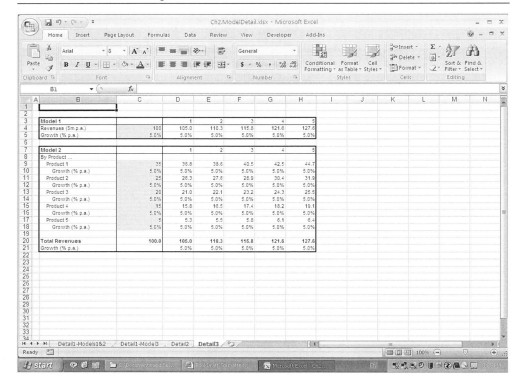

Figure 2.7

different to a more aggregate model in terms of factors such as interest earned on balance sheet cash.

MODEL STRUCTURE AND PLANNING

The structure of a model has a very important role in ensuring not only that it is easy for others to understand but also that it is less prone to errors. This section covers some key aspects of structure, including logical flow, compactness (including the use of multiple worksheets and workbooks), the use of circular references and the use of named ranges.

Logical Flow

For very small models (such as those consisting only of a few rows and columns) the logical flow is usually clear to a new user, or at least can be established quickly by cursory examination. For larger models, a clear logic flow is the key to allowing a third party to rapidly understand it.

The basic principles of good flow are that, ideally:

• The logic should follow a model-as-you-read approach (in other words a left-to-right and top-to-bottom flow).

- There should be a clear (physical) separation of the inputs, calculations and outputs. In other words, a model should consist of input cells (containing numbers only, and no formulae) and calculations and outputs (containing formulae only, and no numbers). The only mixed formulae (if any) should be those that contain universal conversion factors or fixed parameters (such as thousands to millions, pounds to kilograms, miles to kilometres, etc.).

- The calculations should be set up in a modular fashion, with related items grouped close together and in substructures. Each module should be essentially self-contained as far as possible (although typically there will be some formula references (rather like inputs and outputs) to other substructures). In some cases, it may be appropriate to place model inputs locally to where they will actually be used (i.e. within a substructure of the model). A model set up in this way will have an audit trail through it that is as short as possible.

- There should be no change in the formulae in contiguous cells without this being clearly indicated (e.g. by labelling, colour-coding, the use of borders, and comments).

- Appropriate formatting of specific cells and regions should be used to highlight the inputs and key outputs, and to reinforce visually the logical flow (see later for more on formatting).

In many practical situations these principles are not adhered to. This is seldom because the modeller is unaware of their benefits but rather because of the *ad hoc* fashion in which models are frequently developed. Very often, logical structures have been added that may not have originally been foreseen, or an existing model is used and adapted in some way to deal with a new situation (rather than being built from scratch in a single well-planned step). The result is that once an initial model has been built, insufficient attention is subsequently paid to these issues, even as major changes or more detail or functionality is added. Invariably, the flow of such models can be improved rapidly (and the model made more transparent) by a few well-selected cut-and-paste operations to place related logical items closer together, and to improve the formatting to reinforce the structural aspects of the model.

On the other hand, these idealised principles may not be fully achievable in practice:

- Where a time-series forecast is to be produced (such as revenues being calculated along a row of a worksheet by applying an assumed annual growth rate to prior year figures), the historic growth rates may be calculated in the cells immediately below the historic revenue figures, with the same row used for the forecast assumptions of the growth rate. The formulae for the forecast revenue will then be calculated by reference to an assumption below it (rather than only from items above it, as the principle would suggest). The alternative would be to use a separate row for the historic growth figures (placed below the revenue line) than for the forecast growth assumptions (placed above the revenue line). In most practical situations this would probably result in a larger and more confusing model.

- In some modelling situations the relationships between the variables mean that some calculations are required elsewhere before the formulae in the current area can be calculated (especially financial statement models, where, for example, depreciation is generally required both for the Income Statement and for the Balance Sheet calculations). In these cases it may not be possible to follow the idealised logical flow (at least without creating much larger models with highly repetitive structures).

- In many models, it can be easier for the user to understand if it is designed in a modular fashion, with the inputs placed locally to where they will actually be used. This can apply to financial statement and valuation models, for example. In these cases the use of an appropriate formatting to highlight the inputs is especially important. In other words, the inputs are visually separate from the calculations but are not grouped in a separate consolidated input area (though they will generally be in a separate area of each module).

- A model (especially a large one) may contain a summary area at the top (or possibly in a separate worksheet). This could contain key outputs and their sensitivities (e.g. using **Data Tables**; see later). The structure may then be more like: Summary–Inputs–Calculations (where the Outputs are a subset of the Calculations).
- In models with conversion factors (e.g. years to months) or other parameters (i.e. constants that should not be changed), it is arguably acceptable to include such constants within the formulae, rather than treating them as inputs in a separate cell.

Compactness

As a general rule, a model should be structured in a way that is as compact as possible. Compactness should not be interpreted purely in terms of the size of the model, though it is closely related. The principle underlying compact models is that items which are logically related are kept as close together as possible. A compact model can be thought of as one where the total length of all links between all items (if every item were joined to all its precedents and dependents with a line) is as short as possible, and the audit trail is minimised.

Multiple Worksheet Models

Many models are structured over several worksheets (such as when a separate worksheet is used for each of the Income Statement, Balance Sheet and Cash Flow Statement). Such structures may be argued to ease navigation and to facilitate the printing of parts of the model. However, a case can also be made (to which the author strongly subscribes) to aim to build each model in a single worksheet, or at least in as few worksheets as possible:

- The use of many worksheets results in less compactness; by separating items that are closely related, the logical flow becomes fragmented.
- The formula references between worksheets can be hard to follow. Not only do the formulae look larger and more complex due to the explicit presence of worksheet names, but also the auditing of even basic logical paths requires moving between worksheets, which is time-consuming and often confusing.
- Such models are more error-prone, due to the less transparent formulae and longer audit trails. For example, a common mistake is to misalign the year numbers across worksheets, particularly if it is intended in any case to build a time delay into the model (such as the delay between declaring and paying a dividend).
- Where a model is built in a single or a few worksheets, the naming of key areas (e.g. the core outputs) can aid navigation and the printing of parts of it (see later).

The main cases where the use of several worksheets may nevertheless make sense are:

- Where model inputs are derived through calculations, statistical routines or databases. In such cases, the derivation of the input values may be considered as separate to the actual model.

- Where certain inputs are taken from a linked workbook, in which case the links generally should be contained in a separate worksheet (see later).
- Where it is desired to hide confidential data (see later).

Linked Workbooks

Models which are built with linked workbooks are inherently prone to errors (in addition, they suffer from similar disadvantages to those of multiple worksheet models). When the destination workbook is not open, structural changes made to a source workbook (such as the addition or deletion of rows or columns, or changes to names of the workbook or of a worksheet) will not be reflected in the corresponding formulae in the (closed) destination workbook. Unintended consequences and errors can then arise without warning.

When working with a destination workbook, one has no way of knowing whether such changes to a source workbook have been made or not, and therefore of knowing whether the linked cells in the destination workbook refer to the correct cells or not. Since links between open workbooks are, by default, updated automatically, several cases may arise:

- *The source workbook is open.* In this case the linked values used in the destination workbook will be updated automatically (i.e. without any warning message), and would contain values taken from the original (potentially incorrect) cell references in the source workbook.
- *The source workbook is not open.* In this case, a warning of the presence of links is provided, but the fundamental problem of confidence in the links remains, and so any update of the values could lead to unforeseeable errors.

As a general rule, it is therefore best to avoid building models with linked workbooks wherever possible.

On the other hand, where the ownership of several workbooks lies in different hands, then links between them may be unavoidable. Such cases may arise in practice where:

- The source workbook contains standardised data or forecasts that are centrally produced and must be used as the basis for all work by several analysts.
- When the output of a set of individual analysts is collected into a central workbook as a reference database.

The most reliable way to deal with circumstances of fragmented ownership resulting in multiple workbooks is to use mirror worksheets. The objective is to create indirect links so that the owner of each workbook can work independently without having to consider other workbooks. This involves:

- Building destination workbooks so that the links to any source workbooks are contained in a separate (mirror) worksheet of the destination workbook (one such worksheet is required for every source workbook referenced). Any calculations in the destination workbook that require these values should be conducted by taking the required values using cell references to the relevant cells in this worksheet of the destination workbook.
- Building source workbooks so that they contain a copy of these mirror worksheets, whose values are populated by references to the appropriate cells in the other worksheets of the source workbook.

- Making no structural changes to any of these mirror worksheets once they have been created. However, changes to the other parts of the source and destination workbooks can be made independently by the respective owners.
- Updating the values automatically by opening both workbooks (or all source workbooks and the destination workbook if there are several source workbooks).

Another possibility to deal with fragmented ownership is to ensure that all data that is to be taken from a source workbook is done by using named ranges in the source workbook. In this case the correct values would be read into the destination workbook when it is opened.

(As mentioned in the section on Model Auditing, when working with a model with links, one may choose to rebuild or restructure it into a single workbook; formulae containing such links contain a [in the name of the linked workbook, and so can be found using **Home/Find & Select** (or **CTRL+F** or **Edit/Find** in Excel 2003), by searching for this symbol. To avoid finding occurrences when the bracket is used within text labels, use the **Options** submenu and in the **Look in** box select **Formulas**. Links can also sometimes be created through the use of named ranges. **Data/Edit Links** (**Edit/Links** in Excel 2003) can also be used.)

Named Ranges

The use of named ranges is a topic for which there is a wide range of opinions among modellers. Some consider that their intensive use in almost all situations should be considered as best practice, whereas others tend to think that they should essentially be avoided. In this section, we describe key aspects and the advantages and disadvantages of their use, and then provide some examples. It is fair to say that the improved capabilities to manage named ranges in Excel 2007 both eases their use and mitigates some of their potential disadvantages compared to earlier versions of Excel.

Uses and Benefits

In the right circumstances, the use of named ranges can help to create a transparent and robust model. This is especially true where the structure, variables and logic of the situation are precisely understood and clearly defined from early in the modelling process. In this case, the model-building process is essentially one of implementation of an algorithm; modellers who are strong proponents of the wide use of named ranges often implicitly have such an algorithmic (or programming) perspective in mind.

Names can be entered using **Formulas/Name Manager** (**Insert/Name Define** in Excel 2003) or **CTRL+F3**, or in the **Name Box**. (In general, the use of the **Name Box** is quick but does suffer from some disadvantages mentioned below.) Names can have a scope which is either a worksheet or the workbook. The scope of a name is the region of the workbook in which it does not need to be qualified to use it. In general, names that are needed in formula calculations on more than one worksheet should have a workbook scope (if a worksheet scoped named is required in another worksheet it needs to be referred to with the worksheet name as a qualifier, e.g. Sheet1!RangeName). The workbook scope is the default, and would apply when the **Name Box** is used to implement the names. When creating a name with the **Name Manager** in Excel 2007, the scope can be set using the drop-down box (in Excel 2003 a worksheet-scoped name must be created by typing the qualifier (such as Sheet1!RangeName) when the name is being created).

Situations in which the use of named ranges is generally helpful include:

- To quickly navigate, or to print key areas of the model. If names are given to important areas, then **F5** (the short-cut for **Home/Find and Select/Go To**) or the drop-down **Name Box** can be used to move around the model. Ranges can be printed by use of the relevant name in the **Print Area** of the **Sheet** tab of the **Page Setup** menu (under **Page Layout** and then using the **Page Setup** dialog box launcher to go to the **Sheet** tab, or **File/Page Setup** in Excel 2003).
- To simplify the development and presentation of formulae by making them more descriptive than if cell references were used. This can result in increased transparency and reduced errors. When creating a formula in the **Formula Bar**, after typing = the **F3** key (or **Formulas/Use in Formula** or **Insert/Name/Paste** in Excel 2003) can be used to see a list of names that can be inserted. The names shown are those whose scope is the current worksheet or the workbook, but not other worksheets (the same applies to the list of names visible when using the **Name Box**). This can be a more robust way to create formulae than using cell references, where typing or mouse-pointing errors are more likely to occur.
- To simplify database formulae. In particular the use of dynamic or flexible ranges that adjust as data is added or deleted to an existing database can be convenient in some cases.
- To create reusable code that can be copied between models. For example, a formula (such as ProfitOp=Sales−CostsOp−Depn) could be copied from an existing model to a new one, and the range associated with each name then redefined within the new model.
- To link workbooks by naming ranges in source workbooks that are required in a destination workbook. This can help to ensure that the correct links are maintained even if changes are made to the source workbook when the destination workbook is not open (see the earlier section on linked workbooks, where the use of mirror structures is also discussed in this context).
- To create flexible and robust VBA code (see Chapter 6).

Some features to bear in mind when using names include:

- If a named range refers not to a single cell but to a row (or part of a row), then the use of that name in a formula will pick out the value of the element of the range that is in the same column as the one in which the formula is being created. For example, if a name refers to cells A1:A5, then a formula in cell C3 that uses that name will use the value from cell A3. A formula made using several named ranges (such a Profit=Revenue−Cost) will therefore pick up the elements in the corresponding columns for each name. (A **#VALUE!** error message will appear if the current column does not correspond to one in which the named range has an element.) Similar comments apply to a range that consists of a column (or part of a column).
- When using functions with range arguments, it must be borne in mind that **SUM**(Range1, Range2) will sum all the elements of both the ranges, and **MIN**(Range1, Range2) will return the minimum value in both ranges. On the other hand, **SUM**(+Range1, +Range2) and **MIN**(+Range1, +Range2) will refer to the sum and minimum of the two values in the corresponding cells of each range; this is due to arithmetical precedence rules, where the presence of the addition operator forces the individual elements of each range to be picked out. Similar comments apply when using other Excel functions.

- If formulae have been created with cell references that correspond to named ranges rather than with the names (e.g. if the names have been defined after the formulae were created) then the formulae can be rewritten using these names using **Formulas/Define Name/Apply Names** (or **Insert/Name/Apply** in Excel 2003).
- The **Name Manager** can be used to edit, change or delete names. Good practice would suggest that unnecessary or redundant names should be deleted. The use of the **Name Box** to change a name (rename the same range) is generally not recommended as it will result in the original name being retained. (The deletion of all the named ranges in an Excel 2003 workbook is cumbersome, as the dialog box does not allow the use of the **CTRL** key to select multiple names. In this case a fairly simple way to delete all the names is to use VBA code; an example is provided in Chapter 6.)
- Multiple named ranges may be combined as a single name by creating a name (e.g. FinancialStatements) and defining it using the **Refers to** box to list the names of the components separated by a comma but no spaces (e.g. IS,BS,CFS).
- The list of names can be pasted into Excel for reference and documentation purposes by using **F3** and selecting **Paste List** (or **Use in Formula/Paste Names** or in Excel 2003 **Insert/Name/Paste/Paste List**). The names can also be seen from the drop-down names in the **Name Box**. Such techniques can be useful to audit and document a model, to see links to other workbooks and to locate whether a range has been given multiple names (e.g. the pasted list can be sorted using the location of the name as a key, so that names with the same location will be shown next to each other, and the sorted list can be inspected or its elements more formally compared with a formula to check whether consecutive elements are the same as each other). It should not be forgotten that the names shown and pasted are only those whose scope is either the workbook or the current worksheet (but not other worksheets), so that this procedure may need to be repeated in other worksheets. The use of a **SPACE** between the names of a column and row range will return the value of the cell in which these ranges intersect (or a **#NULL!** error if the ranges do not intersect).
- The use of names can help to define ranges which are dynamic, i.e. whose size automatically adjusts according to the size of the data set. However, such names will not be displayed on the drop-down **Name Box**, unlike when using the **Name Manager**.
- Sometimes it is necessary to remove names by replacing the names used in formula with the cell references. This is a little awkward, but can be achieved by selecting **Office/Excel Options/Advanced** and under the **Lotus compatibility Settings for**, checking the **Transition formula entry** box (under **Tools/Options/Transition** in Excel 2003). If one then edits the cell (or cells) in question (or uses **F2**), pressing **ENTER** after editing each cell, and then unchecks the **Transition formula entry** box, then the formula in question will show cell references.

The file Ch2.NamedRanges.Basic.xlsx (Basics worksheet) (Figure 2.8) shows a demonstration of some of these points.

Potential Disadvantages

There are nevertheless some potential disadvantages in using named ranges, including:

- Many modellers or clients of models are not familiar with their use, and may find it difficult to understand the model.

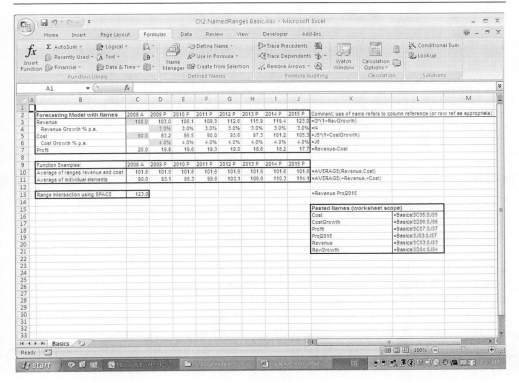

Figure 2.8

- Modelling processes in practice frequently take place in an *ad hoc* fashion. Indeed one of the potential powerful properties of the Excel environment is the flexibility to experiment with different approaches, and to rapidly adapt or extend an existing model. In such cases, the use of named ranges too early in the modelling process can lose the focus on the experimental and exploratory aspects, and therefore be a hindrance.
- The use of named ranges will generally result in a model that contains very many names. In many cases, the set of names that results is poorly structured and uncoordinated, thus negating the benefits, and possibly resulting in a less transparent and more error-prone model. Sufficient attention needs to be given to ensure a careful choice of well-structured and meaningful names, and there may be times where a significant number of names may need to be renamed to maintain clarity.
- The model may give a false impression of the degree to which it is general or flexible. For example where a named range refers to fixed cell references, its range will often need to be extended if new data is added (e.g. a new row of data is added at the end of a database). The need to do this may be less evident to the user who is focusing on formulae with names rather than those built with cell references.
- As mentioned above, **MIN**(Range1,Range2) will refer to the minimum value in both ranges, whereas **MIN**(+Range1,+Range2) will be needed to refer to the minimum of the two values in the corresponding area (e.g. column) of each range. This may be confusing

to some users and result in unforeseen errors that are not immediately apparent (the incorrect values shown will generally appear sensible within the context).
• In Excel 2003 it is possible to create duplicate names by accident, resulting in a model that is complex to audit. For example, the copying of a worksheet containing names would create a new worksheet with names with the same description but of only worksheet scope. Similarly, the copying of worksheets containing named ranges between workbooks may have created links between the workbooks which were unintended and difficult to detect. These problems have largely been overcome with the improved name management tools in Excel 2007.

Choosing Names

The choice of names is important to retain transparency of the model. A large set of poorly planned and executed names will likely create a situation that is confusing, and add complexity. A few points are worthy of consideration:

• Names should ideally reflect the type or role of a variable, as well as any relevant structural and hierarchical aspects (e.g. CostFixedProdOhd could be used to represent the production overhead component of fixed cost).
• There are certain restrictions on the choice of names. For example, names must not contain spaces or &, and cell addresses are not allowed (such as Q1, Q2, YR1, YR2, DCF3, NPV6, etc.). Underscores are allowed, although their use can make names more difficult to read, and generally it is preferable instead to use a mix of small and capital letters to break up the name into components.
• The use of the **Create Names from Selection** menu (or **Create Names** in Excel 2003) to define the names from the adjacent labels is possible, but in many cases is likely to lead to inappropriate names; typically the text labels or descriptions of cells do not represent the full or appropriate structure and hierarchy of names.

Example: Implementing the Black–Scholes Formula

The implementation of the Black–Scholes formula for the value of a European option is a good example of where it would generally be beneficial to use named ranges. In this case their use can simplify the development and presentation of otherwise complex-looking formulae. The formulae are well established and the required variables and calculations are clearly known before the model is built.

There are six input variables (sometimes thought of as three variables and three parameters): S (the current price of the underlying asset), E (the future exercise price at expiry of the option), τ (the time to expiry, or $T - t$ where t is the current time and T the time of expiry), σ (the volatility of the return of the asset), r (the risk-free interest rate) and D (the constant dividend yield).

The formulae for call and put options are usually expressed in terms of intermediate calculations, as follows:

$$C = S\,e^{-D\tau}N(d_1) - E\,e^{-r\tau}N(d_2)$$
$$P = -S\,e^{-D\tau}N(-d_1) + E\,e^{-r\tau}N(-d_2)$$

where:

$$d_1 = \frac{\left[LN\left(\frac{S}{E}\right) + \left[r - D + \frac{\sigma^2}{2}\right]\tau\right]}{\sigma\sqrt{\tau}}$$

$$d_2 = \frac{\left[LN\left(\frac{S}{E}\right) + \left[r - D - \frac{\sigma^2}{2}\right]\tau\right]}{\sigma\sqrt{\tau}} = d_1 - \sigma\sqrt{\tau}$$

$$\tau = T - t$$

and

$$N(x) = \frac{1}{\sqrt{2\pi}} \int_{-\infty}^{x} e^{-\frac{\xi^2}{2}} \, d\xi$$

is the cumulative Normal distribution.

Note that in some implementations, an indicator of the option type is set (positive 1 for a call, negative 1 for a put). The multiplication of the quantities, S, E, d_1 and d_2 by this indicator at the appropriate place in the calculation allows the same formula for the call to be used as for the put, but with this additional indicator as a variable. This is not implemented in this example, but is used in some examples in Chapter 5 and Chapter 6.

The file Ch2.NamedRanges.BS.xlsx (BSFormula worksheet) (Figure 2.9) shows a demonstration of some of these points.

Example: Working with Databases and Dynamic Ranges

When working with database and criteria ranges (see examples in Chapter 1) it can be useful to create dynamic named ranges, i.e. which adjust automatically according to the data set. The **OFFSET** function can be used to do so when using the **Formulas/Name Manager**.

The file Ch2.NamedRanges.Dynamic.xlsx (DynRanges worksheet) (Figure 2.10) shows an example. The ranges named SalesForecastDatabase and SalesCriteria will update to include any new rows of data that are added, provided that such rows are contiguous to the existing data, and that there are no empty rows within the database or criteria range.

Circular References

Circular references arise when the value in a cell requires the value of another cell to be known, but where this value itself requires the first value to be known. A circular reference can arise either by mistake or as an intentional modelling choice.

Assuming that Excel is set on the **Automatic** calculation method (which is the default, but can be changed under **Office/Excel Options/Formulas/Calculation Options** or **Formulas/Calculation Options**; or **Tools/Options/Calculations** in Excel 2003), the presence of a circular reference will be immediately clear: a warning dialog and **Help** menu will appear as soon as the formula creating the circularity is entered. In addition, formulae that are on the circular path will, when evaluated, return zero (one can see this by editing such a cell and pressing **RETURN**).

Where the circularity is unintentional, the model must of course be corrected. Typical causes of such circularities include:

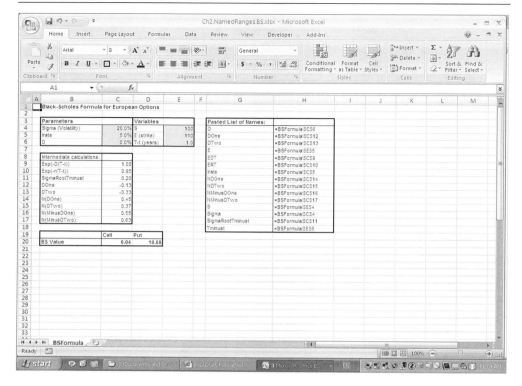

Figure 2.9

- Errors in selecting or typing cell references, resulting in self-referencing formulae such as **B6=SUM (B4:B6)**.
- A model that has a poor logical flow and does not follow the left-to-right and top-to-bottom principle. In such cases a calculation towards the top of the model may refer to a later calculation, which itself require the results of the initial one. In more complex cases, the cause of the circularity can be difficult to identify and it may be necessary (and will in any case often be helpful) to restructure and improve the logical flow in order to identify and eliminate the circularity.

Circularities can also be used as an intentional modelling choice. Examples include:

- The calculation of depreciation, interest and tax items in financial statement models. For example, in interest calculations, one may choose to calculate the cash at period end by including the interest earned during the period, which itself is calculated with reference to the average cash balance, which itself depends on the ending cash.
- In a profit share agreement, where the profit share is determined from the net profit, but the net profit is itself calculated after subtracting the profit share from the gross profit.

Where a model contains circularities, Excel must be set to use an iterative technique to attempt to find stable values of the variables in the model (i.e. values that are unchanged by

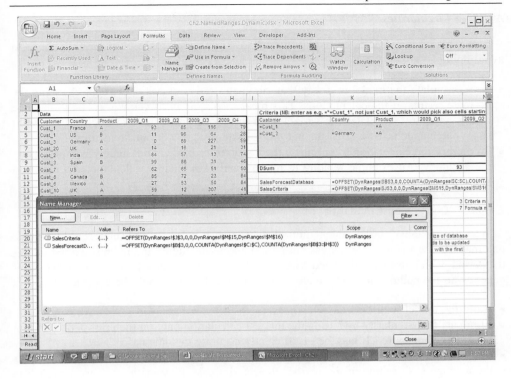

Figure 2.10

further iteration). This is done by selecting **Enable iterative calculation** (under **Office/Excel Options/Formulas/Calculation Options**).

Advantages and Disadvantages

The main arguments for the intentional use of circularities revolve around the case that their use is either more accurate or is unavoidable. On the other hand, there are several reasons to argue that the use of circularities should be avoided wherever possible:

- Models containing circularities may be confusing to others.
- It cannot generally be known in advance whether the circularity is convergent. In theory, a circular reference may be convergent with a unique solution, convergent but with multiple solutions, divergent, or floating (neither convergent nor divergent). While the presence of a divergent circular reference will be clear, the presence of a floating one may not be, and as a result the model may contain unintended errors.
- The model may calculate more slowly due to the iterations required (especially if there is a **Data Table** in the model).
- It is usually possible to avoid the use of circularities while either retaining exactly the same output or accepting only minor changes to the output values.

Avoiding Circularities

Where a model may appear to require the use of circular references, the basic methods to avoid doing so are:

- To reformulate the model in a way that eliminates the circularities without changing the ultimate results of the calculations. This means isolating each variable on only one side of the equation that relates the variables. In the above profit share example, if the profit share percentage is 10%, then the net profit is simply gross profit divided by 1.1.
- To modify the calculation to eliminate the circularities but without unduly compromising the accuracy. An example relating to interest and cash balance calculations is provided below.

Example: Convergent Circularities

As mentioned above, in the calculation of ending cash balances and interest calculations, one may choose to calculate the cash at period end by including the interest earned during the period, which itself is calculated with reference to the average cash balance, which itself depends on the ending cash. There are several approaches that could be considered:

- Build the model with circular references.
- Eliminate the circularity by basing the interest calculation only on the prior period ending balances. This approach may be insufficiently accurate in some cases.
- Eliminate the circularity by basing the interest on the prior period ending balances plus the average cash inflow in the period (the interim cash flow method). This approach is almost always sufficiently accurate.

The file Ch2.CircRef.Conv.Int.xlsx (Figure 2.11) shows the results when each of these methods is used in a simple example (the iterative method is allowed to converge to within a tolerance of 0.001). As is perhaps to be expected in this context, the resulting circular reference is convergent (to a unique value). Although the closing balance for the prior-period (or starting cash) method is fairly different, the circular reference method produces a result that is only marginally different to the interim cash flow method. In addition, the circular reference method in fact makes the implied assumption that interest is earned continually throughout the period, and of course this assumption may be unrealistic, so that the method is in any case not necessarily more accurate. Generally speaking, in situations where a circular reference is uniquely convergent, such convergence will also happen quite quickly. In this example, the first iteration of the iterative method is largely equivalent to the use of the interim cash flow method, and hence the results are similar (the effect of each iteration of an iterative method can be observed by setting the number of iterations to 1, and then pressing **F9** to recalculate the model and perform the iterative calculation).

Example: Divergent Circularities

Many unintentional circular references will be either divergent or floating. A formula such as **B6=SUM(B4:B6),** where cells **B4** and **B5** contain some non-zero values, will generally result in a divergent reference, as each iteration will add the initial total to the new value. Since only a finite number of iterations is possible (the default is usually 100), the numbers displayed may not be obviously wrong.

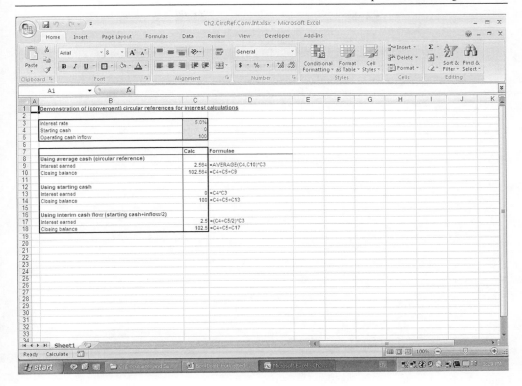

Figure 2.11

The file Ch2.CircRef.DivSum.xlsx (Figure 2.12) provides a simple example. The workbook is set to the iterative calculation method (so no circular reference message appears). The pressing of the **F9** key will result in 100 iterations being conducted, so that 300 is added to the sum each time this is done.

Example: Floating Circularities

Whereas in many cases the presence of a divergent circularity may be suspected due to unexpectedly large or unrealistic values appearing, the presence of floating circular references is likely to be less clear. Such a reference is one that neither converges nor diverges but follows a sequence of values that may repeat at some point. The potential presence of floating circularities is perhaps the strongest argument against the intentional use of any circularities in a model.

The file Ch2.CircRef.Floating.xlsx (Model 1 and Model 2 worksheets) shows an example of a budget which aggregates the cash inflows from three projects and nets them against the cash outflows from three other projects (it is implicitly assumed that these inflows and outflows are the results of other calculations not shown here). The objective is to work out the level of surplus cash that could be withdrawn from the overall portfolio in the first period under the condition that the ending cash balance at any point in time is always non-negative. Model 1 (Figure 2.13) provides a reference point that calculates the minimum cash balances on the assumption that no cash is withdrawn.

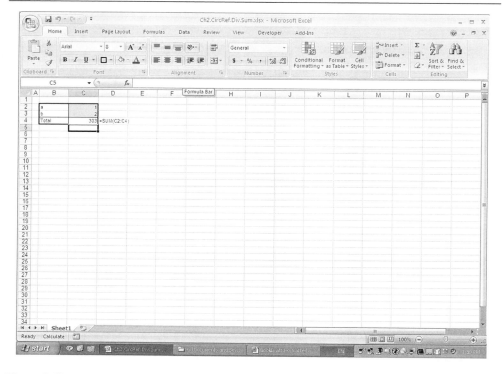

Figure 2.12

In Model 2 (Figure 2.14), it is assumed that at the beginning of the first period an amount of cash is extracted equal to the minimum cash balance over all future periods. The workbook has already been set to the iterative calculation method to deal with the circular reference that arises. The repeated use of **F9** shows that the reference neither converges nor diverges (intuitively: a large amount of cash removed at one iteration will lead to a low cash balance and so only a low level of cash can be removed at the next iteration, which will result in a larger balance, so that more can be removed at the subsequent iteration, and so on). The stable value that is reported depends on the number of iterations used.

MODEL BUILDING

In this section, we cover some principles and techniques that can be applied to the model building process. These include the use of formatting and comments, the use of basic sensitivity analysis techniques to create robust models, and tools to restrict use and protect models.

Formatting and Comments

General Guidelines

The use of appropriate formatting of specific cells or regions (such as the inputs and key outputs) is a powerful tool to reinforce the logic, flow and structure, and hence make the

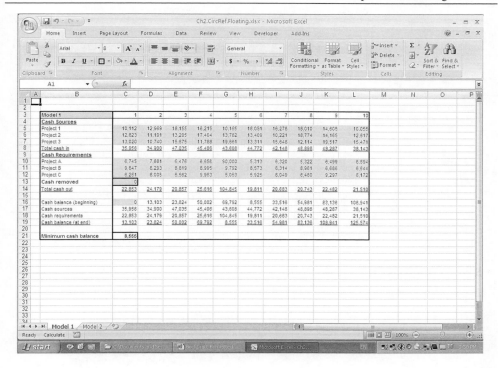

Figure 2.13

model easier to understand. Similarly, improving the formatting of a model is often the single most effective way to rapidly increase its transparency, whereas making structural changes (such as the regrouping of items to minimise the auditing paths), while potentially very effective, generally requires much more work.

The core objectives of formatting are generally:

- To ensure that inputs are clearly distinguished from calculations, and that key outputs are highlighted.
- To distinguish or visually separate different areas, for example, by placing borders around each main calculation module.
- To display values with an appropriate number of decimal places (the significant figures rule). Frequently, too many decimal points are used, which creates a visually overwhelming situation. On occasion, too few decimal points are used, especially for percentage quantities (such as growth rates), in which case it may appear that a calculated quantity of this nature does not vary as some model inputs are changed (e.g. where a cell containing the value 4.6% has been formatted so that it displays 5%, the cell would still show 5% if the value actually changes to 5.2%).
- To format, in a consistent manner, numbers that are of the same type and order of magnitude (e.g. to either always or never use commas to separate 000s).

On occasion it may be desired to use currency formatting for financial quantities, so that, for example, the $ or € symbol is displayed in the cell. To a large extent the use, or not,

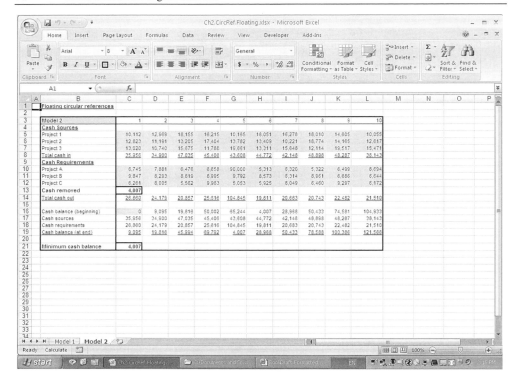

Figure 2.14

of such tools is a personal preference; one disadvantage of doing so is that the display can be compromised, especially when a model is projected onto a screen, printed, faxed or photocopied.

Key tools include the use of:

- Colour-coding and shading.
- Borders and underlining.
- Bold text.
- Comments.
- The **Format Paintbrush** to copy the format of an initially selected range to another range (double-clicking on the paintbrush will keep it activated so that the format can be applied to several ranges in succession, following which it can be deactivated by clicking on it).
- The short-cut **CTRL+1** to bring one directly to the cell-formatting menu.

Conditional and Custom Formatting

Conditional formatting of cells (**Home/Conditional Formatting**, or **Format/Conditional Formatting** in Excel 2003) has a number of uses, such as:

- To highlight cells that contain an error (such as **#DIV0!, #N/A, #VALUE**, etc.). This can be achieved using **Manage Rules/New Rule**, then under **Format only cells that contain** setting the rule description to **Format only cells with** and selecting **errors** (and then setting the desired format using the **Format** button).

- To highlight cells that contain a non-zero value, such as might occur if a cross-check calculation that should evaluate to zero detects an error. Such cells can be highlighted using a similar procedure to the above, but under **Format only cells with** selecting **Cell Value** is **not equal to** zero.
- To highlight cells according to the evaluation of a formula. For example, cells that contain an error can be highlighted by using the rule type **Use a formula to determine which cells to format** and then setting the formula to be **=ISERROR(cell reference)**. (In Excel 2003 this can be implemented by setting the condition to be **Formula is** and using the formula **=ISERROR(cell reference)** in the data entry box.) Similarly, alternate rows of a worksheet can be highlighted by setting the formula **=MOD(ROW(),2)=1** in the data entry box.

Custom formatting of cells allows the creation of bespoke formatting (as well as containing some predefined formats). The menu is accessible under **Home/Number** (using the **Show** icon to bring up the **Format Cells** dialog and choosing the **Custom** category; or **CTRL+1** can be used to show the **Format Cells** menu. In Excel 2003 this is directly visible under **Format/Cells**). New formats can be created by direct typing in the **Type** dialog box, or selecting and modifying one of the existing formats. Examples of possible uses include:

- To display negative numbers in red and with brackets (and with comma separators for thousands and one decimal place use **#,##0.0_);[Red](#,##0.0)**. To simply display negative numbers in brackets (and to one decimal place) use the type **0.0,,;(0.0,,)**.
- To display as thousands values that are actually in millions, create the type **0,** (the comma indicates that the value is divided by 1000 once for display terms). Similarly, the type **0.0,,** could be used to display millions as units with one decimal place (two commas to divide by a million).
- To format a number so that the word "years" appears after it, create the type **0 "years"** in the **Type** dialog box. Other words can also be used ("months", etc.).

A disadvantage of conditional and custom formatting is that their use is not directly visible, so that the ready understanding of the model by others could be partially compromised. Cells that contain conditional formatting can, however, be found using **Home/Conditional Formatting/Manage Rules** (where one then selects to look for all rules in **This Worksheet**) or selected under **Home/Find and Select/Conditional Formatting** or using the **Go To Special** (**F5 Special**) menu.

The Use of Comments

It is usually helpful to the user if there is adequate description and documentation within the model, especially relating to any aspects that could initially appear complex or unintuitive. Comments or other text may be created in a variety of ways including:

- Writing general notes as regular text.
- Making a comment relating to a specific cell in a comment box (**Review/Edit Comment** menu or right-clicking on the cell to insert a comment, or **Insert/Comment** in Excel 2003).

- Placing a comment within a formula using the **ISTEXT** function, such as =**105*ISTEXT** (**"data from 2007"**); the **ISTEXT** function will evaluate to 1 (**TRUE**) since there is text within its arguments. (The **ISNUMBER** function can also be used with an addition operator, as it will evaluate to 0 when its argument is text.)

One of the main challenges in using comments is to ensure that they are up to date. It is easy to forget to update comments when a formula or the input data has changed. Some techniques that can help in the process of keeping comments up to date include:

- Using the **Review/Show All Comments** menu (**View/Comments** in Excel 2003) (or the equivalent toolbar short-cut) to show (or hide) all comments, and the **Reviewing Toolbar** to move between them. This should be done regularly, and as a minimum as a last step before any model is finalised.
- Printing the comments using **Page Layout/Page Setup/Sheet** (in Excel 2003: **File/Page Setup/Sheet**) and under **Comments** selecting whether to print comments at the end of the worksheet or as they appear.

Creating Robust Formulae

It is probably fair to say that the vast majority of models have formulae that contain mistakes. Mistakes are generally easy to detect either where an error message is displayed or where the results are of a different order of magnitude to those expected. However, where the calculations are in fact wrong, but return results of the appropriate order of magnitude, then mistakes can be harder to detect. Similarly, mistakes can be masked by the frequent situation where the calculations work correctly for the base case but are invalid with different input values; this can arise especially where the model contains formulae with conditional statements (**IF, MAX**) or where complex embedded formulae are used. In addition, some models may only be valid when certain input variables are restricted to a range, and often this is insufficiently documented.

Simple Formulae

Most simple formulae (for example, those which conduct arithmetical operations based on the values of two or three other variables), can be created without difficulty. On occasion mistakes can arise, such as using the wrong cell references. The core aspects of ensuring that simple formulae are implemented correctly involve:

- Using the mouse to select cells (rather than typing the cell references).
- Editing the formulae in the **Formula Bar** (or **F2** key) to highlight the cells involved in a calculation.
- Labelling variables clearly, so that cell reference mistakes are not made by referring to a similar but incorrect variable (e.g. sales growth for the wrong business unit).
- Using a common structure in different parts of the model, e.g. the same column for a specific year in multiple worksheet models, or the same description and order for several (e.g. row) labels when they are to be repeated at several places in the model.
- Using formulae for a particular variable which are consistent in adjacent cells (e.g. in adjacent cells of a row where each column refers to a different year). In some cases, the

changing of formulae is unavoidable, in which case colour-coding or other aspects of formatting can be used to highlight such changes.

- Ensuring that, as far as possible, where several arguments to a function are required, these arguments are in a contiguous range of cells. This allows the formulae to be more readily understood and creates a more direct feedback between the inputs and the calculations, so that potential errors are likely to be more visible. This goal may be sometimes hard to achieve in practice because of constraints on the structure that arise from the logical flow, but is a worthwhile objective to keep in mind.
- Avoiding the use of formula references across worksheets (e.g. **SUM**(range), where the range is in a different worksheet). Such formulae are not transparent and therefore error-prone. As mentioned earlier, it can in any case be a worthwhile objective to build the model in as few worksheets as possible (a single worksheet is often achievable).
- Using the tools on the **Status Bar** (such as **Sum** and **Count**) to quickly check the results of formulae without having to build all of these checks explicitly into the model.
- Potentially using named ranges (see earlier).

Complex Formulae

When creating complex formulae, especially those involving several variables, conditional statements (**IF**, **MAX**, etc.) or embedded formulae, extra care needs to be taken to ensure that they are accurate and robust. As a general rule the following principles apply:

- Complex calculations should generally be split into separate logical steps (rather than combined or embedded in a single formula). This ensures that the formulae are transparent and are easy to test and correct. Occasionally the use of compound formulae is appropriate, and in these cases such formulae should generally be built using a stepwise technique (see below for an example).
- Formulae involving conditional statements should be tested in a way that results in all the possible conditions occurring.
- Formulae should be tested so that they work across a range of values. As a minimum they should be valid across the range of values that would be applied when sensitivity analysis is used on the completed model (including the combinations of values that may arise as several inputs vary simultaneously).
- Formulae can be tested across an extreme range of values for the inputs. Where the model becomes invalid in certain cases then one may choose either to document such limitations or to modify the model to make it valid for this larger range of values. One may also decide to restrict the range of values that can be used for such inputs by using **Data/Data Validation** (**Data/Validation** in Excel 2003).
- Build error-checks into the model. For example, where the same quantity can be calculated in different ways (even though only one such calculation may be needed) these extra calculations can be used as a cross-check. It is typically useful to have an error-check calculation (which should evaluate to zero) and then to implement some method (such as **Conditional Formatting**; see earlier) to highlight whenever an error occurs. Where there are many such cross-checks, it can also be helpful to group them together in a single range so that it is easier to scan quickly for errors.
- The use of named ranges can be helpful in some circumstances, as discussed earlier.

- Errors (i.e. calculations that result in an error message, rather than calculation mistakes that nevertheless return a value) can be found using **F5** followed by **Special** and then under **Formulas** selecting **Errors**, with the **Numbers**, **Text**, **Logical** and options deselected. Errors may also be found and highlighted using the tools of **Conditional Formatting** (see earlier).
- Where one wishes to validate formulae by seeing the effect of a change in an input on several calculations, one can set up a **Watch Window** (under **Formulas**, or under **Tools/Formula Auditing** in Excel 2003). Alternatively a one-way **Data Table** with multiple outputs can be created (see later).

Example: One-off Sensitivity Analysis

Sensitivity analysis can be used to facilitate the process of creating formulae, in order that they are robust and flexible. A one-off sensitivity analysis approach involves observing (but not recording) the effect on the calculations of a change in the value of an input, and modifying the formulae as necessary. This approach often works well as an iterative method in which sensitivity testing is conducted after each modification of the formulae, until one has reached a valid and flexible result.

The file Ch2.TaxBands.xlsx (Figure 2.15) shows an example. The objective is to create a formula which allocates a given level of income into several bands, so that a different

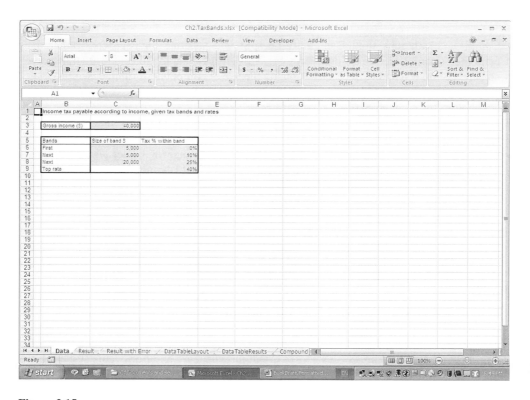

Figure 2.15

tax rate can be applied to the income in each band. Similar applications occur in financing structures, for example where a particular level of borrowing is split into tranches, and where each tranche has a different applicable interest rate, or where a tiered incentive structure is involved in a profit share arrangement. As shown in the Data worksheet, it is initially assumed that the income level is $40 000, but it is desired to calculate the tax payable as the level of income varies. The tax rates that apply are: 0% for the first $5000 of income, 10% for the next $5000, 25% for the next $20 000, and 40% for anything higher.

The following illustrates an iterative process that can be used to generate, test and modify the required formula using a sequence of one-off sensitivity analyses (the key steps are shown in separate worksheets):

1. Take the simplest case (in this case income allocation for the first tax band) and generate an initial hypothesis as to the appropriate formula.
2. Test this initial formula as the input values (i.e. of the income) are varied, adapting the formula as necessary so that it works for all (relevant) input combinations. In particular, in the values tested should cover a range so that each band is unaffected, partially affected, and fully affected, and should also include large positive or negative values.
3. Copy the formula (after setting appropriate absolute or relative cell references) to the cell containing the income for the next band, and use this formula as the hypothesis for the formula that would work for this band, test and modify it as in step 2.

Concerning step 1, with an income of $40 000 it is clear that the income within this band is $5000 (i.e. equal to the size of the band). It will be immediately clear, however, that an approach which sets the taxable income equal to the size of the band is not correct in all circumstances, and this is formalised in step 2.

In step 2, one may consider the case where the income is below the size of the first band, say $3000. In this case the taxable income would be only $3000. So the adapted formula could be:

$$\text{Income in band} = \textbf{MIN}(\text{Size of Band, Total Income})$$

(The formulae here are shown in text form for simplicity of the description, although the formulae in the model have been implemented with the relevant cell references rather than named ranges.) Remaining with step 2, we could check whether this formula works for a wider range of values. For example, while the formula produces the correct result whenever the income is above the size of the band, if the income were negative then it would produce a negative taxable income in the band. Whether this is appropriate would depend on the context (e.g. whether a negative income would results in a tax rebate or not). On the assumption that in such cases we wish not to have any rebates, then the formula would have to be modified so that no taxable income would be within the band:

$$\text{Income in band} = \textbf{MAX}(0, \textbf{MIN}(\text{Size of Band, Total Income}))$$

Moving to step 3, one could copy this formula (with appropriate absolute references) to the next range and then test whether it is valid for tax payable in the range. The worksheet Step3Start contains the initial formulae that would be in the model at this stage (no screenshot is shown, but see Figure 2.16). Once again this formula could be tested for various levels of the total income. One can readily see that the formula would need to be

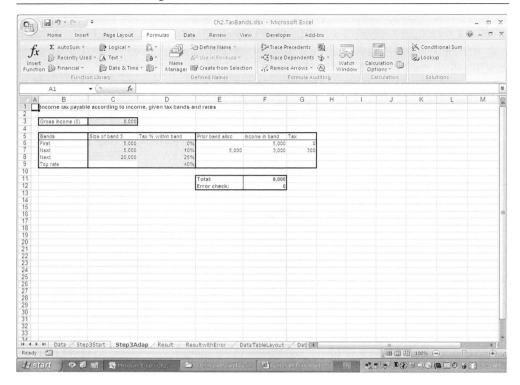

Figure 2.16

adapted as it does not yet reflect that some of the income has been allocated to the earlier band (alternatively using a smaller trial value for the income of, say, $4000 or $8000 would produce values that are clearly wrong). In other words, one could consider a formula such as:

$$\text{Income in band} = \mathbf{MAX}(0, \mathbf{MIN}(\text{Size of Band},$$

$$\text{Total Income} - \text{Income allocated to earlier bands}))$$

The worksheet Step3Adap (Figure 2.16) shows the result of implementing this. A column has been created which shows the cumulative income allocated to the earlier bands. In addition, an error-check has been created which checks that the sum of the income allocated to some band is equal to the total income. (Note that since the formulae have been set up to be valid for only the case where the income is positive, this error-check would detect an error if the income were set to be less than zero. Clearly if it were desired for the model to be valid for these cases, then the formulae would have to be adapted appropriately.)

This formula can be applied to all bands, with the exception of the top rate band. Since the upper limit (and hence the size of the band) is infinite, the expression involving the **MIN** statement can be excluded, resulting in:

$$\text{Income in last band} = \mathbf{MAX}(0, \text{Total Income} - \text{Income allocated to earlier bands})$$

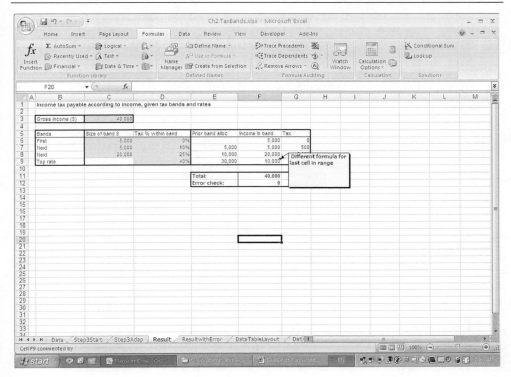

Figure 2.17

The worksheet Result (Figure 2.17) shows the final completed model, including the tax calculations and the error-check. The cell containing the final formula is shown with comments added.

The worksheet ResultwithError (Figure 2.18) implements an error-check that should evaluate to zero and uses the **Format/Conditional Formatting** menu (see earlier) to highlight the occurrence of an error (for example, if a negative income is tried or if one of the formulae is accidentally overwritten).

Restricting Input Values using Data Validation

In some cases, a formula is designed to be valid only for certain input values. Similarly, it is possible that structural aspects of a model determine that certain formulae are valid only within a range of input values (e.g. such a case can arise where an input refers to the row number to be used in a **Lookup** function). Such a situation can be dealt with by:

- Documenting the restriction using comments.
- Placing restrictions on the input values using **Data/Data Validation** (**Data/Validation** in Excel 2003).

Restrictions on input values should only be placed where there are genuine reasons to do so. For example, the occasional practice of limiting a user's choice of discount rate by using

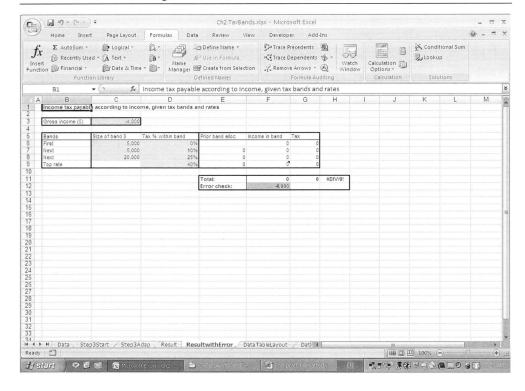

Figure 2.18

a list to define the possible values (so that a project appears profitable under all possible allowed input values!) should in general be avoided.

The use of the **Circle Invalid Data** option of the **Data Validation** menu can allow one to find the cells in a range that do not meet certain criteria. (Where the criteria do not correspond to one of the allowable criteria on the **Settings** tab, the **Custom** criteria on the settings can be used to define a logical formula that should evaluate to **TRUE** for valid data. This can also be used to restrict inputs where there are relationships between several inputs that must hold; for example, that one input value must be larger than another for the validity of the formulae).

Example: Robust Compound Formulae

Although compound or embedded formulae should generally be avoided, their use may nevertheless be necessary or appropriate in some cases in order to build more compact models. In these cases a robust way to build such formulae is to:

- Build and test the separate logical steps using non-embedded formulae (i.e. with every logical step broken out), and ensure that the calculations which represent the result of the individual steps are correct and error-free.
- Work inwards from the outside (of the overall calculated formula) using the **Formula Bar** to copy and then overwrite each argument with the calculation for that argument.

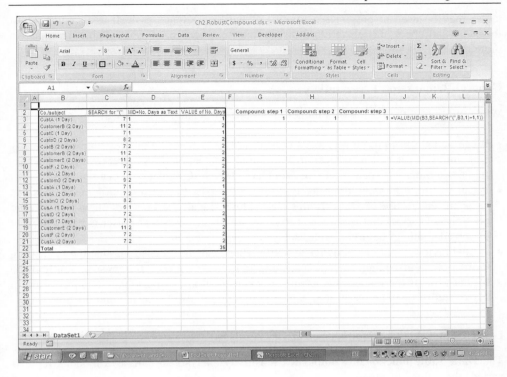

Figure 2.19

The result is an aggregate or compound formula whose individual components have been tested. (Generally one may wish to double-check that the compound formula returns the same value as the one based on individual steps, after which these individual formulae may be deleted.)

- Use a stepwise evaluation of compound formulae **Formulas/Evaluate Formula** (in Excel 2003: **Tools/Formula Auditing/Evaluate Formula**) to see the individual calculations within them.

The file Ch2.RobustCompound.xlsx (DataSet1 worksheet) (Figure 2.19) shows an example (as used earlier in the model Ch1.Text.xlsx (Figure 1.34)). The compound formula has been created by using the **Formula Bar** to copy and paste the end formula (containing the **VALUE** function), and then using the **Formula Bar** to sequentially overwrite the parameters of the functions with the earlier formulae used to calculate them (i.e. first copying the **MID** function and then the **SEARCH** function, and deleting any excess = signs). The individual steps of doing this as well as the original separate formulae are shown for convenience.

RESULTS PRESENTATION AND OTHER USES OF SENSITIVITY ANALYSIS

The main focus of this section is on the use of the **Data Table** feature (under **Data/What-If Analysis** or under **Data** in Excel 2003) to conduct sensitivity analysis. We discuss how such tables may be used to present sensitivities of the key outputs, as well as to build robust formulae and check models. Before discussing this, some brief general comments are in order.

General Remarks on Presentation

When presenting the results of a model, a number of general points should be considered:

- It can be helpful to use a separate summary area which shows the key outputs (typically containing direct cell references to the output calculations). An overall layout such as Inputs–Summary–Calculations (or Summary–Inputs–Calculations) can be useful.
- It can be useful to show the sensitivity of key outputs (in the Summary area). This can be achieved by use of **Data Tables** (see below). Ideally, a range of input values (and possibly scenarios) that is sufficient to cover all of the cases that a user is likely to want to consider should be tested and displayed.
- A final review should be undertaken with particular focus on ensuring that the formatting (borders, colour-coding, etc.) is clear and is used to enhance the presentation and the logical flow of the model, that adequate documentation and up-to-date comments are in place, and so on. The list of any named ranges could also be pasted and documented.

Using Data Tables to Conduct Sensitivity Analysis

The **Data Table** functionality automates sensitivity analysis so that, as a model's input is varied, the values of some outputs (or of key intermediate quantities) are calculated and displayed. The key uses of doing so are to:

- Create and check formulae (including detecting potential errors) by automatically showing the values of key calculations or outputs as some inputs vary. For example, if it is seen that the values of an output are unaffected (or affected in an unexpected way) as the input values change, then this is an indicator of a possible error.
- Display a summary of the sensitivity of key outputs (for example in a summary area of the model). This can be particularly useful to facilitate the use of the model by others (such as senior decision-makers) who may wish to see the results of such sensitivity analysis without having to become familiar enough with the model to confidently change the inputs themselves. When this is an objective it is important that a sufficiently wide range of input values are tested so that displayed values are sufficient to cover all (or the majority) of relevant cases that a user or decision-maker is likely to want to consider. Ideally, the input's base case value should be one of the input values tested, so that a user has a clear reference point for comparison with the other cases.
- Display scenarios, by combining a **Data Table** with a **Lookup** function. In this context a scenario means that several (more than two) variables are required to be simultaneously changed.

Creating and Modifying Data Tables

A **Data Table** can exist in a one-way or two-way form, corresponding to the number of inputs that are being simultaneously varied:

- A one-way **Data Table** shows the value of one or more outputs (or calculations) as a single input varies. Such tables may exist in a column form or in a row form. A key advantage of a one-way table is that the value of several outputs can be displayed. In the column form the values of the input to be varied are arranged in a single column, and cells references to the outputs are made in a row at the top of the table (with the reverse situation for the row form).
- A two-way **Data Table** shows the value of a single model output (or intermediate calculation) as two inputs are simultaneously varied. Since the cell reference to the output calculation is made in the top-left of the table, the results of only one output or calculation can be displayed.

A **Data Table** is implemented by:

- Creating an appropriate range of input values in a column or row (for one-way tables) or in a row and column (for two-way tables).
- Setting the outputs (or intermediate calculations) that are to be calculated in the table by using a direct cell reference from the appropriate point in table area to the relevant calculations in the model (from the top row in a one-way column table, and from the top left cell in a two-way table; see example).
- Highlighting the whole table area (including the top row and left column).
- Using the **Data/What-If Analysis** (under **Data** in Excel 2003) to create the table.
- Creating the appropriate row and column cell reference links (in a one-way table, one of the entry boxes will be left blank). A frequent mistake is to use a row input for a column table or *vice-versa*, but the presence of such mistakes is usually clear from inspection of the values in the table.

Note that because such a table forms an array in Excel, it is not possible to change part of it. For example, if one wishes to add more outputs to a one-way table, or extend the range of values tested in a table, or to reduce the size of a table, then the table will need to be recreated. An extension of the area can be achieved by selecting the new area and effectively overwriting the original table, whereas a reduction is not possible and would require the deletion of the original table and the creation of a new one.

Example: Displaying Sensitivities and Checking Formulae

The file Ch2.DataTables1.xlsx (Layout worksheet) (Figure 2.20) shows the earlier tax bands example in which the required layout of various **Data Tables** has been set up. The DTSens worksheet (Figure 2.21) shows a range of completed tables, which have also been formatted with borders. The tables calculate the value of various quantities, including the total tax payable, the average tax rate, and check for errors as the level of income is varied.

As shown in this example, some techniques that can be applied to assist the process of checking formulae or checking for errors include:

- For models that contain in-built error-checks (e.g. cells that should evaluate to zero), the value of the error-checking cell can be set as an output as shown in the **Data Table**. In this way it can readily be checked whether there is any error as the input values vary. This provides a quick technique to highlight if there are limitations in terms of allowable input ranges. For example, a fairly frequent situation is that no errors are displayed by

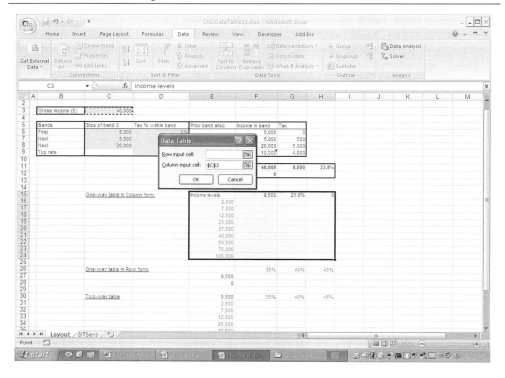

Figure 2.20

an error-checking calculation when the inputs are set to their base values, but that errors arise when some of the input values are varied.

- Setting up a one-way table with several outputs, so that the effect of a change in an input on several calculations can be observed. Alternatively, the outputs or intermediate calculations displayed can be changed (without having to change or reset the whole table) by simply using a formula reference from the table to a different calculated cell. This also applies to two-way tables, where the output reference can be changed. Repeating this process several times for a large range of intermediate calculations allows for a quick general check of the validity in a large range of cases.

Limitations of Data Tables

There are several limitations when using **Data Tables** including:

- The table must be placed in the same worksheet as the inputs that are varied (and so cannot be used on a separate Summary worksheet, although such a worksheet could, of course, contain cell references to a table in another worksheet containing the inputs).
- Although the input to be varied may be an intermediate calculated quantity (rather than a genuine model input), the actual values used for such inputs cannot contain cell references to calculated cells. For example, when running a sensitivity of a cash flow valuation as the discount rate changes (see Chapter 3), if the discount rate is itself based on other

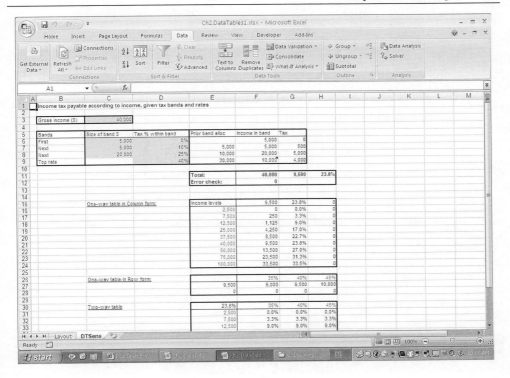

Figure 2.21

calculations (e.g. cost of equity) then the value used as a table input cannot be a cell reference to the calculated discount rate. This may be inconvenient where it is desired (as would normally be the case) to show the base case value of an output as one of the **Data Table** elements. One can of course simply paste the value of the base case input into the appropriate position for the **Data Table**, but this value will not update if any changes are made to the underlying assumptions driving this value.

- Their presence will slow down the recalculation of the model, because any change in the model will cause all the tables to be recalculated. One way to deal with this is to set the model so that **Data Tables** are recalculated only when **F9** is pressed (under **Office/Excel Options/Formulas/Calculation Options** or under **Tools/Options/Calculation** in Excel 2003). Unnecessary tables can be removed; for example, once the model has been checked from a variety of perspectives.

- As for any form of traditional sensitivity analysis, no probabilities are attached to the various outcomes. In general, simulation techniques are required to achieve such a view (see Chapter 4).

- The inputs that are being varied in a particular **Data Table** are not directly visible, and so it may be easy to forget the inputs to which the rows and columns correspond (the inputs can however always be seen by inspection of the array formulae in the table's cells). One-way tables have the advantage that a label can be written in the top-left corner, whereas for two-way tables the labels can be typed in the row and column immediately above and to the left of the table, although this is sometimes a little cumbersome.

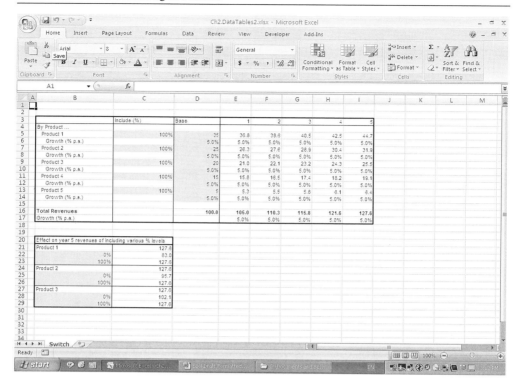

Figure 2.22

Example: Sensitivity to a Switch

In some cases the nature of the sensitivity to test is about whether to include or exclude some factor, or to include it at some weighting (e.g. to represent an average of the inclusion or not of an item). Example applications could be the effect of the inclusion or not of potential synergies from an acquisition, or of a particular product in a portfolio.

The file Ch2.DataTables2.xlsx (Figure 2.22) shows a revenue forecast involving multiple products where it is desired to be able to include or exclude each product from the forecast. Each product is given a weight, which is used to multiply its original revenue forecast (so that when a weight is set to 0 the product would be excluded, and when set to 1 it would be included). The effect, for each of the first three products, of their inclusion or not is captured in the **Data Tables** as the weights of each are varied to be either 0 or 1.

Example: Scenarios using Lookup Functions

The use of a **Data Table** combined with a **Lookup** function can be a powerful way to present several scenarios (i.e. situations in which the values of several inputs are changed simultaneously). The values taken by the relevant inputs can be defined for each scenario, and if the scenarios are numbered with integers (1, 2, etc.), then the scenario number can be used as an argument of a **Lookup** function to feed the relevant input values into the model. A **Data Table** can then be created in which the input variable is the scenario

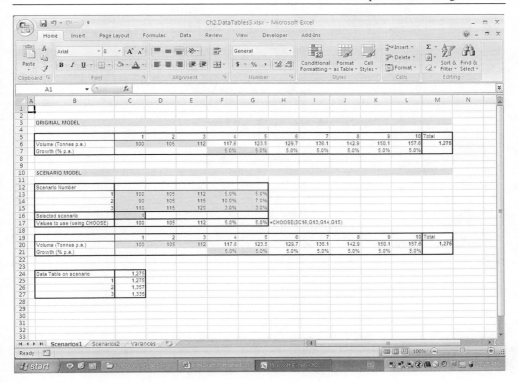

Figure 2.23

number, with the table then showing the values of the model's output for each scenario. Excel's **Scenarios Manager** (**Data/What-If Analysis** or under **Tools** in Excel 2003) can also be used to create scenarios, but has the disadvantage that the scenarios are not as explicitly visible or computationally accessible in the worksheet, and so are not used in this text.

The file Ch2.DataTables3.xlsx (Scenarios1 worksheet) (Figure 2.23) shows an original model with five input assumptions that calculate the total volume for a 10-year period. A copy of this model is also shown and has been extended by the use of three scenarios, and the **CHOOSE** function is used to pick out the relevant values for each scenario that are to be fed into the main part of the model.

The file Ch2.DataTables3.xlsx (Scenarios2 worksheet) (Figure 2.24) demonstrates that other **Lookup** functions can be used, including **VLOOKUP**, **INDEX** and **OFFSET**, and shows an example of the implementation of each (the cell inputs are restricted using **Data Validation**, as discussed earlier). As a check that the results are the same in all cases, a two-way **Data Table** showing the value of the result for each scenario for each method has been created. The **CHOOSE** function is often the preferable **Lookup** function to use in such cases, as it can be applied when the input cells for the different scenarios are not contiguous. In addition it may sometimes be computationally quicker, as the lookup process is more direct than when using the indirect matching that takes place with the other functions.

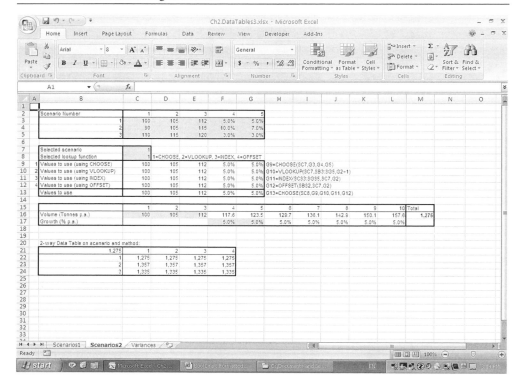

Figure 2.24

Example: Variance Analysis

Variance analysis aims to isolate the effect due to each input when a set of inputs are simultaneously changed (e.g. when moving from a base case to a worst case). This can be achieved by using the above scenarios approach, where a sequence of scenarios is set up. Each scenario in the sequence involves changing the value of the next variable from its original (base case) to its final (worst case) value while retaining the changes made to previous variables (the impact of each variable calculated in this way will depend slightly on the order in which the variables are used in the sequence of changes, due to interaction effects).

The file Ch2.DataTables3.xlsx (Variances worksheet) (Figure 2.25) shows an example.

Hiding and Protecting Models

On occasion one may wish to hide parts of a model or to protect it in some way so that it cannot be changed. Some of the possibilities include:

- *Locking cells (or an entire worksheet) so that their contents cannot be changed.* For example, one may wish the user to be able to change the input values but not any of the formulae. The locking of cells is the default position of Excel, but is often not directly

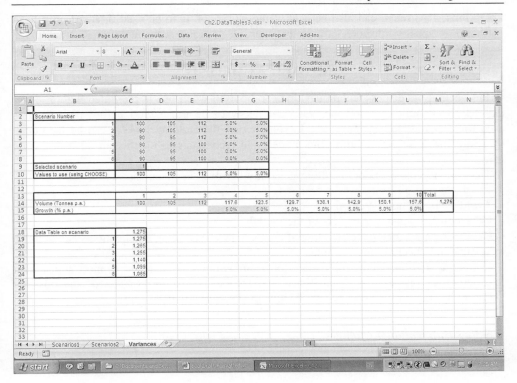

Figure 2.25

apparent because it only has an effect when the worksheet is protected with a password. In other words, to lock a range of cells one must unlock all cells in the worksheet, select the range to be locked, and then relock the worksheet and protect it. The unlocking of all the cells in a worksheet can be performed by selecting all cells (clicking on the top-left square of the worksheet), using **CTRL+1** to bring up the **Format/Cells** menu (also under **Home**, followed by clicking on one of the dialog box launchers), selecting the **Protection** tab, unchecking the **Locked** box and clicking **OK**. The cells to be locked can then be selected (e.g. to select all formulae one may use **F5 (GoTo) Special**). One must then return to the **Protection** tab, check the **Locked** box and click **OK**. The final step is to protect the worksheet with a password under **Review/Protect Sheet** (**Tools/Protection/Protect Sheet** in Excel 2003).

- *Hiding a worksheet.* Examples include where a worksheet has been used to perform data analysis to calibrate or calculate input values, but where certain information in the detailed data set is confidential. A worksheet can be hidden by right-clicking on the **Sheet** tab and selecting **Hide** (**Format/Sheet/Hide** in Excel 2003), following which the workbook must be password protected (using **Review/Protect Workbook**) to prevent the user from being able to unhide the worksheet (in Excel 2003: **Tools/Protection/Protect Workbook**).
- *Requiring a password to open or modify a workbook.* This can be done using **Microsoft Office Button/Save As** (in Excel 2003: **File/SaveAs**), then selecting **Tools/General-**

Options. This menu can also be used if the workbook is to be used in **Read-only** form (that is not password protected), so that the user does not accidentally change anything.

MODEL AUDITING

In this section we discuss techniques that can be used when one is presented with a model that has been built by someone else, and needs to be understood before perhaps it is used for decision analysis purposes. In some cases, the auditing process can be facilitated by restructuring or reformatting the model, and techniques to do this are also discussed here.

The core aspects of model auditing generally involve such steps as:

- Avoiding unintentional changes.
- Developing a general overview of the model.
- Generating a detailed understanding of the logic flow, including the the inputs and outputs.
- Testing and checking the formulae.
- Correcting and improving the model, for example to create a clearer or more transparent structure, or one in which sensitivity analysis can be readily conducted, and possibly improving the presentation of sensitivities of the key outputs.

Avoiding Unintentional Changes

To avoid unintentional changes the following general rules apply:

- Work with a copy of the model, rather than the original model. Regularly save the work under a new name (perhaps with part of the filename indicating the date of the last change), in order to create a sequence of models and a rapid recovery trail if necessary.
- Do not update linked values when opening the model if a warning of the presence of links to other workbooks is provided. The presence of links will generally require specific further work to ensure that a robust procedure is created to update links (see earlier section on Linked Workbooks).
- Set up a **Watch Window** (under **Formulas**, or under **Tools/Formula Auditing** in Excel 2003) to show the values of a range of key variables (especially outputs and other key calculations). Ensure that any changes made do not affect these values (except, of course, deliberate changes to input values or corrections to formulae, both of which in any case should not normally be undertaken at this early auditing stage).
- Do not run any macros, press any buttons that might run macros, or change any other aspect of the model at this stage.

Developing a General Overview

When developing a general overview of the model, the following tools can be helpful:

- Ensure that all worksheets are visible. If under the **Review** menu there is an option to **Unprotect Workbook** (under **Tools/Protection** in Excel 2003), then it is possible that there are hidden worksheets that may only be accessible with a password (see earlier). If any formulae in the visible part of the model refer to cells in these hidden worksheets, then it would clearly be necessary to make these worksheets visible to create a full understanding of the model.

- If there are circular references, set the workbook on manual recalculation and establish the role of the circularity and whether it is likely to be intentional or not (see earlier).
- Check for the presence of **Lookup** functions. Where such functions are present, one must be particularly careful in making any structural changes that affect the ranges of these functions (see below).
- Check for the presence of named ranges (see earlier). The **Name Manager** can be used and the list of names whose scope is the workbook or current worksheet can be pasted into Excel by using techniques covered earlier.
- Check for the presence of **VBA** code (macros) or user-defined functions. The presence of macros in Excel 2007 will be clear from the file extension (.xlsm), whereas in Excel 2003 one may check for macros by using **Alt+F11** to invoke the Visual Basic Editor. Any such code is an integral part of the model, and knowledge of VBA (see Chapter 6) generally will be required to proceed further.

Understanding the Details and Logical Flow

Once an overview has been established, it is important to find the outputs and inputs and to generate a detailed understanding of the logical flow. At this stage it is preferable to avoid making any changes to the structure or calculations until the model is understood in more detail. Techniques that can help to understand and follow the logical flow include:

- Following the forward and backward paths from a particular cell using the **Formulas/Trace Precedents** and **Formulas/Trace Dependents** toolbar (found in Excel 2003 under **Tools/Formula Auditing**, etc.). The end point of a sequence of forward-tracing paths should generally correspond to an output (or potential output), and the beginning to an input. Of course not all such end points may be relevant outputs, and some intermediate calculations could also be relevant outputs, so some judgement is still required. Double-clicking on a tracing line will allow the paths to be followed.
- Using the short-cuts **Ctrl+[** and **Ctrl+]** to go to a cell's direct precedents or dependents.
- Using **F5** followed by **Special (Home/Find & Select/Go To Special** or **Edit/Go To** menu in Excel 2003) to select cells according to various criteria. Useful objectives include the selecting of constants, which are by definition a subset of the inputs to the model (the **Text**, **Logical** and **Errors** options should be deselected), the selecting of direct (or all) precedents and dependents of a cell, or the selecting of errors. Since this process selects the relevant cells, it can often be useful to immediately apply a formatting to the cells (e.g. colour-coding the inputs).
- Searching for all cells containing mixed formula (e.g. =E4*1.3) or fixed values arising from formulae (e.g. =5*300). This is easiest to do by visual inspection of the formulae using **Formulas/Show Formulas** (or **Tools/Formula Auditing/Formula Auditing Mode** in Excel 2003), or the short-cut **CTRL+`**.
- Using formatting (e.g. colour-coding) or comments to record inputs, key outputs or areas that require further investigation or checking.
- Checking that no formulae have arguments that are blank cells. This can be done using **Office/Excel Options/Formulas/Formulas Referring to Empty Cells** (under **Tools/**

Options/Error-checking in Excel 2003) and ensuring also that **Enable background error checking** is chosen. The other error-checking options must be deselected. Such cells will then be shown with error markers. A perhaps better alternative is to select all such cells simultaneously (so that they can be colour-coded as potential errors and then investigated individually). This can be achieved by highlighting the entire worksheet, using the **Go To Special** menu, searching for **Blanks**, then using **Ctrl+]** to trace dependents of such blanks (and then colour-coding such cells).

- Exploring any links to other workbooks. Formulae containing such links contain a [in the name of the linked workbook, and so can be found using **Home/Find & Select** (or **CTRL+F** or **Edit/Find** in Excel 2003), by searching for this symbol. To avoid finding occurrences when the bracket is used within text labels, the **Options** submenu in the **Look in** box select **Formulas** can be used. Note that links can sometimes be created through the use of named ranges (see earlier) and such links are visible in the **Name Manager** in Excel 2007. **Data/Edit Links** (**Edit/Links** in Excel 2003) can also be used.
- Cells that contain conditional formatting can be found using **Home/Conditional Formatting/Manage Rules** (where one then selects to look for all rules in **This Worksheet**) or selected under **Home/Find and Select/Conditional Formatting** or using **Go To Special** or **F5 Special**.
- Cells that use **Data Validation** can be found under **Home/Find and Select/Data Validation** or using **Go To Special** or **F5 Special**.

Testing and Checking the Formulae

The accuracy of the calculations can be checked using some of the techniques discussed earlier, including:

- The basic inspection of formulae and their ranges.
- The use of one-off sensitivity analysis and **Data Tables**, as well as the use of a **Watch Window** to see the effect of a change in an input on several calculations.
- The finding of cells that contain errors (i.e. calculations that result in an Excel error message) by using **F5** followed by **Special** (**Home/Find & Select/Go To/Special** or **Edit/Go To** menu in Excel 2003), and selecting **Errors** under **Formulas** (the **Numbers**, **Text**, and **Logical** options should be deselected).
- To find and highlight errors, the tools of **Conditional Formatting** may be used (see earlier), in which the rule type **Use a formula to determine which cells to format** is used, the formula being =**ISERROR(cell reference)**. (In Excel 2003 this can be implemented by **Format/Conditional Formatting** setting the condition to be **Formula is** and using the formula =**ISERROR(cell reference)** in the data entry box).

Improving the Model

Often, even the process of checking or validating a model requires it to be substantially rebuilt, meaning that model auditing in practice cannot always be separated from model rebuilding. This is particularly the case when an initial review of the model finds it to contain errors (formulae errors or implied assumptions that are not valid when considering sensitivity analysis), or when the model is so poorly structured that its complexity renders it essentially incomprehensible in reasonable time without it being rebuilt, so that is has a simpler and more transparent structure and improved or corrected formulae.

Some important aspects of this process include:

- Document any changes that are made.
- Use appropriate formatting to highlight key structural aspects of the model. The improvement of the formatting is usually the single most effective way to rapidly improve it, because other types of changes (e.g. of a structural nature), although also very effective, are generally much more complex to implement. Formatting (especially colour-coding and comments) can also be a useful work-organisation tool to highlight any potential errors or areas requiring further review if they are not immediately changed or corrected.
- Restructure and rebuild the model according to best practice principles where possible. In practice the amount of effort that is worthwhile to invest in such restructuring will depend on the modelling context and objectives. For example, it may be worthwhile to rebuild some mixed formulae so that key inputs are separate and can be easily varied to conduct a sensitivity analysis, but it may be unrealistic to rebuild all formulae to eliminate mixed input-calculation cells. Similarly, it will generally be worthwhile to eliminate errors and to rewrite some of the more complex formulae, where doing so would create more transparency. The rebuilding of multiple worksheet models to reduce the number of worksheets can be particularly effective, but also generally requires significant effort.

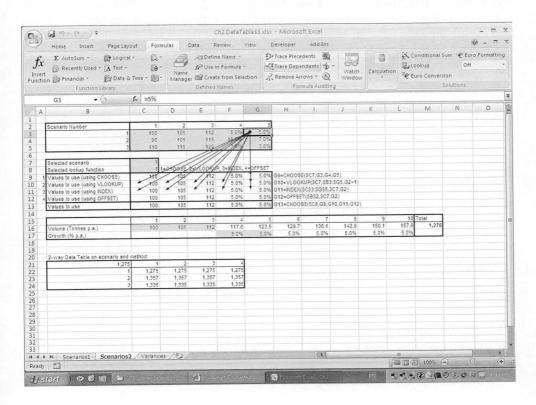

Figure 2.26

- Generally, use cut-and-paste (rather than copy-and-paste) to retain the cell references when formulae are moved around.
- Take extra care in restructuring models that contain **Lookup** functions (see below), as well as those with named ranges and macros (see earlier comments).
- Where a model is linked to another workbook or model, consider integrating them into a single workbook. If this is not possible, the links can be restructured to be placed on separate mirror worksheets or by the use of named ranges as appropriate (see earlier).
- Selectively apply named ranges where appropriate.

Auditing and Restructuring Issues with Lookup functions

As mentioned above, where a model contains **Lookup** functions great care needs to be taken before making any structural changes that affect the range of such functions. For example, the addition of a column within the range of a **VLOOKUP** function would result in the wrong values being looked up (and this error might not be clear if the wrong values are of similar magnitude to the correct ones). In this case the entire lookup range may need to be cut before the column is inserted and then pasted back in after the column has been inserted. The **OFFSET** function requires even more care in this regard.

The **OFFSET** and **INDIRECT** functions can also be problematic in that their lookup ranges may not appear as precedents to the functions. The use of **Formula/Trace Dependents (Tools/Formula Auditing** in Excel 2003) may result in a misleading conclusion, with cell values that do affect the model's output not appearing to be inputs, as the cells do not feed directly into the function as arguments.

The file Ch2.DataTables3.xlsx (Scenarios2 worksheet) (Figure 2.26) shows an example.

3
Financial Statement, Cash Flow
and Valuation Modelling

The modelling of financial statements is required frequently in corporate finance contexts, such as profit and cash forecasting, assessing financing requirements, analysing credit risk, and valuation. This chapter focuses on the modelling issues related to this application. We assume that the reader understands the key principles of financial statements, including having a basic understanding of the Income Statement (or IS, i.e. that it shows sales, costs, taxes and profits, etc., as recognized in a period), of the Balance Sheet (or BS, i.e. that it summarises the assets and liabilities at a point in time) and of the Cash Flow Statement (or CFS, i.e. that it describes the cash flows that actually occur in a period, whether from operations, investments or financing activities).

From a modelling perspective, there are essentially only a few core common themes that occur across the majority of cases, and it is on these that we concentrate. These include:

- The choice of model structure and logic.
- Techniques to achieve a balance sheet that balances.
- The appropriate use of circular references.
- The creation of error-free models.
- Feasibility checking and ratio analysis.
- Aspects of more advanced cash, debt and tax modelling.
- Cash flow valuation, including the calculation of terminal values and sensitivity analysis.

In practice, modellers may be faced with more sophisticated accounting issues, such as dealing with associated companies or minorities, reflecting proceeds and gains from asset sales, dealing with goodwill write-offs, topics related to off-balance-sheet obligations, and so on. Whereas the accounting treatment of these topics can be complex (and is generally beyond the focus of this text), from a modelling perspective their implementation generally poses little difficulty once their accounting treatment is understood. Readers who are comfortable with implementing the fundamental modelling principles described in this chapter should be able to add any additional accounting issues or other features that may arise in practice.

FINANCIAL STATEMENT MODELLING: CORE POINTS AND EXAMPLE

As in most other modelling situations, there are potentially many ways to build a financial statement model. Since even a basic model requires the forecasting of several variables (e.g. sales, costs, tax, dividends, cash, fixed assets, investment levels, borrowings), there are thousands of possible modelling variations that exist.

The file Ch3.BasicFS.xlsx (Figure 3.1) shows a completed basic model, which is used in this section as the basis for a line-by-line discussion of the key modelling issues that

100   Financial Modelling in Practice

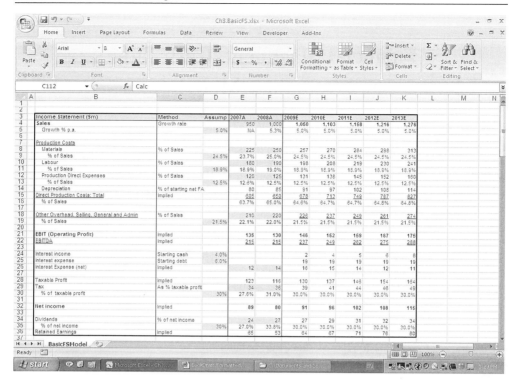

Figure 3.1

arise when building a financial statement model. Later in the chapter we discuss some generalisations of this basic model.

General Comments

Before discussing the individual items of the basic completed model, some overall comments are in order:

- An important difference between the modelling and accounting approaches to financial statements is that accounting essentially concerns itself with historic numbers, whereas modelling is a forward-looking (forecasting) activity. This has implications for the calculation and roles of equity and debt. Whereas in traditional accounting, equity serves as a residual value to achieve a BS that balances, in forecasting the balance is generally best achieved through the use of excess cash or short-term borrowing. This is one of the most important issues in the modelling of financial statements and is discussed extensively later in the chapter.
- For financial statement models it can often be very difficult to fully obey the standard best practice principle of top-to-bottom flow. The presentation of the order of the items in a financial statement largely follows predefined standards. On the other hand, ensuring that a forecasted BS balances usually requires the calculation of balancing items, which itself

requires knowledge of all other BS items. The idealised logic flow would be possible to achieve by use of a final BS presentation which used direct cell references from the initial BS and the balance calculations, but in general this repetition would create a large model. Therefore a single BS is generally more appropriate with the balancing items placed within it after calculation of the balance of each side excluding these items, resulting in a compromise of the top-to-bottom principle.

- As discussed in Chapter 2, it is generally good modelling practice to keep related items as close together as possible and to use as few worksheets as possible. Also, it is often necessary to build parts of the model more or less in parallel. For example, the depreciation calculation for the IS will require information about the fixed assets on the BS and the calculation of interest expense and income will also require information from the BS and in some cases also from the CFS. This is partly why it often helps to keep such models in a single worksheet.

- In practice it is often convenient to place many of the assumptions locally to where they will be used (rather than consolidated in a separate area of the model). This approach can optimise transparency in terms of keeping the assumptions clear and reasonably separate from the calculations, while minimising the logical and auditing paths in the model. In practice this can result in there being several columns for assumptions; for example a different growth rate may be used for the first few years of a forecast to the one that will be used for later years. As discussed in Chapter 2, appropriate formatting or colour-coding can be used to make clear which cells are inputs and which are calculations. In other words, the assumptions are separated visually from the calculations but may not necessarily be contained in a single input area.

- The potential use of circular references arises in a number of areas, including depreciation and interest calculations. As described in Chapter 2, it is generally possible to build models to the required degree of accuracy without the use of circular references, and this is the approach taken in the basic example model in this section. Later in the chapter we provide an example of the use of circular references in such models. Readers may also wish to refer to the more general discussion of the topic in Chapter 2.

- When historic data is available to calibrate a model (e.g. by the calculation of material costs as a percentage of sales, labour costs as a percentage of sales, etc.) one must be careful not to overemphasise the validity of continuing recent trends (or apparent trends) into the future. For example, the continuation of a recent decline in a cost-to-sales ratio could result in a model where margins increase indefinitely over time, which is likely not to be realistic, as in competitive markets margins are more likely to hold constant or decrease in the long-term. Even when a large set of historic data is available, the calibration is usually subject to judgement, as business conditions or the precise definitions of the measured quantities are likely to have changed over time.

- The credibility of the assumptions can be partially checked by considering ratio analysis. Particularly for valuation models based on long-term forecasts, measures such as the forecast return-on-capital are important to ensuring credibility. For example, if this measure tends upwards in the long-term, it may be that the margin assumptions are too aggressive (or that the capital expenditure forecast is too low). This is discussed in detail later.

- Some modellers prefer to use negative signs for costs and other cash expenditures or investments. This can be argued to be more aligned with some accounting conventions. The key is, of course, that any such approaches are used consistently and are clear to the user.

Income Statement Forecasting

There is a large variety of methods that may be used to forecast each of the IS items, and the key issues that are involved for each are discussed below.

Sales Forecasts

In the basic example (Figure 3.1), it is assumed that the sales figure is determined by applying an assumed growth rate to the most recent historic figure. In general, the sales figure could be forecast using different methods, including:

- Using a different growth rate for each time period.
- Developing a detailed forecast by product, business unit, customer or geographic market and aggregating these.
- Forecasting the unit price and volume, with sales calculated as the product of these.
- Forecasting cost items first and applying a margin assumption to derive sales. This could be appropriate in a low-margin business where most of the cost is represented by variable cost of commodity inputs, where the price of the end product may closely track the input cost.
- Forecasting the total size of the market and applying a market share assumption to calculate the sales.

The selection of the method arguably may have little effect on the values in the base case (as the assumptions would generally be recalibrated to historic data or judgement), but is important when considering sensitivity analysis. As discussed in Chapter 2, a key consideration is to choose the method that will best allow the required sensitivity analysis to be conducted on the completed model.

Nominal or Real Values

In some situations, expressing values in real terms can help to clarify the focus of the thinking. For example, one may wish to disaggregate the effect of productivity increases (which reduce unit cost), and inflation (which tends to increase it). However, there are many reasons why nominal values are ultimately required for accurate calculations:

- A model in real terms will overstate depreciation (e.g. relative to revenues or cost) and hence understate the profit and taxes.
- A model in real terms will underestimate the required investment in working capital (e.g. with no revenue growth in real terms, a real terms model will generally show no such investment, whereas a nominal model with positive inflationary growth will show that investment is required).
- Where the discount rate used in a cash flow valuation is estimated from the market (such as observed bond yields), such information already includes an inflation expectation; so a real terms model could use an inconsistent discount rate.
- A decision-making process conducted in real terms may lead to a misleading conclusion. For example, if one has purchased a house with 10% equity and a 90% mortgage, then with general inflation at 2%, an increase of 1% in the house's value is still likely to

represent a good return on the capital invested, even though the house's value has fallen in real terms.

Inflation may be built into a model in two main ways:

- As an explicit assumption, where many of the values that are initially expressed in real terms are converted to nominal terms for the relevant calculations. In these cases, the model will need to have an explicit inflation assumption (sometimes several inflation assumptions for different components are used, such as for materials prices, labour costs, etc.).
- As an implicit assumption, where it is directly assumed that all figures are in nominal terms. For example, the growth rate of sales could be assumed to be a nominal figure. Note that where this approach is used to forecast some variables (such as sales), with other variables derived by applying ratios (e.g. costs as a percentage of sales), the cost figure is automatically a nominal figure.

The implicit approach is the one used in the basic example. Its advantage is that it makes the model smaller, and potentially easier to compare with historic information (which is measured in nominal terms). Its disadvantage is that there may be less clarity on some of the underlying driving factors in the model (e.g. what determines cost productivity, or the ability to raise prices in the future?), and of course that sensitivity analysis of the model's outputs to the inflation rate would not be possible. In addition, if one were to be in a situation where multiple currencies are used in the model (or to compare the outputs of various models, each in a different currency), then one may need to explicitly know the assumed inflation rates in each currency in order that a fair comparison can be made.

Cost Forecasts

In the basic example (Figure 3.1), costs are split into different types (materials, labour, etc.), but no distinction is made between fixed and variable costs. In general, a variety of approaches are possible:

- Forecasting main items, such as materials, labour and other expenses.
- Forecasting each item as the sum of individual components (such as fixed and variable, or salary and personnel overhead, and so on).

The appropriate level of detail and nature of the assumptions will depend on the situation at hand and the objectives. For example:

- For long-term forecasting and cash flow valuation, a fairly aggregate model is generally sufficient; a cost-to-sales ratio assumption may provide adequate accuracy. It may be reasonable to assume (implicitly) that if costs were to become misaligned, then management would take action to reduce the cost base. In addition, in the long term, all costs are essentially adjustable, and so there may be little added benefit in making a distinction between fixed and variable costs.
- For short-term forecasting (such as if there are potential liquidity or cash flow issues to be considered), a pure variable-cost approach would underestimate the true sensitivity to a reduction in sales (and hence understate the risk of a liquidity problem). For such analysis a distinction between fixed and variable costs would generally be more appropriate.

Depreciation and Fixed Assets

In the basic example (Figure 3.1), depreciation is derived as a percentage of starting net fixed assets, with capital expenditure (capex) derived as a percentage of sales. This is the simplest approach that can be taken. Note that this would, over the long term, lead to the net fixed asset level tending to a constant proportion of sales,

Note also that even where a simple approach has been used to forecast cost items, it is usually nevertheless necessary to forecast depreciation explicitly:

- As a non-cash item, it is usually required when creating cash flow forecasts by the indirect method (i.e. calculating cash flow by using net income as the starting point).
- It is usually more logical to calculate depreciation from the value of the fixed assets, rather than by using a depreciation-to-sales ratio.

When forecasting depreciation based on the value of fixed assets, there are a number of further potential options and issues that may arise:

- Whether the level of depreciation is likely to be more closely related to gross or net asset values. In most cases, as long as the asset base is reasonably stable (and the ratios used in the model are calculated from historic data in a way consistent with how they are used in the forecast), then this issue is unimportant.
- Whether depreciation should be forecast using a ratio of the starting value of fixed assets, or of the average value. The latter approach would create a circular reference, with the options to deal with such a situation being essentially the same as those discussed in Chapter 2 (and later in this chapter) in the context of interest calculations.
- Whether to use more complex depreciation calculations, such as those based on an explicit fixed asset list, possibly involving separate depreciation schedules for different assets or asset classes. Some of the examples in Chapter 1 are relevant in this context, such as the use of **Lookup** functions to create a flexible time axis, the **TRANSPOSE** function to link a capital expenditure forecast to the depreciation schedule, and the implementation of a range of choices for the depreciation method using the **VDB** function. In many long-term forecasting models (such as cash flow valuations), such a level of detail may not however provide any more accuracy or insight.
- The method used for the fixed asset forecast. Since, by definition:

$$\text{Net Fixed Assets (ending)} = \text{Net Fixed Assets (starting)} + \text{Capex} - \text{Depreciation},$$

  then once two of the items on the right-hand-side are forecast, the other item in the equation becomes a derived quantity (since starting values in the next period are the prior period ending values, and so are already known).
- For long-term forecasting (especially cash flow valuations) it is often appropriate to build in an extra checking mechanism (e.g. adjusting the capex levels) to ensure that the business is not undercapitalised (thus helping to avoid overvaluation of the business by underestimating capex requirements and overstating the free cash flow). This is discussed later in the chapter.
- The calculation of depreciation for the IS will require some information about fixed assets. In simple cases, the fixed asset calculations may be performed directly within the calculation area for the BS, but often it may be preferable to conduct these in a separate area (as shown in Figure 3.1).

Operating Profit

Once the sales and operating cost items have been forecast, the operating profit can be directly calculated. For the purposes of this section we assume no distinction between operating profit and EBIT (earnings before interest and tax). More complex models may require additional line items or adjustments, such as for foreign exchange losses (which may be considered to be non-operating losses but should nevertheless be reflected in the EBIT figure). For forecasting purposes, many such one-off items are often assumed to be zero in future even where the historic values are non-zero (unless one is explicitly considering risk analysis, for example using the techniques of Chapter 4).

Interest Expense and Income

In the basic example (Figure 3.1) we use separate interest rates for cash and debt, and calculate the interest using prior-period ending values (to avoid circular references). In general, however, the calculation of interest expenses and income involves several decisions:

- Whether to use a single interest rate for interest expense (on debt) and interest income (on cash), or separate rates for each. Often there can be a significantly lower interest rate on cash than on debt. Especially where net debt is low (but results from significant levels of cash and gross debt that more or less offset each other) a small change in cash flow or interest rate differentials could have a large impact. One can generalise this further to allow for different interest rates for each type of debt. Often this extra detail is not necessary, but the methodology to do so in a flexible way is covered later in this chapter.
- Whether to build the model with circular references or not. This has been covered extensively in Chapter 2, where we showed that it is usually possible and sufficient to avoid circular references. Some implementations of the various possibilities are shown later.

In practice the calculation of interest may require items from the BS and CFS (BS when only starting balances are used to calculate interest, and from the CFS when considering period average non-interest cash flows in the calculation). As discussed later, the basic (planned) cash asset line will usually include an additional asset line to represent excess cash (or short-term investments) beyond the planned level. This excess cash or debt will generally also result in interest income or expense, and so should be included in the interest income formulae.

Taxable Profit, Tax and Net Income

Taxable profit can be calculated after subtracting the net interest expense from the operating profit (EBIT), and the net income will result directly once tax has been calculated. The core calculations on the IS would then be complete (assuming that there are no other line items, such a minority interests).

For the basic example, tax is assumed to be a percentage of taxable income (irrespective of whether the income is positive or negative), from which post-tax profit or net income is derived. There may be situations where more sophistication is desirable or necessary in tax calculations. For example:

- The application of a simple tax rate would result in a negative tax payable figure (i.e. a tax rebate) in the case of a loss. Such a rebate could be a fair reflection of the reality in some cases; however, in other cases it might be that no taxes would be repaid; rather a deferred tax asset would arise on the BS (see later).

- One may choose to model the difference between taxes recognised on the IS and those actually paid. Where assets are depreciated for tax purposes more quickly than on the financial statements, a deferred tax liability would arise on the BS (see later).

Once again, the choice of whether this type of extra functionality is required will be a combination of the objectives and context and after consideration of the sensitivity analysis that will need to be conducted on the completed model, as discussed in Chapter 2.

Dividends and Retained Earnings

These items are arguably not directly part of the IS (belonging rather to the BS and CFS). However, their calculation at this point is usually appropriate within the modelling process. First, the appropriate dividend assumption may be influenced by the level of net income. Second, the calculation of retaining earnings on the BS requires the dividend level to have been calculated.

In the basic example, it is assumed that forecast dividends are a percentage of net income. More generally, there is a variety of other methods that could be considered. The most accurate attempt to take into account the actual behaviour and decision-making patterns of companies when setting dividends, includes reflecting that:

- The key measure is usually dividend-per-share rather than the total level of dividend paid in absolute terms.
- Companies often have a target pay-out ratio, such as 25% to 35% of net income (possibly after adjusting the net income for one-time items).
- The rate of dividend growth is often fairly steady, with companies following a sticky dividend policy. Companies try to avoid adjusting their dividends to perceived short-term fluctuations in their performance (whether these fluctuations are on the positive or negative side). The aim is to reduce any potential overreaction in the financial markets (where dividend levels are assumed to potentially contain inside information on the future performance of the business; the so-called signalling theory of dividend policy).
- Dividends can sometimes be estimated by following whole number trends. For example, dividends-per-share that have been £1.50, £1.60, £1.70, for the most recent three periods could often reasonably be assumed to be £1.80 in the next period.

As always, whatever assumptions are made, it will be possible to conceive of situations where these can be questioned or would be invalid. The important question from a modelling perspective is whether their violation would have any material impact on the subsequent analysis and its conclusions.

Other Items

Financial statements may also contain other line items that are not shown in the basic model. Examples include one-off items, the inclusion of earnings from associated companies, minority interests, and so on. As mentioned earlier these items generally pose little challenge from a modelling perspective once their accounting treatment is understood, and so are not covered further here.

Balance Sheet Forecasting

Perhaps the single most important topic in the implementation of financial statement models is the mechanism to ensure that the BS balances. Techniques to do this are discussed below, following the discussion of the individual line item forecasts.

Figure 3.2 is a screenshot of the completed BS for the basic example.

Fixed Assets

The issues involved in forecasting net fixed assets have essentially already been covered in the depreciation forecast for the IS, so no further comments are made here.

Inventory, Receivables and Payables and Planned Cash

The basic example forecasts these items using a mixture of a days-equivalent measures (e.g. inventory of 8% of sales would approximate to one month or 30 days of sales) and percentage-of-sales approaches (cost-of-goods sold measures are also often used in practice for inventory). Similar approaches apply for variables such as accounts receivables and payables on the liabilities side of the BS.

Balance Sheet ($m) (and Fixed Asset Calculations)	Method	Assump	2007A	2008A	2009E	2010E	2011E	2012E	2013E
Fixed Assets, Capex and Depreciation									
Net Fixed Assets									
Starting	Implied		520	550	590	625	660	697	735
(+) CapEx	% of sales		110	125	128	132	139	146	153
% of Sales		12.0%	11.6%	12.5%	12.0%	12.0%	12.0%	12.0%	12.0%
(-) Depreciation	% of starting net FA		80	85	91	97	102	108	114
% of starting Net Fixed Assets		15.5%	15.4%	15.5%	15.5%	15.5%	15.5%	15.5%	15.5%
Ending	Implied		550	590	625	660	697	735	774
ASSETS									
Net Fixed Assets (ending)	See fixed asset calc		550	590	625	660	697	735	774
Inventory (Stocks)	Days of sales		35	45	43	45	48	50	52
Days of sales		15.0	13.4	16.4	15.0	15.0	15.0	15.0	15.0
Accounts receivable (Debtors)	Days of sales		85	94	98	103	108	113	119
Days of sales		34.0	33.8	34.3	34.0	34.0	34.0	34.0	34.0
Cash (planned)	% of sales		54	60	50	53	56	58	61
% of Sales		4.8%	5.7%	6.0%	4.8%	4.8%	4.8%	4.8%	4.8%
Short-term investments/Balancing item	Implied		0	0	42	71	103	138	178
Total current assets	Implied		177	199	233	272	314	360	409
Total assets			727	789	857	932	1011	1094	1183
LIABILITIES									
Short-term debt/Balancing item	Implied		0	0	0	0	0	0	0
Accounts payable (creditors)	Days of sales		56	60	62	65	68	72	75
Days of sales		21.5	21.5	21.9	21.5	21.5	21.5	21.5	21.5
Taxes payable (current)	Implied		34	36	39	41	44	46	49
Dividends payable	From IS		24	27	27	29	31	32	34
Current liabilities	Implied		114	123	128	135	142	150	159
Long term debt									
Starting	Implied		310	310	310	310	310	310	310
(+) increases	assumed		0	0	0	0	0	0	0
(-) reductions	assumed		0	0	0	0	0	0	

Figure 3.2

One can, of course, always conceive of situations where these (or any other assumed relationships) would not hold. For example, if a company grew more quickly than a base forecast by selling to lower credit customers or to larger accounts (which used their power to negotiate later payment terms), then the level of accounts receivable would generally increase to a higher proportion of sales than in the base forecast. However, the simpler methods are usually adequate providing that there is consistency between them and the calculation of the ratios from historic data their use in the forecast.

The forecast of (planned) cash is simply to reflect that some cash liquidity will always be required (such as short-term bank deposits to pay forthcoming wages). To some extent this item is unnecessary, as its net result is to reduce the level of the short-term investment balancing item (or to increase the level of short-term borrowings). On the other hand, some liquidity is always necessary, and there may be occasions when this short-term liquidity is itself financed by short-term borrowing, resulting in offsetting entries on both sides of the BS, rather than neither entry appearing.

Other Assets

More general models could include a range of other assets, such as equity investments or associated companies. As stated earlier, the inclusion of such items generally poses little challenge from a modelling perspective, once the accounting technicalities have been understood. (Generally the cash flow forecast will not reflect the cash associated with such assets, and so for valuation purposes the value of these assets will need to be added to the value derived from a cash flow forecast.)

Short-Term Investments, Short-Term Debt and Balancing Items

These are plug numbers to make the BS balance, and are discussed extensively later.

Taxes and Dividends

The basic example uses the simplest approach, which is that taxes payable will be identical to the value calculated on the IS. On the assumption that the cash outflow of taxes occurs in a later period, taxes payable represents a liability at the end of the period. Similarly, the declared dividends will generally be paid after the BS closing date and therefore represent a liability at the period end. Some more advanced approaches to tax calculations are discussed later.

Long-Term Debt

For the basic example, we assume that the level of long-term debt is fixed as the base case, but the capability to change it is included.

Note also that a corkscrew approach has been used to achieve transparency of the calculations. In this approach, starting values are taken from prior period ending values, and the inter-period calculation is broken out into separate line items showing changes during the period. Such corkscrews are useful for the modelling of many BS items (including fixed asset calculations, more complex tax situations, long-term debt and equity).

In practice, the levels of long-term debt depend on financing decisions made by the company:

- The benefits of the interest tax shield on the debt (i.e. because interest is deductible from earnings before the taxable income is calculated).
- The risk of bankruptcy if too much debt is used and business conditions deteriorate.

There are therefore several possible approaches that could be taken:

- Assume that the long-term debt is fixed. An advantage of this approach is that it does not force the financing decision within the logic of the model. A disadvantage is that it may result in an unrealistic financing structure, especially over longer forecasting horizons. As a general rule, long-term debt levels would increase in line with the free cash flow of the business (and hence with its value).
- Assume that long-term debt changes in line with the free cash flow or the value of the company. A simple proxy assumption is to set the level of long-term debt to be related to the level of operating assets or sales, and this is often sufficiently accurate.
- Explicitly build in line items that represent changes to the long-term debt. For example, one could create the flexibility to experiment with different maturities of long-term debt and with separate interest rates for each maturity. This approach is, of course, more complex, but may be necessary where an analysis of the financing decisions and its implications is an inherent part of the reason for building the model, or where a cash flow or financing structure is to be imposed.

Equity

In the example model, the basic share capital (and changes to it, using a corkscrew structure) is shown separately to the accumulated retained earnings. Once the equity calculation is complete, the level of total liabilities can be calculated from the individual line items. Equity is derived using already calculated quantities:

Retained Earnings (ending) = Retained Earnings (starting) + Net income − Dividends

In general, additional line items may be required, such as those associated with increases or decrease in equity from stock issuance, the retirement of treasury shares, the inclusion of preference shares and minority interests, and so on.

Other Liabilities

As for the asset side, in general there could be other liabilities (such as minority interests), that need to be included in a forecast and adjusted for in a cash flow valuation. Once again, any challenges here are usually of an accounting nature, not a modelling one.

Balancing the Balance Sheet

One important difference between the modelling and accounting approaches to financial statements is that accounting concerns itself with historic numbers, whereas modelling is a forward-looking (forecasting) activity. This has implications for the calculation and the roles of equity and debt. In traditional accounting, equity serves as a residual value to achieve a BS that balances. In forecasting, the balance is usually achieved through the use of excess cash or short-term borrowings, with equity not treated as a residual value, but rather is fully determined from the starting equity and explicit changes to it (as in the above formula, for example).

In other words, since the line items on each side of the BS are forecast individually and essentially independently, there is no reason for the BS initially to balance. It could be argued that this non-balancing results from some of the items being incorrectly forecast, and that some of the individual line item forecasts should be corrected (for example, by finding the level of receivables or of payables that would create a balancing BS). The use of excess cash or short-term debt as the balancing item is, however, generally the most appropriate approach, as it imposes the least restriction on assumptions about specific aspects of the firm's operations or of managers' decisions.

So a BS forecast will involve:

- Forecasting all line items essentially independently (including an initial forecast of planned levels of cash and/or short-term debt). This creates an initial trial BS which generally will not balance.
- Working out the initial trial (or interim) sums of the assets and liabilities.
- Adding an additional line item to the asset or liability side to force the balance. In practice, the most robust method is to create two balancing items, one for each side of the BS, where in practice one of them is zero and the other non-zero, as required.

In other words, a trial difference is calculated consisting of the difference between the sum of the forecasted assets less the sum of the forecasted liabilities (where these sums are not calculated by referring to already calculated BS asset and liability totals, but are rather directly calculated, to avoid circularities). When this difference is positive, the amount must be added to the liability side (as extra borrowings above the initial forecasted level), and when it is negative then its absolute value is added to the asset side (as excess cash above the initial forecasted level). That is:

$$\text{Trial Difference} = \text{Assets (excl. balancing item)} - \text{Liabilities (excl. balancing item)}$$

$$\text{Amount to add to assets (as excess cash)} = \textbf{MAX}(-\text{Trial Difference}, 0)$$

$$\text{Amount to add to liabilities (as excess borrowing)} = \textbf{MAX}(\text{Trial Difference}, 0)$$

Note that there are other ways to implement these formulae. For example the amount to be added to the assets could also be expressed as:

$$-\textbf{MIN}(\text{Trial Difference}, 0) \quad \text{or as}$$

$$\textbf{IF}(\text{Trial Difference} > 0, 0, -\text{Trial Difference}) \quad \text{and so on.}$$

Cash Flow Statement Forecasting

The CFS is usually structured into operating, investing and financing sections, where the sum of the cash flow from each should equal the net change in cash calculated on the BS. Roughly speaking, operating cash flow is the cash flow counterpart to net income from the IS (which means that interest paid and taxes are regarded as operating cash flows, as they are claims which are senior to those of shareholders, whereas dividends paid are reported as a financing cash flow).

In general, once the IS and BS have been forecast, the items on the CFS can be derived directly and without further assumptions. For example, the operating and investing cash flow items (such as changes in working capital and capital expenditure) will have been forecast within the asset part of the model.

In some modelling situations, it is required to forecast certain CFS items directly; this arises most frequently in situations where the financing cash flows are assumed or imposed from the context or from contractual obligations. In these cases the logical flow will be slightly different, with the related BS items determined from the CFS. The slightly more complex logical flow may require additional care and documentation, but there are usually otherwise no issues of particular relevance from a modelling perspective.

The operating cash flow part of the CFS may be presented in one of two ways:

- The direct method shows the actual cash receipts and payments e.g. cash received from customers, cash paid to suppliers etc. This is not frequently used in financial statement reporting, but in some cases can be useful in forecasting due to level of transparency it creates about the cash flow sources.
- The more frequent indirect method starts with net income and derives operating cash flow by adding back any non-cash items that would have been included in the net income calculation. Such items include depreciation, amortisation, and other write-offs that may have been made on the IS, increases in working capital (amounts owed by customers or decreases in amounts owed to suppliers) which will also have used cash but not have been reflected in the net income, and the difference between the taxes recognised in the IS and those that were paid this year (which in the simplest case would be the taxes recognised in the prior period). Similar arguments in terms of timing apply to dividends paid (cash outflow in financing section) versus dividends declared. In other words, the model's formulae will reflect that taxes and dividends are quantities where the cash flow usually occurs in the next period, and so the periodic declared amounts become end of period current liabilities.

Note that in more complex statements, there may be other quantities that need to be adjusted for, such as:

- The gains from the sale of an asset will generally have been recognised in net income, and should be subtracted in the operating cash flow calculation, whereas the proceeds from the sale are recognised in the investing section.
- An accrual (non-cash liability) made on the BS for some possible future event may have been charged to net income, and so would need to be added back as a non-cash item.

A screenshot of the completed CFS for the basic example is shown in Figure 3.3.

ERROR CHECKS AND FEASIBILITY CHECKS

General Error Checking Tools

Using the Cash Flow Statement

As well as the construction of the CFS in its own right and for general completeness, one of the main purposes of doing so is as a cross-check of the rest of the model. The fact

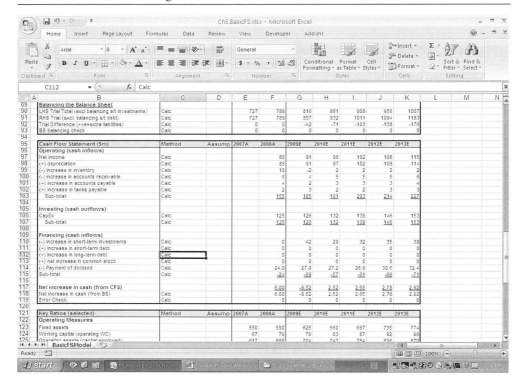

Figure 3.3

that a forecast BS balances provides little information about whether a model is error free, because the balancing has been forced (when using the earlier methodology). Rather, the most basic such check is whether the total cash flow derived in the CFS is the same as the change in planned cash shown on the BS.

Note that the occurrence of an error in this context would mean that one or more of the line items is missing, or is incorrectly or inconsistently calculated (rather than say that the ratio assumptions are realistic).

Other Error Checking Tools

In some cases it can take considerable time to trace and diagnose errors. The following techniques can help:

- Using a cross-check row to calculate the difference between the forecast of cash from the CFS and the change in cash forecasted on the BS. The elements should all be equal to zero, and conditional formatting (as discussed in Chapter 2) can be used to highlight clearly when they are non-zero. This approach is used in the basic example.
- Starting with a simple model and making this error-free before adding more detail or complexity. Whenever additions are made, always make only one change at a time, each

time checking that the model remains error-free. It is much harder to diagnose and correct an error when it is first noticed after several changes have been made.

- Working with a copy of the model and experimenting with simple input assumptions (for example, by changing inputs into round numbers or zero, such as setting the dividend or the tax rate to zero, and so on). It can then be easy to visually identify errors. This process may need to be repeated several times, with individual errors eliminated one after the other.
- Checking for the consistent modelling of the time treatment of tax and dividend payments between the IS, BS and CFS.
- Checking for the presence of non-cash items in the CFS (or that cash items were excluded).

Feasibility Checking and Ratio Analysis

General Points

A financial statement model which is error-free may nevertheless contain unrealistic input assumptions. Techniques that can be used to help to create credible assumptions include:

- Ensuring that the direct forecast assumptions are broadly aligned with judgement, historic experience or comparable companies.
- Checking that profit margins and other key calculated quantities do not show unreasonably large levels or changes, and that the effect of short-term trends (such as recent cost reduction initiatives) is not unreasonably extended into the future.
- Checking that the short-term balancing items on either side of the BS are relatively small. Large balancing items are an indication that other aspects of the forecast may be unrealistic (e.g. excess cash is accumulating because the cost, investment or growth assumptions are optimistic) or that if such a forecast were to be realised, then the business would likely perform some additional future actions that are not captured in the model (e.g. return cash to shareholders with a one-off dividend, reduce long-term debt levels below those that are assumed).
- Generally speaking, it is better to make any required changes to the input assumptions by first changing those assumptions that affect operational and investment quantities (cost of working capital, or depreciation ratios), before dealing with any financing assumptions. In general, if short-term balancing items remain large after cross-checking and adjusting the operational and investment assumptions, one has a choice as to whether or not to build in changes to the financing side of the business. Whether to do this or not must be considered on a case-by-case basis, as often it is preferable not to reflect such decisions in the base case of a model.
- Conducting ratio analysis on a variety of the model's calculations and key outputs, and using the ratios to compare with those of other companies, as well as a check of the general credibility of the absolute levels of these ratios.

Key Ratios

The following key ratios are typical of the ones that may be relevant in many applications:

- Operating and investment measures, such as:
  — Working capital/sales.
  — Sales/operating assets (= asset turn).

— Depreciation/sales.
— Capital investment/sales.
- Profitability measures, such as:
  — EBIT/sales, EBIT/operating assets.
  — NOPAT/sales, NOPAT/operating assets (see later).
  — Economic profit (see later).
  — Free cash flow (see later).
- Financing, gearing, and liquidity measures, such as:
  — Net debt/EBITDA.
  — Interest cover (EBIT/interest payable; EBITDA/interest payable).
  — Cash interest cover (e.g. NOPAT+depreciation/interest payable).
  — Net debt/equity.
  — Payables period (days) =365 × accounts payable/cost of goods sold.
  — Current ratio (= current assets/current liabilities).
  — Quick ratio (= current assets (excl. stocks)/current liabilities).

This list is not intended to be fully comprehensive, and the modeller may be able to find other ratios that are relevant in specific circumstances. In addition, many variations exist, and there is often no precise definition of whether certain items should be included or not in the calculation of a particular ratio. For example a sales-to-asset ratio or a profit-to-asset ratio could be based on starting, average, or end of period asset balances. Similarly, although working capital is crudely defined as current assets less current liabilities, one may discuss in certain contexts whether to include planned cash or the short-term balancing items (sometimes the term operational working capital is used to designate when these terms have been left out). The principle in defining such ratios in particular cases is to make sure that the definition is logically consistent within itself, with other comparisons, and in relation to the context in which it will be used.

The focus here is on the use of such ratios from a modelling perspective, and in particular in the creation of credible forecasts. Readers can also refer to standard texts on financial statement analysis for a more thorough presentation of such ratios.

Figure 3.4 shows the ratio analysis for the basic example.

The following describe some measures and ratios in more detail. The focus here is on measures that are important in the discussion of valuation later in the chapter.

NOPAT and Economic Profit

An important quantity is the net operating profit after tax (or NOPAT), defined as:

$$NOPAT = EBIT(1 - Tax\ rate)$$

A few comments are in order about NOPAT:

- It is in some sense a conceptual rather than actual quantity, as of course in reality tax is calculated after interest.
- It represents the net income that the business would generate if it had no debt. It is important in cash flow valuation calculations in order to avoid double-counting the cost of finance (which is reflected in the rate that is used to discount cash flows).
- It is also used in the calculation of economic profit. This is one of the most powerful cross-checks on the credibility of long-term forecasting models, and as such is often used

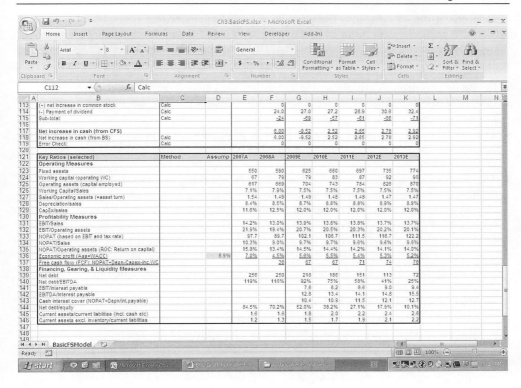

Figure 3.4

in cash flow valuation. It is defined as:

$$\text{Economic profit} = \text{NOPAT} - \text{Capital employed times cost of capital}$$

The economic profit would usually be calculated with reference to annual quantities, and is often converted into a percentage by dividing through by the capital employed; in this sense it can also be thought of as an excess return. It is of course a post-tax quantity, as is NOPAT. (The estimation of the cost of capital is discussed later.)

The importance of economic profit is that it can provide a powerful cross-check as to the credibility of the model's assumptions:

- In competitive markets the return-on-capital of a company should in theory in the long term tend towards its cost-of-capital, so that economic profit tends to zero.
- Valuation models that do not conduct a cross-check on economic profit typically over-value a business, by implicitly assuming that high levels of economic profit continue for ever. Such a situation is also typified by a valuation that is extremely sensitive to assumptions on the growth rate used for the terminal value calculation (whereas the value of a business that earns only a small economic profit in the terminal period would in reality be fairly insensitive to such an assumption, with any additional growth creating little value due to the extra capital required to achieve that growth).

In a forecasting model it may therefore be desirable to ensure that economic profit adjusts (generally: reduces) over time to some long-term equilibrium level (perhaps to zero or marginally above). Some judgement is usually required when considering the level and time-frame over which this adjustment should take place:

- In practice companies are often able to sustain such excess returns over many years.
- Generally speaking, many businesses may be currently earning an economic profit, and in reality markets may not be perfectly competitive.
- The role of management is to create economic profit; also, entrepreneurs and venture capital investors would neither create nor develop businesses if they expected zero economic profit on average.
- The level of capital in the capital base. Strictly speaking the capital employed for the economic profit calculation would need to be expressed at market value, or at least at current equivalent value. However, the capital taken from the BS will often be an understatement of the true capital relevant for an economic profit calculation. Some adjustment to the definition of capital could create a more realistic calculated level. However, such adjustments will typically require much judgement. Examples include:
  — The capital on the BS will not only have been partially depreciated but also will be expressed at historic prices.
  — R&D development costs and marketing expenditures (e.g. used to create brand awareness) are likely to have been expensed, and therefore not recorded as capital in the BS. Such items nevertheless contribute to profit through the continuing existence of the business, the volume of sales, and the prices achievable for the products sold. Similarly, the measured capital base is affected by the choice of inventory valuation policies, the existence of goodwill, the value of capital implicit in leased property, and of intangibles.

Once the long-term level for return-on-capital has been decided, the required input values (such as the long-term capex-to-sales ratio) can be found either by manual manipulation of the model's input assumptions or by creating a more automatic adjustment process, such as by using **Solver** or **GoalSeek** (see Chapter 1). This is discussed in more detail in a later section on valuation.

ADDING GENERALITY

In practice, a financial statement model may have further aspects to it than those shown in the basic example:

- There may be a requirement to have different assumptions for a short-term forecast (say the first one to three years) than for the long term:
  — A public company may have given specific guidance to the market on certain line items for some period of time into the future.
  — A company may have a budget for fixed costs that is pre-planned and largely known. It may be desired to implement these assumptions, by splitting out fixed cost separately from variable cost.
  — The modeller may be faced with a situation where the recent actual historic ratios (e.g. accounts receivable-to-sales) are out of line with medium or long-term expectations. In such cases, the assumptions for each year can be overwritten with the assumption required for the expected forecast to be met. This approach poses no real modelling

challenges, but it is important (for example, by formatting, colour-coding or shading) to clearly indicate that the assumptions are time-varying.

- It may be necessary to add further line items. Examples include earnings from associated companies, foreign exchange gains or losses, or other one-time items, provisions for future losses, and minority interests. As mentioned earlier, these items generally pose little challenge from a modelling perspective once their accounting treatment is understood. On the other hand, certain aspects can pose challenges from a modelling perspective, and these are the issues discussed below:
  - The use of several layers of debt or cash with different interest rates (including for the balancing items).
  - The inclusion of deferred tax assets and liabilities.
  - The use of more complex depreciation calculations.
  - The use (or avoidance) of circular references.

Example: Debt or Cash Waterfalls and Financing Structures

One of the most important financial modelling applications is the allocation of a quantity across various layers or tranches (sometimes referred to as creating cash waterfalls). An example was presented in Chapter 2 for tax calculations (see Figures 2.15–2.18).

The file Ch3.LayersAlloc.xlsx (Figure 3.5) shows an example in a BS context, where the aim is to allocate the balancing amount (after the calculation of the initial totals of

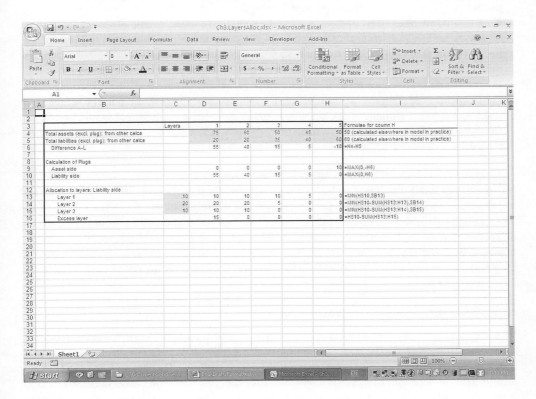

Figure 3.5

each side of the BS, as described earlier) between either a single asset balancing item or several liability balancing layers. In practice, once this allocation is complete, an interest rate specific to each layer could be applied in order to work out the total interest expense.

Example: Deferred Tax Assets and Liabilities

In reality there may be many reasons why the tax shown in the IS will be different to the taxes that are actually due or paid. In such situations it may be necessary to reflect deferred tax assets or liabilities in the model.

Examples include:

- Deferred tax liabilities can arise when the depreciation of assets for tax purposes (sometimes called capital allowances) initially occurs more quickly than the depreciation recognised on the financial statements. In such cases the initial cash taxes paid to tax authorities are lower than the tax recognised in the financial statements. At some point in the future this position would be reversed, and the depreciation related to these assets in the financial statements will become larger than that for tax purposes. The initial difference that arises must be recorded as a liability that will theoretically be due at a later date. Often, if a business continues to grow and invest in new assets (which themselves are likely to be depreciated more quickly in their early life), then this liability may never be realised. For this reason, deferred tax liabilities are often treated as quasi-equity and positioned in the BS appropriately (i.e. between debt and equity). Deferred tax liabilities can also arise if certain items have been treated as capital expenditure in the financial statements but as expenses for tax purposes, thus temporarily reducing taxable income and the immediate tax payment. This may apply to items such as software development costs, but of course this ultimately depends on the actual tax regime that is in place.
- Deferred tax assets may arise if taxes paid or due are larger than those recognised in the financial statements. This may occur, for example, if a loss in the current year would result in no direct reclaim of tax but would rather generate a tax loss that would be carried forward and offset against future taxes, i.e. the future tax savings generated by this loss would be a deferred tax asset.

The file Ch3.DTA&DTL.xlsx (Figure 3.6) shows an example of the modelling of deferred tax assets and liabilities. The taxable profit recognised on the IS is used to work out that for tax purposes by replacing the originally recognised depreciation by the capital allowance. The net balance is then allocated (after taking loss carry-forwards into account) as either a deferred tax asset or liability, depending on whether the amount to be allocated is positive or negative. Note that splitting the taxable amount into an asset or liability in this way is the same process as working out balancing items on the BS after an initial trial balance, as described earlier.

Example: Depreciation and Debt Schedules

In some cases it may be necessary to model a depreciation profile or a debt repayment schedule in more detail. The structural and modelling aspects required to do so were covered in Chapter 1. In the file Ch1.Lookup.xlsx (OFFSET1 worksheet) (Figure 1.28) we showed how a generic schedule of bond repayments after the year of issue could be changed into a specific schedule once the issue date is decided or known. The same technique could be applied to work out the total depreciation charges from a list of assets with different

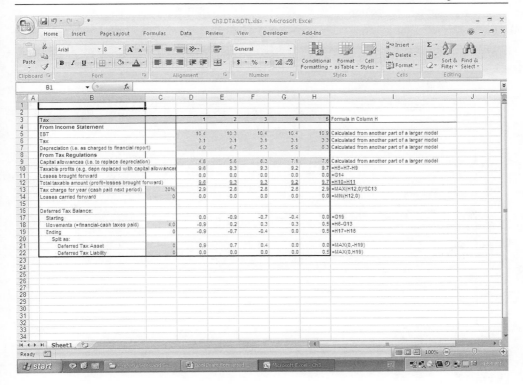

Figure 3.6

purchase dates and lives. In the file Ch1.Array.xlsx (Transpose worksheet) (Figure 1.39) we showed how a capital expenditure profile could be linked to a depreciation calculation, and also implemented the possibility of applying different depreciation methods. Many practical cases can be dealt with by using variations of these methods.

Example: Avoidance of Circular References

In Chapter 2 we discussed extensively the topic of circular references, in particular comparing the result of a method using circular references with that obtained with an interim cash flow method (where the interest calculation not only used prior period cash and debt levels, but also reflected the average periodic cash inflow).

The file Ch3.IntTaxLayers.xlsx (Figure 3.7) shows an example in which both methods are implemented, and where the user can select which one to apply. For completeness of presentation, the model also includes some of the other generalities discussed above, including multiple debt layers, and deferred tax assets and liabilities. Note that when using the periodic cash inflow in the interest calculation, the calculation of this cash inflow includes all line items except those relating to the interest calculation (otherwise a circular reference would be created); this calculation is rather like producing a partial cash flow statement, but excluding items related to interest.

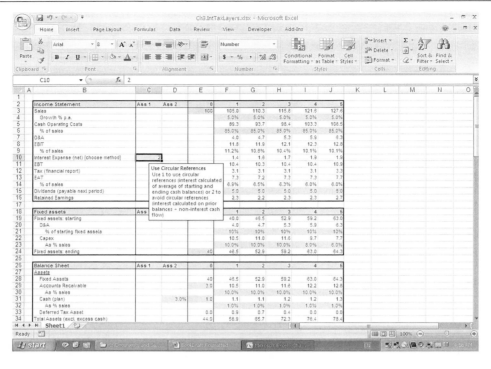

Figure 3.7

CASH FLOW VALUATION

This section focuses on the cash flow valuation of a business or project. It assumes knowledge of the ideas covered earlier in this chapter relating to economic profit, and the calculation of NOPAT and free cash flow. Other approaches to valuation exist, including those based on comparables. As use of alternative approaches can often complement a cash flow valuation by providing additional insight, cross-checks and benchmarks, some of these methods are also briefly mentioned.

Cash flow methods are sometimes thought of as fundamental methods because they usually involve a detailed modelling of the key factors that will affect the asset's (or company's) cash flow and its value (such as sales, sales growth, costs, taxes, investment requirements, etc.). The advantages are that the modelling process helps to structure clear thinking on the value drivers, it allows changes to the assumptions and sensitivity analysis, and it also means that proprietary aspects of valuation can be included (e.g. the inclusion of the effect of merger synergies, such as cost reduction opportunities). The disadvantages include that the detailed modelling required is more time-consuming than some other methods, such as those based on comparables.

The key steps in a cash flow valuation are:

- To create a forecast of free cash flows.
- To discount the forecasted free cash flows to reflect the time value of money and their risk, and to form the sum of all the discounted free cash flows (i.e. their net present value).

- To estimate the value associated with the continuing operations of the business after the forecast horizon, and discount that value to present terms.
- To make any further adjustments that may be required for the specific situation at hand. For example, for the valuation of equity, the starting level of net debt would need to be subtracted from the total enterprise value (using the period beginning net debt, if this period's cash flows are included in the valuation). It may also be necessary to add back the value of associated companies or equity investments, or subtract the value of minority interests, to the extent that the cash flow from these has not been included in the cash flow forecast.

Calculation of Free Cash Flow

Free cash flow (FCF) is the cash flow produced after taking into account any reinvestment (capital expenditure) required to keep the asset base forecast consistent with the revenue and operational forecast. FCF represents the cash available to repay debt and other liabilities and for distribution to shareholders (hence the term 'free'). FCF is defined as:

$$FCF = NOPAT + Depreciation - Capital\ Investment - Increase\ in\ Working\ Capital$$

A few observations can be made about this:

- Since FCF calculations are based on NOPAT, interest is not subtracted in its calculation. When using FCF to conduct cash flow valuation, the cost of finance is reflected in the discount rate; the subtraction of interest from the FCF would double-count the cost of debt finance.
- It requires only that the IS be modelled to the EBIT level. However, it is generally good practice to model the full statement: First, the extra effort in doing so is usually small. Second, doing so provides an additional error-checking possibility. Third, where other valuation methods are used for comparative purposes (such as price–earnings or dividend methods) then the corresponding lines for these items will be needed in any case.
- The working capital item is the operating working capital as discussed earlier, i.e. excluding cash and short-term balancing items. The inclusion of these items would represent double-counting. However, the starting value of these items would of course need to be taken into account in the final valuation of the overall business (e.g. such as when net debt is subtracted from enterprise value to provide an equity value).
- The term FCF is sometimes used in different contexts (or incorrectly). For example, the earnings before interest, tax, depreciation and amortization (EBITDA) is sometimes used as a proxy measure of cash generated by business operations. However, since EBITDA is a statement of cash flow before required reinvestment, it is not free. Sometimes the term 'operating free cash flow' is also used to represents cash produced from operations (but before investment in fixed assets). Therefore one may need to take care in interpreting the term in certain contexts.

Discounting Free Cash Flow

Since cash in hand today could potentially be put to a large variety of uses, and future cash flows are by definition uncertain (as business conditions could change and the forecast may not be realised), any valuation based on future cash flows needs to reflect their risk and timing. This is achieved by discounting them at an appropriate discount rate.

The Average Cost of Capital

Since FCF is available to repay any source of finance, the discount rate must represent the aggregated (or averaged) cost of the sources of finance, usually called the weighted average cost of capital (WACC):

$$\text{WACC} = w_e r_e + w_d r_d (1 - t)$$

In this formula r_e and r_d represent the cost of equity and debt, and the weights (w's) reflect the target capital structure at market values (and of course total 100%). In other words:

$$\text{WACC} = \frac{E}{D + E} r_e + \frac{D}{D + E} r_d (1 - t)$$

The use of the target capital structure in the weighting reflects the mix of capital that will be used in the long term. It also creates comparability between companies that are operationally identical but choose to finance themselves differently. The use of the actual capital structures for two otherwise identical businesses would result in a lower cost-of-capital for the one with the higher level of debt, since the WACC would be lower, and hence the valuation would be higher.

For fairly mature businesses, it can often be assumed that the existing capital structure is a good representation of the target structure, but this may not be an appropriate assumption for businesses at an early development stage. In addition, in some cases, a public company may make statements as to its own estimation of the target structure. Generally the target (optimal) capital structure results from balancing:

- The higher risk of bankruptcy that would result from higher levels of debt.
- The lower cost of debt. Debt is cheaper than equity for several reasons:
  — Interest is charged before tax, so that the use of debt creates a tax shield.
  — Debt coupon repayments are contractual obligations that have priority over dividend payments to equity holders, so that the risk of non-payment of debt obligations is lower.
  — The cash costs of issuance (e.g. fees to bankers) are generally lower for debt than for equity.
  — The issuance of equity may signal that insiders (i.e. management) believe that equity is overvalued. This creates extra implicit costs associated with equity issuance, and a risk that the share price might fall on the announcement of the issuance.

The Capital Asset Pricing Model and the Cost of Equity and Debt

The most important framework (or model) to guide the calculation of the cost-of-capital sources is the Capital Asset Pricing Model (CAPM). This is summarised briefly here; readers wishing more detail may refer to standard texts in corporate finance such as Brealey and

Myers (see Further Reading). The CAPM states that:

- The price of any financial asset should adjust so that the expected return from holding the asset compensates investors for both the time value of money and the risk.
- Compensation should be expected (in asset pricing or returns) only for risks that cannot be offset by holding a well-diversified portfolio.

In this approach, the risk of an asset is measured as the covariance of its return with the market's return. Denoting the risk-free rate by r_f, the expected return on the asset by $E(r_s)$, and the expected return on the market by $E(r_m)$, and using ρ_{sm} to represent the correlation coefficient between the asset's and the market's returns, and σ_s and σ_m to represent the standard deviation of the asset's and market's return, CAPM can be written as:

$$E(r_s) = E(r_f) + \beta_s(E(r_m) - E(r_f))$$

$$\beta_s = \frac{\text{cov}(r_s, r_m)}{\text{cov}(r_m, r_m)} = \frac{\rho_{sm}\sigma_s\sigma_m}{\sigma_m\sigma_m} = \frac{\rho_{sm}\sigma_s}{\sigma_m}$$

The β (beta) of an asset is used as a relative measure of its non-diversifiable risk, with the market having a β of 1, and an asset with a β of less than (greater than) 1 being less (more) risky than the market. The difference between the expected return on the market and the risk-free rate can be thought of as the market risk premium.

The CAPM results in some initially counter-intuitive results. For example, it implies that investors generally should receive no premium for projects relating to oil exploration, drug development or to many generally insurable events (such as fires and car crashes); these (project specific risks) generally are uncorrelated with asset markets, so the variability associated with such projects at an individual level can be offset by holding a large number of such projects in a portfolio.

When estimating the cost of equity, providing that appropriate historic data is available, the β can be derived from data on equity returns and market returns, either by regression analysis or by using the appropriate Excel functions (see Chapter 1). When doing so, the β calculated will correspond to the historic capital structure (and will also be subject to statistical error, due to the typically relatively small sample sizes of truly comparable data). If the target capital structure is different to the historic one, then the cost of equity at the target capital structure can be calculated by first unlevering β from the historic structure and then relevering it to the new structure, for each calculation using the standard formula:

$$\beta_l = \beta_u(1 + D(1 - t)/E)$$

This formula assumes that the beta of debt is zero; sometimes an alternative is used:

$$\beta_l = \beta_u + (1 - t)\frac{D}{E}(\beta_u - \beta_D)$$

Once the β is estimated, the cost of equity can be calculated, by using further assumptions on the risk-free rate and the market risk premium:

- The risk-free rate can be reasonably estimated from the yield on government debt. In Chapter 1, we showed how the **IRR** function (or the **YIELD** function) could be used to calculate the yield of a bond from the price, coupon and maturity. Note that the yield on debt varies (typically increases) as the maturity lengthens. For example, at the time of writing the yield on US government bonds was 2.96% p.a. and 3.77% p.a. for 5 and 10 Year bonds (the corresponding figures for UK government bonds were 4.39% p.a. and 4.59% p.a., and for German government bonds they were 3.76% p.a. and 3.99% p.a.). One could therefore consider whether to use a different risk-free rate (and therefore a different cost of capital) for each year. This is perfectly possible, and poses little challenge from a modelling perspective, simply requiring the calculation of yields over a wider range of maturities, and also meaning that future cash flows need to be individually discounted with different discount rates (so that the **NPV** function could not be used for the whole range of cash flows). On the other hand, in practice such a procedure may not be worthwhile: first, the cost of capital that is associated with doing so largely averages out compared with the case where a single figure is used based on medium maturity debt (in this latter approach, the cost of capital would be slightly overstated in the earlier years and understated in the later years when the yield is increasing over time); second, the cost of capital is ultimately an estimated figure, and the uncertainty surrounding it is usually dominated by the assumption used for the cost of equity, and in particular that used for the equity risk premium (see below).

• The appropriate level of the equity risk premium is a subject of much academic research. For example, studies have shown that it has varied quite significantly over time and across geographic markets. The details of this are beyond the scope of this text; interested readers may refer to Dimson, Marsh and Staunton (see Further Reading). Ultimately, one will need to make an assumption that is credible and explicit, so that one can perform a sensitivity analysis on the assumption if desired (often, of course, such sensitivity analysis is implicit in that performed on the aggregate cost of capital).

The calculations for the cost of debt are typically slightly more straightforward than those for equity. Generally, one may consider either using the yield on existing debt issued by the company (or comparable companies), or using a CAPM approach (in which case the β of the debt must estimated, with 0.2 often used as a starting point).

The file Ch3.Val.BasicFS.xlsx (Figure 3.8) shows the earlier completed basic financial statement with the aggregate cost-of-capital calculation included. (We use a risk-free rate of 5% p.a., an equity-risk premium of 5.5% p.a., with a cost of debt of 6% p.a.)

Terminal Value Calculations

When building a forecasting model for a project with a defined life, it would be typical to construct an explicit forecast for the entire period of the project. In contrast, a business does not have a defined life, and will typically have some residual value at the end of the explicit forecast period (the terminal value). In some cases, the terminal value can represent a large proportion of the overall value; this situation can be unsatisfactory in the sense that it is value associated with a non-explicit or detailed forecast. In addition, many models result in valuations that are also excessively sensitive to the growth rate assumption used during the terminal period. The consequence is that the results appear to be either less credible or not worthy of further consideration (as most of the value appears to be determined from a factor that is uncertain and over which there is very little control). Some approaches that can be used to provide a better estimate of the terminal value include:

• Extending the forecast period. The larger model that is created by doing so is usually manageable with modern computing power and the extra columns available in Excel

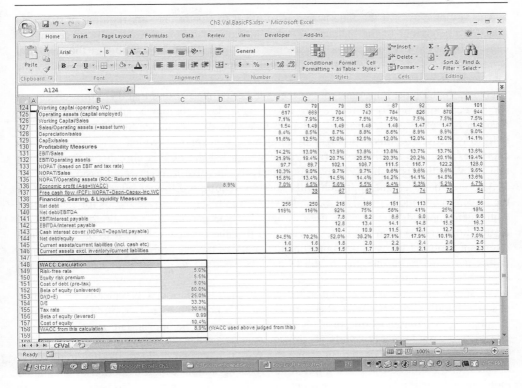

Figure 3.8

2007. There can nevertheless sometimes be a reluctance to do this, as the nature of the business and relevant assumptions at some future distant time are highly uncertain. On the other hand, even simple terminal value approaches (such as those based on valuing perpetuities of cash flows, as discussed later) use implicit assumptions, and making those explicit can be useful.

- Ensuring that the forecast during the terminal period is credible. In particular, this includes checking that the level of economic profit during the terminal period is appropriate.
- Testing a variety of approaches to the calculation of value, in order to generate a comparison of the results.

These methods are not exclusive of each other, and indeed one may choose to use all three for any particular valuation. For example, where the forecast period has been extended, perpetuity formulae will still be applicable, but will simply be applied after a longer period.

The Use of Fade Periods and the Return on Capital

The modelling horizon could be extended beyond the initial forecast period, with the initial period being regarded as the formal forecast period, and the extended period being the fade period (for example, each of the explicit forecast and fade periods might typically be 5 or 10 years).

The key objective of the fade period is to use it to ensure that any required or expected long-term behaviour of the business or relevant ratios is reflected, especially its return-on-capital. Its purpose is not *per se* to generate an explicit forecast credible at the line item level (unlike for the forecast period), but rather to provide a basis to check and modify the long-term assumptions.

Generally the most important role of the fade period is to ensure that the return-on-capital (or its economic profit) converges to a reasonable level, before a subsequent perpetuity formula is applied to the terminal (i.e. post-fade period) cash flows. Such an approach can help to remedy a common problem in many valuation models, which is to understate the capital expenditure requirements (in turn, meaning that the FCF is unrealistically high and that the valuation is both too high and excessively sensitive to other input assumptions).

A model that uses this approach will generally require a different set of assumptions for the forecast and fade periods, for example with different capex-to-sales ratios for each. Other adjustment methods can also be used during the fade period, such as modifying the cost assumptions (rather than the capex levels), so that the profit level is set to an appropriate return-on-capital. However, one potential advantage of the use of the capital base adjustment is that it retains more integrity in the IS calculations (say to the level of EBITDA) at the expense of a potentially less realistic BS.

An appropriate return-on-capital at the end of the fade period will typically be one that is some margin above the WACC (i.e. that there is a positive economic profit). A potential assumption that the economic profit is precisely zero may be appropriate in some circumstances, but would often be overly pessimistic (see the earlier discussion of economic profit). Once a reasonable level of margin above the WACC has been decided, the required capex-to-sales ratio could be estimated approximately using simple experimentation or calculated more formally using **Solver** or **GoalSeek** (see Chapter 1). One must also bear in mind that this level would need to be reset each time any of the other input assumptions are changed (which can limit the possibilities to perform automated sensitivity analysis, as discussed later).

Valuation of a Perpetuity for the Terminal Value

In order to value the cash flows after the fade period, we need a method to value cash flows that are growing in perpetuity. Further, we will assume that the return-on-capital in this terminal period is constant, and is one that we wish to explicitly set.

The assumption of constant return-on-capital leads to the conclusion that the net investment requirement is equal to the capital base multiplied by the growth rate for the free cash flows. In other words:

$$FCF_1 = NOPAT_1 - CE_0 g$$

Also:

$$NOPAT_1 = CE_0 \ ROCE$$

(where g is the growth rate in the terminal period, CE_0 denotes the capital employed at the beginning of the terminal period (end of fade period), and FCF_1 and $NOPAT_1$ represent the FCF and NOPAT during this first period, and ROCE the (constant) return-on-capital employed.)

When discounting FCF_1 to the beginning of the terminal period, its value is:

$$\text{Discounted FCF}_1 = \frac{CE_0(\text{ROCE} - g)}{1 + \text{WACC}}$$

In each subsequent period, these cash flows grow, but must also be discounted to the beginning of the terminal period, so that:

$$TV = \frac{CE_0}{1 + \text{WACC}}(\text{ROCE} - g)\sum_{t=0}^{\infty} \frac{(1 + g)^t}{(1 + \text{WACC})^t}$$

Using the standard formula:

$$\sum_{i=0}^{\infty} x^i = \frac{1}{1 - x}$$

results in:

$$TV = CE_0 \left(\frac{\text{ROCE} - g}{\text{WACC} - g}\right)$$

Several other points are worthy of note when using this:

- The formula represents the terminal value at the beginning of the terminal period, which needs to be further discounted to the present (failure to do this is a common mistake).
- When ROCE is equal to WACC, the formula shows that the terminal value is equal to the capital employed at the end of the fade period (beginning of the terminal period), independent of the growth rate. In other words, in such circumstances, growth produces no additional value (as should be expected).
- The assumed terminal growth rate should be one that is sustainable in the long term. Many economists recommend a figure of about 4.5% to 5% p.a., reflecting the economic opportunity created from the combined effects of population growth, inflation and general productivity increases. A growth figure that is too high would implicitly assume that the company under consideration is gaining an increasing share of the world's economy in the long term, and is likely to be unrealistic. Where there is an explicit long-term inflation forecast in the model, then such a growth figure can be disaggregated and varied automatically if the sensitivity to inflation were to be tested.

Note that one may ask whether it is still necessary to model the fade period when one uses this terminal value formula; one could instead just apply the formula directly at the end of the forecast period. Such an approach is valid, but the additional advantage of a fade period is that it allows the return-on-capital to adjust gradually to the assumed level at the end of the fade period, and also allows the return-on-capital assumption for the terminal period to be different to that at the end of the fade period. This extra flexibility provides an extra layer of accuracy and confidence in the forecast.

Example: Valuation of the Basic Financial Statement Model

The file Ch3.Val.BasicFS.xlsx (Figure 3.9) extends the forecast contained in the earlier model to include a 10 year fade period. An additional column has been added for the fade

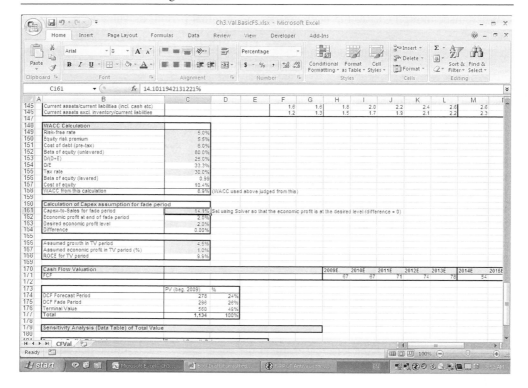

Figure 3.9

period assumptions. The fade period has been visually separated from the forecast period using bordered formatting to highlight that there is a change in the formulae along some rows due to the change in the reference cell of the assumption. The capex-to-sales ratio for the fade period has been adjusted (using **Solver**) to a level that results in the economic profit at the end of the fade period being 2.0. A long-term growth rate of 4.5% p.a. and a return-on-capital for the terminal period that is 1.0% above the WACC has been assumed for the terminal value calculation.

Further Adjustments

In most practical applications, the enterprise value that is calculated from a cash flow valuation will need adjusting before the results can be used for a specific decision. For example:

- The entity being valued may also own assets or have liabilities whose cash flows have not been included in the cash flow forecast. Possible examples include starting levels of cash or debt, associated companies or equity investments, off-balance-sheet obligations or other non-debt liabilities, minority interests (i.e. external interests in the consolidated cash flow), or the effect of pension obligations or capital leases.
- The potential dilution effects of share options, warrants, or convertibles.

- When valuing equity, the net debt will need to be subtracted from the enterprise value that results after the above adjustments.

Once again, there may be some detailed accounting-related issues here, but from a modelling perspective such adjustments are generally straightforward, and are not covered further in this text.

Sensitivity Analysis

In most valuation contexts it is worthwhile to conduct of a range of sensitivity analyses, not least because an accurate valuation is clearly important in most practical decision situations, and because knowledge of the potential uncertainty can inform better decision-making.
In this context, sensitivity analysis refers both to:

- Changing the assumptions used in a given model, such as varying the growth rate or assumed level of economic profit in the terminal period.
- Considering different modelling and valuation approaches, in order to provide an additional cross-check or benchmark with which to view the results.

Long-Term Growth and Economic Profit Assumptions

The file Ch3.Val.BasicFS.xlsx (Figure 3.10) shows a sensitivity analysis to the assumptions on the terminal growth rate and to the level of economic profit during the terminal period, and uses a two-way **Data Table** (as covered in Chapter 2). Note that when varying the growth rate, it is implicitly assumed that this variation is due to real growth in the business, not to inflationary effects (changes in growth due to inflationary effects would also need to affect the WACC and would reduce the overall sensitivity).

Comparison with Other Valuation Methods

The use of other valuation methods is a valuable cross-check on the results produced from a cash flow valuation. Such alternative methods are briefly mentioned here, but are not covered in detail as they mostly pose little difficulty from a modelling perspective.

- Dividend-forecasting models are sometimes used to conduct equity valuation. These involve discounting a forecast of dividend payments to equity holders. The simplest such approach is to forecast dividends by applying a growth rate to a recent or assumed figure. While the approach can be useful in certain circumstances, it may not be clear if such dividend levels would be sustainable (the dividend is itself a residual value, resulting both from general business performance and from management decisions). Further detailed modelling in this regard may be needed, which would then usually require the construction of a full cash flow model in any case. So this approach generally represents a quick guide and potentially valuable cross-check, rather than a fundamental one.
- The comparables approach relies on finding assets which are similar to the one being valued, and whose value is known (such as a set of publicly quoted companies). The advantage of this approach is that the required data is often readily available and the analysis is easy and quick to implement. For example, if it is determined from market prices that a comparable company's value is equal to twice its annual revenues,

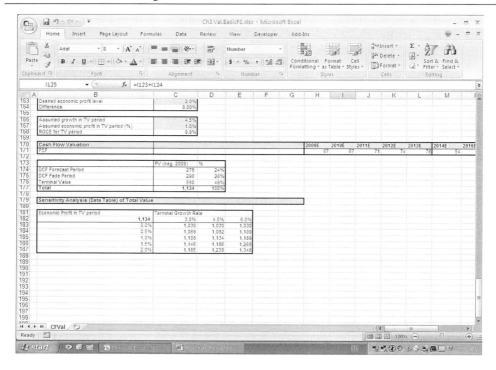

Figure 3.10

this same ratio could be applied to the company being valued. Ratios such as price-to-earnings or enterprise value-to-EBITDA are other common methods in this category. The disadvantages of the comparables approach include that:

— Perfect comparables are rare, and there is often no easy mechanism to correct for differences between such assets. For example, companies operating in different geographic markets may be subject to different market conditions and growth rates, tax rates, or legal and regulatory structures, all of which could affect the value of the business for strategic, operational and financing reasons. The multiplier will not reflect these differences. Even for companies in the same environment, the price–earnings measure is affected by leverage in the capital structure of each business.

— Circular reasoning could arise, i.e. where each asset in a group is valued with reference to the same group of assets (e.g. the cheapest asset in a set of comparables is revalued as a result of the comparison, resulting in it no longer being the cheapest, and the new cheapest asset is itself revalued upwards; this potential circularity can work downwards as well as upwards, of course).

— The method is not very satisfactory when used to estimate terminal values. Future multiples are likely to be very different to current ones. For example, a sector experiencing rapid growth today will generally currently have larger multiplies than a stable sector. The multiples that would apply at some time in the future when the sector is mature would be lower. The approach may therefore result in reinforcing upwards the valuation of growing sectors.

- The arbitrage approach to valuation involves finding another asset whose value is known and whose changes in value are perfectly correlated with the original asset. The most frequent example is in derivatives, i.e. the value of a traded derivatives contract is determined from the value of the underlying asset with changes between the two being perfectly correlated. In this way, portfolios of alternative assets can be created whose movements mirror those of the original asset, and hence there must be a direct relationship between the known values of the portfolio and that of the original asset. Such methods are very powerful when they are available, but they usually apply only in special circumstances, such as the valuation of options and other derivatives. In some ways, a comparables approach can be considered to be a crude example of this type of thought process.
- The options approach is sometimes cited as a possible method to conduct equity valuation. In this approach, the firm's equity is regarded as a call option on the assets of the firm, and the option's exercise price is equal to the debt and other liabilities. The Black–Scholes formula (or other option pricing techniques) is then applied with assumptions on the value of the required parameters. This is a theoretically enticing argument, but is rarely useful in practice, partly due to difficulties in estimating the parameter values required for options models (such as volatility) and partly because the full theoretical framework required for most options valuation techniques does not in fact apply to general assets (e.g. the time to exercise is unclear, as is the optimal exercise strategy, and the valuation of embedded options inherent in ongoing business operations).

4
Risk Modelling

The topic of risk modelling (or uncertainty modelling) can be considered to be a natural extension of sensitivity analysis. The outcome of a process will almost always be different to that predicted by any single point forecast or to the limited set of possibilities identified through a sensitivity analysis. In addition, risk analysis examines not only the potential occurrence of outcomes (as does sensitivity analysis), but also their likelihood.

In this chapter we cover the benefits that may be achieved by conducting an explicit modelling of uncertainty, demonstrate some tools that are available to do so, and use example models from a range of applications. We make extensive use of the add-in @RISK (from Palisade Corporation). In Chapter 5 we extend the topic of risk modelling to options and real options situations, and in that context also make use of Palisade's PrecisionTree to implement decision trees. A free (time-limited) trial version of these products may be downloaded from www.palisade.com. We provide some brief guidance on their use, which should be sufficient for the reader to work with the example models in this text. The Palisade website also provides tutorials for these products, which can be used by readers who wish to reinforce the knowledge or explore specific points in more detail. Those modelling examples in Chapters 4 and 5 which use Palisade software are built in Excel 2003 (but still presented in the screenshots in Excel 2007); this is due to some backward compatibility issues with the Palisade software that were present at the time of writing, meaning that models built in Excel 2007 would not be immediately readable by users of Excel 2003.

BENEFITS AND CHALLENGES OF RISK MODELLING

Reflection of Uncertainty in Decision-Making

There may be cases where it is possible to make an appropriate decision without explicitly reflecting the uncertainty of the outcome in the decision process. A possible example is a go/no go decision for a project. To the extent that the project can be considered to be representative of the type of project that is frequently encountered, the decision to proceed should in theory be based on whether the average (mean) benefit (or net profit) of doing so is positive. As long as the project is of this repetitive nature (and the mean can be estimated) then further analysis of uncertainty may be unnecessary.

On the other hand, in practice the following benefits may be achieved by explicit consideration of the uncertainty:

- The estimation of the mean of the output may in practice require some form of uncertainty modelling. The inputs to a static model are likely to be populated at their most likely values (because the choice of any other value represents a less likely case for that particular input), and so the output will in general not show its mean, especially where the uncertainty is non-symmetrically distributed or the model has a non-linear behaviour.
- Uncertainty analysis forces a clearer definition of what the static (base case) forecast is intended to represent (something that is usually not explicitly otherwise addressed). It

will generally lead to any particular forecast being viewed in the context of the range of possible outcomes. Biases that are introduced unintentionally (due to most likely value assumptions for the inputs) or intentionally (for motivational or political reasons) should have less of an influence in the decision-making process (which can focus on the average, the range and the likelihood of various outcomes).

- The modelling of uncertainty allows the reflection of personal risk preferences and tolerances in the decision process. Especially where the decision is regarded as non-repetitive (for example, where failure could result in a loss of status for the decision-maker or bankruptcy of the business, etc.), then the mean outcome may not be the key decision criterion, rather the distribution of the outcome needs explicit consideration. For example, a project which is profitable on average may be rejected because of the possibility (and consequences) of some of the negative outcomes. Alternatively, a senior manager may be willing to accept a project which allows the possibility of a large gain albeit with some chance of loss, whereas a junior manager may decide that the occurrence of the loss would not be acceptable to his or her career prospects, and hence reject the project. Similarly, in project budgeting, the total budget may be set (e.g. by a project manager) not at the original base planned cost, but at a value that will be achievable in say 90% of cases.

Robustness of Modelling Process and Improved Communication

The process of conducting an uncertainty analysis is generally a more structured and rigorous one than that for static forecasting. Typically, one needs to explicitly identify the factors that could cause variability in a model's output, estimate their likelihood and impact, and develop mitigating actions where appropriate. The process of identifying the drivers of risk is in many ways similar to the process of sensitivity analysis thinking described in Chapter 2. Such a process may work in an iterative fashion in which additional factors are brought into the model, these actions having some cost and benefit (e.g. a reduction of uncertainty elsewhere in the model). A risk model is therefore likely to include additional factors that were not in the original base case static model. For example, event risks would generally not be included in a base case model, but would be included in the risk model, as would potential measures (where worthwhile) to mitigate the probability or impact of such events.

The risk modelling process generally facilitates a greater involvement of working groups in the design and functionality of the model. It can therefore aid communication and consensus building. It can help to make explicit those areas where people may be making different assumptions, and allows a wide set of points of view (often all generally valid) to be incorporated into the modelling.

Combinations and Probabilities

Where a model contains several important variables, sensitivity techniques can become impractical to implement due to the number of possible combinations. For example, a model with five inputs, each of which could take only one of three values, would have up to 243 possible values for the output. In addition, the outcomes identified by such a sensitivity analysis would not have any probability explicitly associated with them. The process to generate a large (sufficiently representative) set of the possible output values and associated probabilities will generally require automation through simulation techniques.

Contingent Claims and Non-linear Behaviours

Some modelling situations explicitly require the consideration of variability for them to be meaningful. This particularly applies where the outcome varies in a non-linear way with other model variables or the inputs. Examples include contingent claims analysis, as is found in insurance, contract penalty clauses (e.g. a penalty is payable whenever some condition is not met), and options and real options situations. In such cases, a static model may have very limited or no relevance.

Limitations of Traditional Excel Structures

The basic Excel environment (i.e. without add-ins or VBA code) can also be inadequate where a modelling situation contains sequences of decisions. For example, if one is taking a decision as to whether to proceed with a project whose scope could be redefined (e.g. abandoned, expanded, or modified) after some initial information has been gained in its early stages (such as the results of a test which provides an imperfect indicator of the likely future success of the project), then the embedded logical structure is one involving branching to different project structures. In some cases, it is possible to reflect the logic and branching of tree structures in an Excel model (without using other software). However, in many cases it can be necessary or more appropriate to augment the Excel environment with additional software (as we do in Chapter 5 when discussing some real options models).

Challenges in using Risk Analysis Results

In practice there may be many challenges in using the results of quantitative risk analysis models. The organisational context (in terms of culture, management, structure and processes) can have a large impact on the willingness to integrate the results of risk analysis within corporate or group decision processes. Typical objections include:

- That the analysis appears too complex, and therefore suspect.
- That the results are too difficult to communicate to others in a clear way.
- That the responsibility for risk should be internalised within the project under question and not considered as part of an overall decision and planning process that surrounds a project.

Such views, while understandable, are likely to become less tenable as the benefits of such analysis and the capabilities to rapidly implement simple yet powerful risk models become more widespread.

THE RISK MODELLING PROCESS

Defining Risk and Risk Analysis

For some, the term risk evokes a notion of negativity (such as the likelihood and impact of a specific adverse event), whereas for others it may suggest the possibility to create value through exploitation of variability. At its core, risk analysis makes no assumption on whether the various outcomes in a situation are good or bad. Such a judgement is dependent on the impact on the particular subject. In this text, we will use the term in a general sense;

that is simply to represent a situation where an outcome of interest could have multiple possible values. This could be the weather tomorrow, someone's arrival time at work, the future value of a house, and so on.

Sometimes a distinction is made between the terms *uncertainty*, *variability* and *risk*. In such contexts, uncertainty is used to refer to a lack of knowledge (e.g. if we tossed a coin 10 times and produced three heads, how likely is it that the coin is a fair one?), variability is used to refer to the random (or stochastic) nature of a process (e.g. the tossing of a coin can produce one of two outcomes), and risk is used specifically to indicate the potential occurrence of an event. Philosophically, some may argue that there is no difference between uncertainty and variability; for example that once a coin has been tossed, whether it lands heads or tails is not random but fully determined by the laws of physics (with the outcome being simply unknown to the observer and therefore uncertain). There are some cases where it may be necessary to make a formal distinction between these concepts, but in many practical situations it is not, and so we do not emphasise it.

Building a Risk Model

The basic aim of risk modelling is to calculate or estimate the range and likelihood of the possible values of the output (i.e. the probability distribution of the output), and to use this to inform decision-making. Risk modelling will often be part of a wider process of risk management, often thought of as consisting of stages such as:

- *Risk identification and prioritisation.* As for other modelling activities, the identification of drivers of risk requires an understanding of the situation. Some common sense can be augmented with the use of formal brainstorming techniques where appropriate.
- *Risk analysis and modelling.* This includes the modelling of risk using probability distributions, the capturing the dependencies or other relationships in the model, and the calibration of the model. Risk models using simulation allow one to capture a wide set of dependency relationships, including correlated sampling and parameter dependencies (see later).
- *Risk monitoring and controlling.* This is the process of managing risks as they occur and of updating the model to reflect any changed circumstances (e.g. the materialisation of risk factors, new estimates for model parameters and so on).

A risk model may contain a larger or augmented set of variables than a static model. It results from an iterative process consisting of the above steps conducted several times. It would generally include all risk mitigation measures that are worthwhile (and their impacts on other variables in the model), but exclude potential mitigation factors that are not worth while (because they are judged too expensive to implement). In some sense the risk model reflects a new base case, which can be thought of as an optimised one, with the resulting uncertainty in the outcome being a residual uncertainty.

AN INTRODUCTION TO SIMULATION TECHNIQUES

Simulation techniques are essentially automated ways to generate many samples or scenarios for a model's output (as the inputs vary). Each individual outcome may be thought of as a scenario i.e. it answers the What If? question for a particular combination of input values. The basic process involves:

- Construction of a model which is valid as the relevant inputs are varied. The use of the sensitivity analysis principles of Chapter 2 can be particularly important here.
- Generating samples for each of the input variables, recalculating the model and recording the results for the value of the outputs. Typically the sampling of values used is based on the assumption that the input uncertainty follows a probability distribution.
- Repeating the above step many times.
- Analysing the results. In particular the data set of results will have statistical properties and can be considered as representing the samples from a probability distribution of the outputs.

Simulation techniques are generally quite easy to set up, and are intuitive to understand, with the modeller generally not required to have any advanced knowledge of mathematics, probability theory or statistics. The results are usually also fairly readily understandable, easy to share and communicate. The disadvantages are that simulation techniques can be time-consuming to run if very accurate results are required, and they may not pick up rare events (e.g. worst and best case combinations). In some circumstances, analytic techniques or other numerical methods are required instead, but these are generally beyond the scope of this text.

The Language of Probability Distributions

Probability distributions are a key aspect of risk analysis, and can be used to represent uncertainty both in model inputs and outputs.

Continuous and Discrete Distributions

Distributions can broadly be classified into two categories, according to whether the variable represents a continuous quantity (e.g. time, space, money) or a discrete one (e.g. the occurrence or not of an event, the number of goals in a soccer match, the outcome of throwing a dice, whether one arrives late for work or not, etc.). It is usually clear from the context whether a distribution is discrete or continuous.

More complex (compound) distributions can exist, such as would arise where there are event risks (i.e. events which may or may not occur), whose occurrence is associated with an uncertain impact.

Density and Cumulative Curves

Distributions can visually be displayed in two formats:

- As a density curve, in which the y-axis represents the relative likelihood of the particular value. The advantage of this display is that key properties of the distribution (e.g. the mean, standard deviation and skew) can be more or less seen visually. One subtlety is that the y-axis of a density curve for a discrete distribution represents the actual probability of occurrence, whereas for a continuous distribution it represents the relative likelihood, with a probability being associated only with a range of outcomes.
- As a cumulative curve. The advantage of this display is that the probability of a range of values can be read from the y-axis, whereas it would have to be visually estimated when

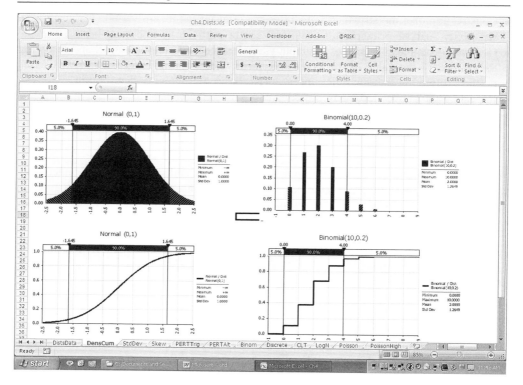

Figure 4.1

using the density curve. The y-axis shows the probability that an outcome less than or equal to a particular value is achieved.

The file Ch4.Dists.xls (DensCum worksheet) (Figure 4.1) shows an example of the density and cumulative curves for some continuous and discrete distributions.

Measures of the Central Point

The key statistics that can be used to describe the central points of a distribution are:

- The mode represents the most frequently occurring value. As mentioned earlier, when providing a point (static) estimate of a value or model input, very often the mode would be given, as the occurrence of any other value would be less likely.
- The mean (or expected value) represents the average (sometimes referred to as a probability-weighted average because the process of calculating an average involves including points which occur more frequently with this same frequency in the calculation):

$$\mu = E(x) = \sum p_i x_i$$

Visually, the mean can be interpreted as the x-coordinate of the centre of gravity (i.e. the point on the x-axis where the distribution balances). In financial calculations the net present value (NPV) of a series of cash flows is the mean of the discounted cash flows.

- The median represents the point at which 50% of the values are on either side of it (i.e. the 50th percentile or P50). It can be a useful measure in population statistics (e.g. to represent the average political opinion, or the average salary of a group of people when looked at from the perspective of individual perceptions of wealth).

Note that these three measures will be the same for distributions which are symmetric and single-moded (such as the Normal distribution), but in general will be different to each other.

Measures of the Spread and of Risk

Often one requires a single measure of risk. Broadly, there are two possible approaches to this, one providing some measure of the spread, and the other a probability as to whether a certain outcome or outcomes within a range would be achieved. The key measures of spread are:

- The standard deviation is a standardised measure of the spread around the mean. It has the same units as the variable under consideration, and is calculated as the square root of the variance, which itself is calculated as the weighted average sum of the squared distances of every value from the mean:

$$\sigma = \sqrt{\sum p_i (x_i - \mu)^2}$$

(This formula assumes that the data represents the whole population; a small correction term can be applied when sample data is used to estimate the population's standard deviation; this is the difference between Excel's **STDEVP** and **STDEV** functions mentioned earlier. More details can be found in the function's description in Excel's **Help** or in standard statistical texts). For many distributions, the standard deviation crudely represents the size of the band around the mean which contains approximately two-thirds of the values (although this rule of thumb does not apply in all cases). For a Normal distribution, the one standard deviation region either side of the mean contains around 68.3% of the outcomes, and the two standard deviation region around 95.4% of the outcomes.

- The size of a range between two percentiles (e.g. the difference between the P90 and P10). The minimum–maximum range (i.e. P0 to P100) can also be considered, but this is often not a good measure in practice, either because many distributions are unbounded (in theory) or because simulation techniques can never produce a good estimate of this range (as the end points generally have very low probability of occurrence and are not picked up by simulation).

Measures of risk which use spread sometimes do not directly answer specific questions that the decision-maker may have. In many cases, more appropriate risk measures may be those that do so, such as:

- What is the probability that the base case will be achieved?
- What is the probability that losses will exceed a certain amount?

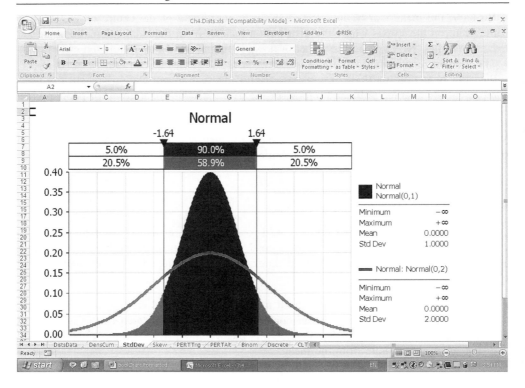

Figure 4.2

Note that in cases where the results are approximately Normally distributed (see later for examples), then the knowledge of the mean and standard deviation (or of the probabilities associated with any two outcomes) would formally provide the same information, although not necessarily in the form most directly relevant for communication purposes.

The file Ch4.Dists.xls (StdDev worksheet) (Figure 4.2) shows an example that compares two Normal distributions of different standard deviations.

Measures of Symmetry

An important topic in risk analysis is that of non-symmetry. The skew (or skewness) is a measure of symmetry; a symmetric distribution has zero skew. The skew is a non-dimensional quantity, essentially calculated as the weighted average cube of the distance of each point from the mean divided by the cube of the standard deviation (as for the calculation of standard deviation a small correction term may be included depending on whether the sample represents the whole population or not). Since the calculation involves the cube of the distances from the mean, for a symmetric distribution, such deviations offset each other, resulting in zero skew.

In many real-life applications the most relevant distributions are positively skewed (i.e. crudely they have a tail to the right-hand side that is longer than that to the left, or the outcomes are biased towards larger ones rather than smaller ones; a distribution with negative

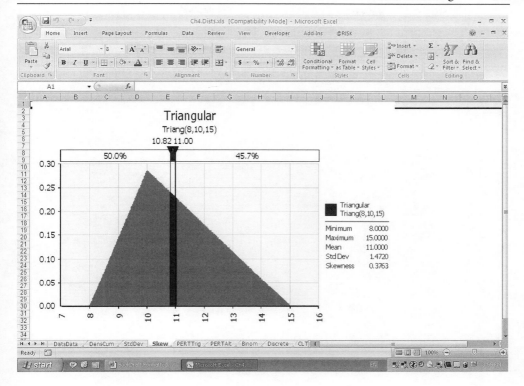

Figure 4.3

skew has the reverse property). Roughly speaking when the skew is above about 0.25, the non-symmetry of the distribution is immediately visually evident. For positively skewed distributions the mean will be larger than the median, which will itself be larger than the mode. Static value models using modal values for skewed inputs will not provide a good guide as to the mean of the output, and so potentially could be misleading.

The file Ch4.Dists.xls (Skew worksheet) (Figure 4.3) shows a positively skewed Triangular distribution. The positive skew results in the mean being larger than the mode, with the median (or P50) point lying between the mode and the mean.

Measures of Peakedness and Fat Tails

In certain applications (notably financial markets and insurance) one is often concerned with a fourth property of a distribution, known as the kurtosis. This is a non-dimensional quantity (essentially calculated as the weighted average fourth power of the distance of each point from the mean divided by the fourth power of the standard deviation). Kurtosis provides a simultaneous test of the peakedness of the distribution around the mean and of the extent to which the distribution has fat tails. Distributions with high kurtosis often arise when event risks are present in a situation, particularly where the probability of occurrence of such an event is low but its impact is high.

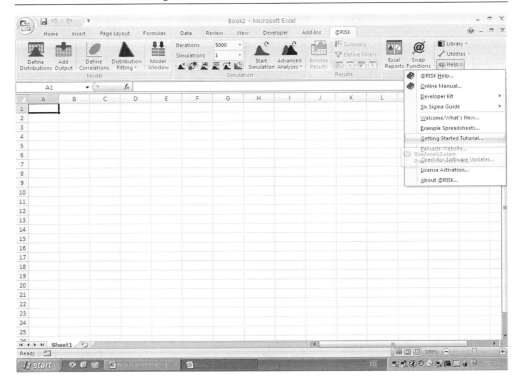

Figure 4.4

A Normal distribution has a kurtosis of 3; such distributions are known as mesokurtic. Distributions with a kurtosis greater than 3 are known as leptokurtic (or platykurtic when less than 3). When using the function **KURT** (and in some other contexts), the quoted kurtosis figure refers to the excess kurtosis, that is the one that arises by subtracting 3 from the original figure (so that a Normal distribution has a **KURT** value of zero).

Quick Guide to using @RISK

The Palisade website provides a tutorial that explains how to get started with @RISK; it is broken into sections so that different topics can be quickly reviewed (Figure 4.4). It is hoped that readers of this text will nevertheless be able to understand and work with the essentials of this chapter and the example models without reference to the tutorials. However, some readers may prefer to refer to the tutorial before working through the examples in this chapter, or alternatively to refer to specific topics in the tutorial if the need arises when working with the examples.

The key icons that are required for the purposes of getting started with @RISK and for using the models in this text are:

- **Define Distribution** can be used to place a distribution in a cell; the parameters of distributions may be cell references.

- The **Add Output** icon is used to define a cell (or a range of cells) as an output, whose values will be recorded during the simulation and be available for post-simulation analysis.
- **Define Correlations** allows the implementation of correlated sampling of input distributions.
- **Distribution Fitting** finds a distribution that best fits a given data set (including a set of simulation results).
- The **Model Window** gives an overview of the inputs, outputs and defined correlations within the model.
- **Iterations**. A single simulation consists of repeatedly calculating the model for a set number of iterations (recalculations). Typically, around a thousand iterations are required for stability of basic statistical values (such as the mean and standard deviation), and several thousand for the graphical presentations to be stable. The number of simulations will usually equal 1, but multiple simulations can be conducted (e.g. two simulations may be run with different values for the distribution of a parameter, so that the results can be compared; this requires the use of the **RiskSimtable** function). Alternatively the **Simulation Settings** icon can be used to set the number of iterations and simulations.
- The **Random/Static Recalculation** icon can be sued to switch the values shown in the distribution functions between fixed (static) values or random values. When random values are shown, the repeated pressing of **F9** can be used to gain a crude idea of the range of values that would be produced during a simulation, and to test the model.
- **Start Simulation** to run the simulation.
- The **Summary** window allows one to view the simulation results. Thumbnails can be dragged and dropped to create a larger visual display. Overlays can be created by dragging one graph on top of another.
- Statistics about simulation results may be placed in the workbook by use of the **RiskStatistics** functions, such as **RiskMean** (or **RiskStddev**) to return the mean (or standard deviation) of a simulated value, **RiskPercentile** to return the percentile value of the distribution and **RiskTarget** to determine the probability associated with a particular value; these functions can be found under the regular Excel **Formulas/Insert Function** menu (under the category **@RISK Distribution**).
- **Swap functions** can be used to remove all @RISK functions and replace them with static values.
- **Utilities** can be used to perform various operations, including defining settings for the application, removing simulation data that have been saved with a workbook, and performing various additional operations.

Example: Cost Budgeting and Contingency Planning

In order to demonstrate a basic practical application of risk analysis, we consider a budget for a project, made up of the addition of a number of individual cost elements.

The file Ch4.CostBudget.Triang.xls (Figure 4.5) shows a base case model and a risk model in which the possible values for each item are defined using a Triangular distribution. Following the simulation, the results show that the average (mean) cost of the project is in fact £15 667 (rather than the original base of £14 000); the difference is due to the assumption of the non-symmetry of the risk, which skews the results to the right-hand side. The probability of being able to deliver the project for less than or equal to the original budget is about 0.5%, and a figure of about £16 902 would be required as a budget in order to be sure that the project is delivered within budget in 95% of cases (this is the P95 of

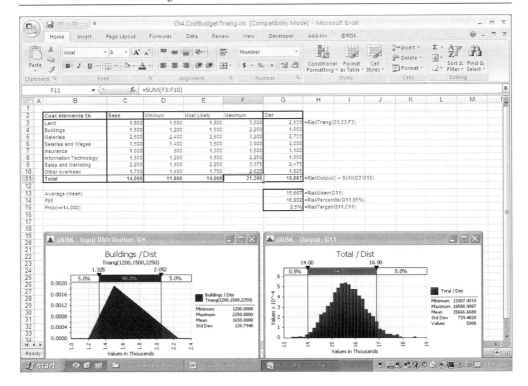

Figure 4.5

the distribution of costs). These results can be seen from the graphs or by use of @RISK's **RiskMean**, **RiskTarget**, and **RiskPercentile** functions (as also shown here). For the P95 budget point, the extra budget (contingency) of £2902 required above the base case can be broken down into the difference between the base case and the mean (of £1667), and the difference between the P95 and the mean (of £1235) (these components may be thought of as static model calibration error and genuine risk contingency).

Types of Dependency Relationships in Risk Models

The building of accurate and flexible models requires that the correct relationships be established between the variables. This is true for regular Excel models but is even more so for simulation models, as every iteration generated by the simulation must represent a valid scenario.

In regular Excel models, variables are essentially either independent or dependent (the independence of variables is often implied by default, whereas dependency results from the value of a variable being fully derivable from others through Excel formulae). In simulation models, two additional generic types of possible relationship arise: semi-dependency (or parameter dependency) and correlation (or correlated sampling). The correlation relationship is generally weaker than a semi-dependent relationship, but the relationships are not exclusive of each other and may be used in combination (i.e. the sampling of semi-dependent random variables may also be correlated).

Very often, the introduction of dependency relationships may have little or no impact on the mean of the results. However, it will have an impact on the spread of the distribution of results, for example as measured by the standard deviation. The most significant effect is, however, on the tails of the distribution. For example, the probability of exceeding a fixed value in the tail of a distribution is very sensitive to any change in modelling assumptions that affect the spread, such as a change in the dependency relationships. More generally, when a model shows that a fixed outcome of particular interest (such as a base case) has a low probability of being achieved, then this calculated probability is sensitive to the quality of the model, that is to choice of variables, their relationships, model calibration and general model error.

Semi-Dependence and Parameter Dependency

This type of relationship (also known as partial dependence) describes a category of relationships in which at each iteration the value drawn in the sampling of one variable influences the parameters of the distribution of another variable to be used in that iteration. Examples of this type of relationship include situations such as:

- In a sequence of projects, the realised (i.e. sampled) value of the cost of one project may provide the best guess as to the most likely value for the cost of the next project in the sequence.
- Where the probability of an occurrence of an event is determined from whether another event has occurred or not.
- Where the parameters which define the range for the volume sold of a product (e.g. minimum, most likely, maximum) are derived from the price level (which is independently sampled at each recalculation of the simulation).

Correlation and Correlated Sampling

In some cases it may be appropriate to capture the relationship between variables using correlation. The correlation coefficient between two data sets of equal size can be calculated, for example using the **CORREL** function (see Chapter 1). Of course, the existence of a non-zero correlation coefficient between two variables does not imply that the process that generated their values was one of correlation (nor that correlation is the correct relationship to implement in the model). For example, a relationship of parameter dependence would typically result in a fairly large correlation coefficient between the variables.

The use of correlated variables may be considered as a proxy for a more complex relationship, which either cannot efficiently or accurately be determined, or where doing so would involve excess complexity. Correlation can be considered to be a way of relating variables where the ultimate causal factors that determine each variable is not modelled (i.e. is outside the model). For example, correlation is typically used in situations such as modelling the changes in the price of two quoted stocks, or possibly between those of commodities or currencies, where it is known that a general relationship must exist but its exact nature is hard to explicitly specify.

When using correlation, there is no notion of an independent or of a dependent variable, rather it concerns the (joint) sampling of the distributions for each variable. In other words, a correlated sampling essentially affects the order in which the set of sampled values from the distributions are used in the simulation; a higher correlation would correspond to the situation where the high values from the distributions tend to be used together and also the low values tend to be used together. Simulation techniques generally use the rank correlation method to implement this forced ordering of the sampling. This method also provides flexibility when selecting the values of the points to sample. For consistency the coefficients for use in a simulation model should generally be calculated from historic data using the rank correlation approach (see Chapter 1).

Note that the implementation of a correlation relationship may have some consequences that are initially unexpected, until reference is made to the notion of correlated sampling. For example, in a model in which advertising expenditure is correlated with sales volume, the addition of a fixed amount to the base advertising budget would have no effect on the sales volume, because the addition of this amount would not affect the sampling of the distribution for advertising and hence not affect that for sales volume. One could conclude (perhaps incorrectly) that advertising has no effect on sales, but this would be a statement of the logic contained in the model rather than the reality of the situation.

Example: The Effects of Dependency Relationships

The file Ch4.LinkedPriceChanges.xls (Figure 4.6) shows different possible implementations of these relationships. In the model, the materials and sales prices are changing over time.

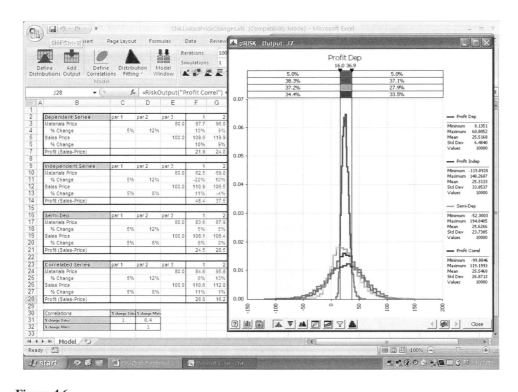

Figure 4.6

For a particular one of these items the changes from one period to the next are independent of each other. However, various possibilities for the relationship between materials price changes and sales price changes in each period are shown, including independence and dependence, semi-dependence and correlation. Because the output shown is the profit (i.e. the difference between the prices), the dependent approach has the narrowest range; the use of such a relationship would severely reduce or eliminate risk as it would have the property that an increase in raw materials prices would lead to an automatic increase in sales prices. For similar reasons, the approach that uses independent changes results in the largest spread, with the spread of the correlated and semi-dependent models being in between these. Of course, variants of these relationships can be built, for example: where the sales price change is independent of the materials price change, except when there are large changes in materials prices (either very low or very high), in which case the sales changes could be reset to a different amount (such as being equal to the materials price changes in these extreme cases). The modeller must of course decide which relationship is appropriate in their specific case.

THE SELECTION AND USE OF DISTRIBUTIONS

When building a risk model, the possible range and frequency of values that could occur for an input variable is described using distributions. The selection of an appropriate distribution for each input is of course something that needs consideration. The screenshot (Figure 4.7) shows the distributions available in @RISK (using the **Define Distribution** icon.)

Generally the selection of the appropriate distribution to represent the uncertainty of a model's input involves the use of one (or more) of several possible approaches:

- Pragmatic approaches, whose main objective is the ease of communication of the model. Distributions used are those that rely on simple parameters (mostly commonly the minimum, most likely, and maximum). The use of the most likely value as a parameter allows a direct reference to what is typically the base case model. Typical distributions used here include:
  — Uniform (continuous form)
  — Triangular
  — PERT
  — Binomial
  — Discrete
  — Any distribution when used in @RISK's alternative parameter form. This means that some or all of the parameters are replaced by percentile values (e.g. by specifying the P5, P50 and P95 points), which can make a distribution simpler to use and communicate in many practical cases.
- Data-driven approaches, whose objective is to use a set of historic data in selecting or creating a distribution. Two common approaches apply here:
  — The fitting of distributions to historic data (using **Distribution Fitting**).
  — The re-sampling from the data using the discrete form of the Uniform distribution.
- Scientific approaches, whose objective is to use knowledge of the underlying (but non-modelled) process which generates an uncertain variable to match this process with one that corresponds to the processes described through distribution science. These will potentially be the most accurate methods, but not always required nor appropriate. The notion of

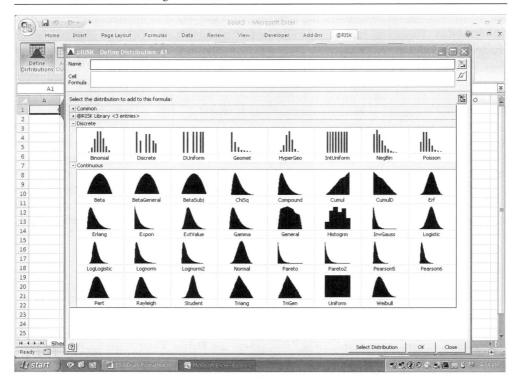

Figure 4.7

there being a correct (rather than appropriate or sufficiently accurate) distribution depends on the existence of some underlying conceptual (or more detailed) process that produces this input. Examples include:

— Additive processes will tend to generate symmetric distributions and become close to a Normal distribution as the number of added processes increases.
— Multiplicative processes will tend to generate positively skewed distributions and become close to a Lognormal distribution as the number of processes increases.

In addition, some industries (especially finance, insurance and oil and gas) have adopted their own standardised distributions for certain variables, such standards typically having arisen from consideration of the data-driven and scientific approaches in some combination. For example, the Normal, Lognormal and Poisson distributions occur frequently in financial market and insurance applications, the Pareto distribution is also frequently used in the insurance industry to model severity of loss, and the oil, gas and mining sectors tend to use the Lognormal distribution for the level of reserves or deposits.

Pragmatic Approaches and Distributions

As mentioned above, when pragmatic approaches are used, the key continuous distributions are the Uniform, Triangular and PERT (Program Evaluation and Review Technique) distributions, and the most important discrete distributions are the Binomial and (general purpose) Discrete.

The Uniform Continuous Distribution

This distribution (sometimes called the no-knowledge distribution) can occasionally be used to model uncertainty. Some real-life processes that essentially follow this distribution include the position of a particular air molecule in a room, the point on a car tyre where the next puncture will occur, the number of seconds past the minute that the current time is, or the length of time that one may have to wait for a train (assuming that trains arrive in regular intervals but that we have no knowledge of the current time). One of the reasons that such a distribution is not of frequent occurrence in the natural world is that in many cases it is readily possible to establish more knowledge of a situation (in particular there is usually is a base case or most likely value).

The distribution is nevertheless a key factor in risk modelling, not least because it is often used as an intermediate step in the generation of random numbers from other distributions (by inversion of the cumulative distribution, as mentioned in Chapter 1 and also in Chapter 6).

The Triangular Distribution

The Triangular distribution has a number of desirable properties from a pragmatic perspective, including a simple set of parameters and the existence of a modal (most likely) value as a parameter.

The two main disadvantages of the distribution are:

- When the parameters result in a skewed distribution, the distribution will generally overemphasise the outcomes in the direction of the skew. This is a consequence of the fact that the area under any distribution is 100%, and that the straight lines of the Triangular distribution constrain its shape; as skew is increased (e.g. by moving the right-hand boundary further to the right), then the relative likelihood of the modal value must drop (e.g. with the consequence that the frequency of outcomes at or below the base case reduces).
- It is bounded on both sides. In reality most real-life process are bounded on one side but unbounded on the other (e.g. travel time to work, level of the stock market, the possible oil price, etc).

The PERT Distribution

The PERT distribution is in fact a special case of a scaled Beta distribution. Its use from a pragmatic perspective is to partially overcome some of the limitations of the Triangular distribution with skewed parameters. As a smooth curve, it has a more flexible shape than the Triangular. At the same time, it has the same simple min-most likely-max parameterisation. For positively skewed distributions with the same input parameters, the PERT distribution will have a lower mean and standard deviation than the Triangular distribution. Of course, the PERT distribution still suffers from the issue that it is bounded on both sides.

The file Ch4.Dists.xls (PERTTrig worksheet) (Figure 4.8) shows an example.

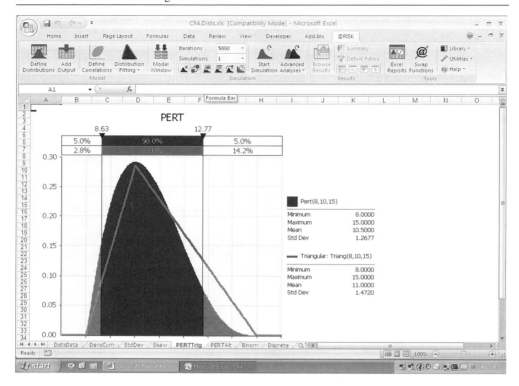

Figure 4.8

Alternate Parameter Methods

One potential disadvantage of the use of continuous bounded distributions is that the end points of the range have a relative likelihood of zero and hence could not actually occur in practice. From a pragmatic perspective, this is often unsatisfactory. For example, assuming that such a distribution were used to represent someone's travel time to work and that the person was asked to estimate a minimum journey time, it is likely that the response would be a value that corresponds to an observed journey, rather than a theoretical non-achievable value. In other words, the data provided would understate the true range. The alternate parameter formulation in @RISK allows the use of percentile values in place of standard parameters, and hence to overcome this problem. For example the minimum could be reinterpreted as the P5 point (rather than P0) and the maximum as the P95 (rather than P100).

The file Ch4.Dists.xls (PERTAlt worksheet) (Figure 4.9) shows an example.

The Binomial Distribution

Perhaps the most fundamental distribution in the real world is the Binomial distribution. It has two parameters, n (representing the number of independent trials), and p (the probability of occurrence per trial). For example, Binomial(10,20%) would represent the number of

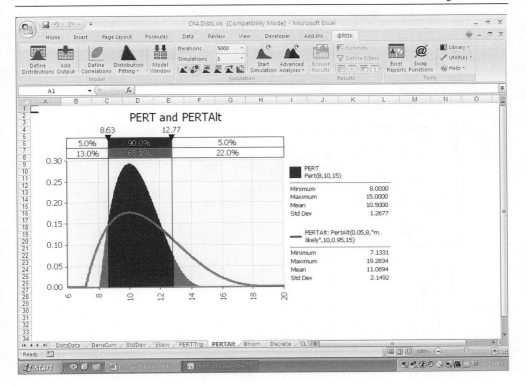

Figure 4.9

discoveries of oil from a portfolio of 10 prospects, where each prospect has a 20% chance of having oil. The most important modelling application is when n is 1, so that there are two possible outcomes (0 or 1), where 1 has a probability p of occurrence (and 0 has probability $1 - p$.) With $p = 0.5$, it is equivalent to tossing a fair coin. More generally, the Binomial distribution can be used to model event risk.

The file Ch4.Dists.xls (Binom worksheet) (Figure 4.10) shows an example.

Example: Risk Registers

The file Ch4.EventandOpRisks.xls (Figure 4.11) shows an example of the use of the Binomial distribution to model event risks and to aggregate a register of risks. Each row represents a potential event that may or may not occur with a given probability in a given time period (implicitly assuming that there is either 0 or 1 occurrence of each event). The impact of each event is also uncertain and is modelled with PERT distributions. One of the convenient properties of the 0 or 1 outcome of the Binomial process (with n equal to 1) is that this outcome can be multiplied by a sampled impact (or severity) of that outcome, without recourse to **IF** statements. In this example, there is a 31.5% chance of no adverse events happening, but in 5% of cases the impact would be more than around $1m.

Note that such a model is of very wide applicability, and by a change of terminology can represent other situations. When applied to the oil and gas sector, it could be a model for the potential level of reserves that may exist in a portfolio of prospects. When applied

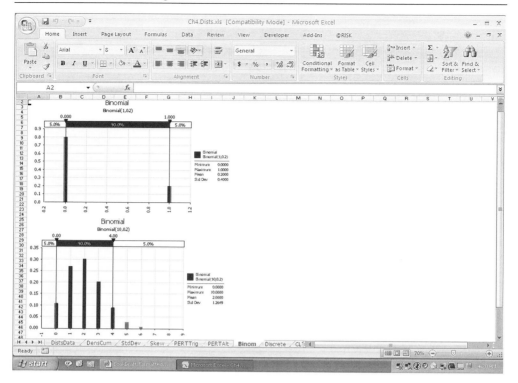

Figure 4.10

to sales forecasting it could be used to estimate the range of sales that may be achievable from a portfolio of new customer prospects. Finally, it may be used as a more generic form of cost model, where the probabilities are set to 100% for those costs that will definitely occur and to less than 100% for those items which are intended to represent additional costs resulting from potential adverse events.

In addition, there are many ways that dependency relationships could be built into this model. For example, the probabilities of occurrence of one event could depend on the outcome of another; this example of parameter dependence could be implemented by the simple addition of **IF** statements to the column containing the probabilities and adapting the probability according to the outcome of the previous event. Similarly, dependencies between the impacts could be implemented. Note that in this type of situation (i.e. when the probability of occurrence is fairly low) the effect of dependencies or correlations between the distributions of occurrence is generally more significant than the effect of such dependencies on the distributions of impact.

The Discrete Distribution

The Discrete distribution is effectively a user-defined distribution; that is, the user specifies all possible outcomes and their probabilities. It can be used to model the possibility of a

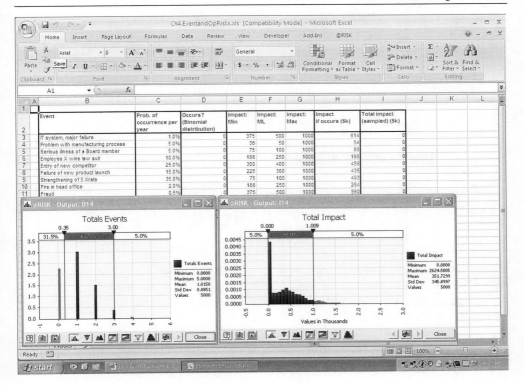

Figure 4.11

few outcomes (e.g. low, medium, high), and to replicate some other discrete distributions (such as the Binomial distribution), as well as to model discrete scenarios.

The file Ch4.Dists.xls (Discrete worksheet) (Figure 4.12) contains a basic example. It is essentially self-explanatory, although a more complex example of the use of the distribution is given later in the context of the modelling of Markov chains.

Data-Driven Approaches and Distributions

Distribution Fitting

Where historic data is available, the **Distribution Fitting** tool in @RISK can be used to find distributions which fit this data. There are several implicit assumptions that are being made when using a fitting approach:

- That the data set represents samples that are from the same random process. For example, it would not be appropriate to fit a distribution to data on the absolute level of the stock market for the last 20 years (because the earlier values are much lower), whereas fitting a distribution to the set of inter-period percentage changes (e.g. daily changes) would be more appropriate (the daily percentage changes themselves could more reasonably be considered to have come from the same distribution).

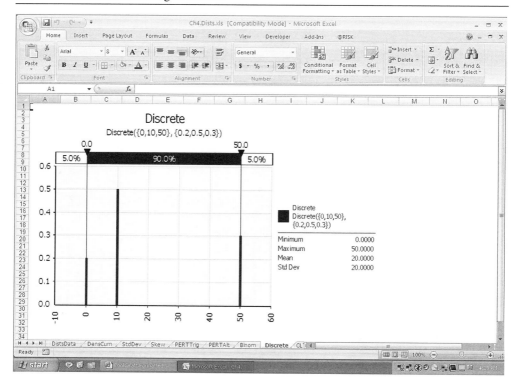

Figure 4.12

- That the underlying distribution that generates the data set is one of those available in the fitting software. Fitting may not be appropriate where the data arises from compound processes, such as those involving several possible event risks.

When using a data-driven approach (in isolation) to select a distribution, one would always use the top fitting distribution. However, in practice one may wish to combine the approaches and choose a well-fitting distribution (even if not the top fitting) if there are further reasons to do so.

Example: Goals in a Soccer Game

The file Ch4.SoccerGoals.xls (Figure 4.13) shows the number of goals scored in each match of a particular team's soccer game for a season, and shows a range of fitted distributions (using the **Distribution Fitting** icon, once the data is selected). The top fitting distribution is the Poisson distribution (there is also a theoretical reason to expect this; see later).

Re-sampling of Historic Data

In many cases, the data set may not be smooth, or one may simply not know the nature of the process that has generated such data. In this case a resampling method can be used. This involves using the historic data as the parameters of the discrete Uniform distribution

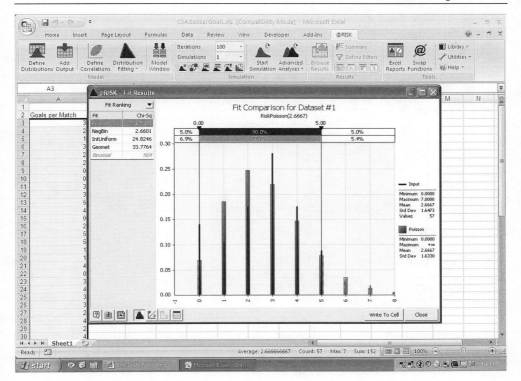

Figure 4.13

(DUniform), from which sampling is directly done. The sampled points are simply a resample of the historic data set (but in a different order). This can be a powerful method, partly because it does not make any further assumptions other than that the past is representative of the future possibilities. Where a data set contains rare events, these events would occur in a resampling method, whereas their frequency may be reduced if a fitted distribution were used.

Example: Stock Market Daily Changes

The file Ch4.Resampling.xls (Figure 4.14) shows the re-sampling method applied to changes in the stock prices of companies using the historic data on prices and changes. An individual resampling method uses a separate (independent) distribution for each stock. A variant also shown is a multi-dimensional resampling. In this case, a sample drawn from of a set of integers is used as an argument to a **Lookup** function in order to simultaneously sample the historic data points for each stock on the relevant day (thereby preserving some relationships – such as correlated daily changes – that may be in the historic data).

Scientific Approaches and Distributions: The Basics

One approach to selecting a distribution for a model input is to use the science of distributions. This means combining some knowledge (or assumed behaviour) of the underlying

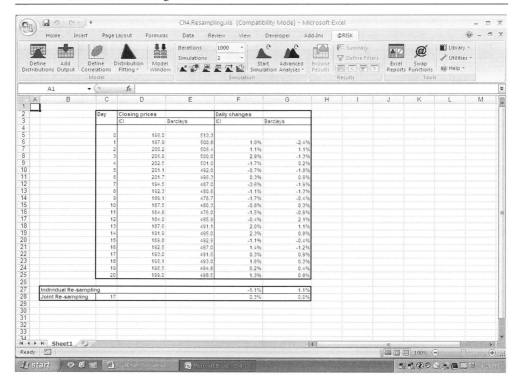

Figure 4.14

process which generates that input (even by definition if this process is not explicitly modelled), with an understanding of how such a process would result in a particular type of
distribution according to distribution (or mathematical) theory. It may be argued that such an
approach is the most accurate method, but of course in some sense it is also more complex
because a more fundamental understanding of distribution theory must be gained, and its
accuracy also ultimately depends on the validity of the underlying conceptual model.

The basic results of distribution science are summarised as follows:

- A variable that results from the addition of many independent and identical random
  processes will follow a distribution that is approximately Normal. This result (called the
  Central Limit Theorem) suggests the use of the Normal distribution whenever the process
  in the real world results as the additive effect of more detailed (non-observed) random
  processes.
- A variable that results from the multiplication of many independent and identical random
  processes will follow a distribution that is approximately Lognormal. This result follows
  from the Central Limit Theorem, as the logarithm of the product of variables is equal to
  the sum of their logarithms.
- The number of events that occur over a continuous domain (usually considered to be
  a period of time) follows a Poisson distribution, whenever the likelihood (intensity) of
  occurrence is constant over that domain.

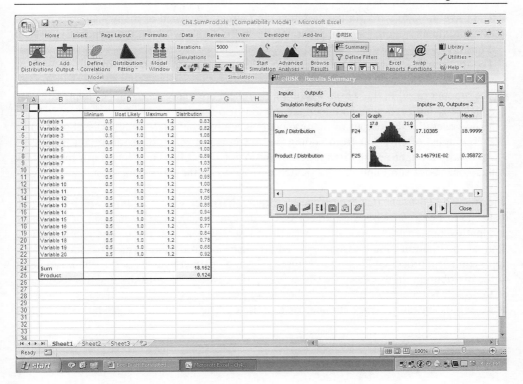

Figure 4.15

Example: Sum and Product of Distributions

The file Ch4.SumProd.xls (Figure 4.15) demonstrates by simulation the results relating to the Normal and Lognormal distributions. It shows a set of negatively skewed PERT distributions, with the outputs of the simulation model being the sum and product of these. The results clearly show the approximate symmetry and positive skew of the sum and product distributions.

The Normal Distribution

The Normal distribution is a symmetric continuous distribution which is unbounded on both sides, and described by two parameters (μ and σ, i.e. its mean and standard deviation). As described earlier, it can be used to represent the uncertainty of a model's input when it is believed that the input is itself the result of many other similar random processes acting together in an additive manner. Of course, it is implicit that it is neither necessarily, efficient, nor practical to model these detailed driving factors individually. Some possible examples of processes that may be expected to be represented with a Normal distribution could include:

- The total electricity used by a town at a particular point in time during the day (the mean and standard deviation will be time dependent).

- The travel time to work, in the case that the journey consisted of many segments of road of approximately equal length, separated by traffic lights working independently of each other.
- The total goals scored in a soccer season, adding up the (Poisson distributed) number of goals in each game.
- The amount of oil in the world, assuming that there are many reservoirs of approximately equal size, but each with an uncertain amount of oil.
- More generally, the output of many models is approximately Normally distributed since such outputs often result from adding the outcomes of many other uncertain processes. An example might be the distribution of discounted cash flow in a long-term forecast, as this consists of summing the discounted cash flows of the individual years.

The file Ch4.Dists.xls (CLT worksheet) (Figure 4.16) shows an example of a Binomial distribution that represents the number of events that would occur from a set of 100 independent events, each of probability 20%. It is visually clear that the results approximate a Normal distribution. Some insight into why a distribution that is formed by adding many non-symmetric processes is close to symmetric can be gained by considering the mean point of the distribution. In this case, for illustrative purposes, we can consider that the occurrence of the event is thought of as a head when a coin is tossed. Clearly, the average number of heads is 20, and the average number of tails is 80. The likelihood of deviating from this

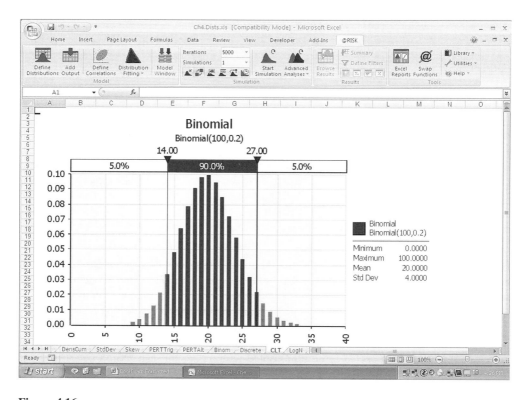

Figure 4.16

central point can be considered in two cases: to increase the number of heads, we have a pool of 80 tails, each with a 20% chance of switching if they were tossed again, whereas to decrease number of heads, we only have a pool of 20, but each of which has an 80% chance of switching to a tail if tossed again. So the probability of a deviation in either direction is the same.

The assumption of a Normal distribution is of course an approximation. For example, the distribution has a range of $-\infty$ to ∞, whereas many of the processes above cannot be negative. In practice, such differences are often unimportant. For example, where the mean of a process is much larger than its standard deviation (e.g. 4 times or more) then a negative sampled value of the Normal distribution would occur only rarely (about 3 times in 100 000).

The Lognormal Distribution

Like the Normal distribution, the Lognormal distribution has two parameters (μ, σ) corresponding to the mean and standard deviation. As shown earlier, the effect of multiplying many random processes is to generate a distribution with positive skew, and specifically one that tends to a Lognormal distribution as many such processes are included in the calculation.

To provide further intuition here, consider the example of an apartment initially valued at $100 000, and where it is assumed that its value could either increase or decrease each year by 10%. After one year the price would be either $110 000 or $90 000. After two years, the price range will be $81 000 to $121 000, after three years the range will be from $72 900 to $133 100. In other words, the range becomes non-symmetric. When continued over several periods the low and high values of the possible price curve are decreasing and increasing geometrically; when thought of as a process in which the time axis is continuous, the boundaries are of exponential rather than geometric nature. The future distribution of values is then Lognormal, i.e. a skewed distribution whose values are such that their logarithm is distributed Normally, or equivalently a distribution formed by calculating the exponential of every value of a Normal distribution, i.e. a Lognormal distribution can be considered as Lognormal = exp(Normal).

The Lognormal distribution has a number of desirable properties, i.e. ones that are also found in real-world processes. These include that it is skewed, and that it has a positive and unbounded range, i.e. from zero to infinity. More subtly, because it can have a high level of kurtosis, it is flexible at representing a large variety of situations, such as a distribution of losses with relatively heavy tails. Another useful property is that when σ is small compared to μ, its skew is small and the distribution approaches a Normal distribution; so any Normal distribution can be approximated by a Lognormal distribution by using the same standard deviation, but increasing the mean (so that the ratio σ/μ is small), and then shifting the distribution by subtracting a constant amount so that the means are matched.

The distribution is very frequently used in practice in the following contexts:

- As a representation of the future value of an asset whose value in percentage terms changes over time in a random fashion, and where the nature of the randomness is constant (and independent) over time (e.g. a large change at one point in time has no effect on the subsequent changes). The key point is that we are dealing with percentage changes (not the value itself), and so the asset's future value is the product of many random changes.

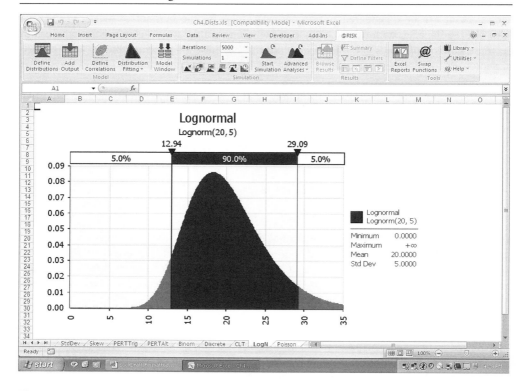

Figure 4.17

Examples would include forecasting the level of a stock, or the stock market, the size of an economy (e.g. GDP), the level of property prices, or the price of oil.

• As a model of oil or mineral reserves, following geological studies whose results provide an imperfect guide as to the true volume. For example, the total amount of oil is calculated by the multiplication (with certain adjustments) of the uncertain values of the spatial dimensions of the field, the porosity and water saturation, a formation factor and the recovery rate. Of course, this is an approximation because the amount of oil in any particular field is limited within some bounds (such as the size of the planet).

The file Ch4.Dists.xls (LogN worksheet) (Figure 4.17) contains a basic example of this distribution.

Example: Price Forecasting

The forecasting of future prices, asset values, or other time-varying quantities is an important application of risk analysis. A key application is the forecasting of future values based on the assumption that the percentage change from one period to the next is random, and drawn from the same distribution.

The file Ch4.AssetPriceForecasts.xls (Figure 4.18) shows an example of the time development when periodic changes are assumed to be Normally distributed. The future distribution

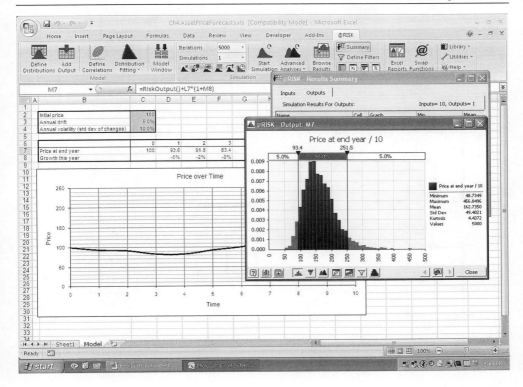

Figure 4.18

from such a process is determined by the compound effect of multiplying several random changes together, and therefore we should expect it to be approximately Lognormally distributed. The results graph shows the skewed future distribution that arises from a multiplicative process (which is approximately Lognormal, and this could be verified through a fitting procedure).

The Poisson Distribution

The Poisson distribution generally arises as a model for the number of events that occur in a given time period, although it can be applied to processes over other domains (such as space). It is essentially an extension of the Binomial distribution in which the domain of the modelling (e.g. time) becomes continuous instead of discrete. It has a single parameter, λ, which represents both the mean and the variance (so that its standard deviation is $\sqrt{\lambda}$).

For example, if there were a 5% chance of a car breaking down within a given month of the year, then one could consider various models for the total number of breakdowns in a year:

• Using a discrete time model of monthly possible breakdowns, in which there is either zero or one breakdown every month. The total number of breakdowns per year would be given by Binomial(12,5%).

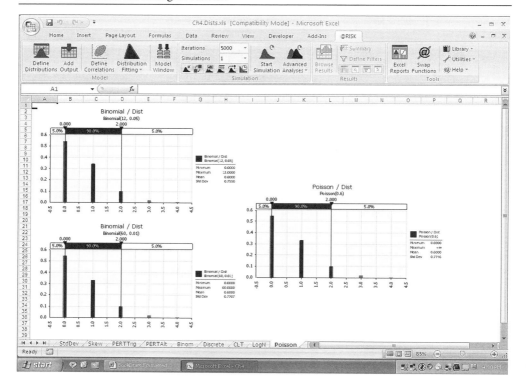

Figure 4.19

- Using a discrete time model with shorter time periods, and adjusting the probability of a breakdown per period accordingly, so that the mean is unchanged. The total number of breakdowns per year could be Binomial(60,1%), for example.
- Using a continuous time model i.e. with the time axis being divided into smaller and smaller segments, with a corresponding decrease in the probability, but an increase in the number of periods, and an increase in the maximum number of breakdowns that could occur. The limiting case of such a process would result in a Poisson distribution.

The file Ch4.Dists.xls (Figure 4.19) (Poisson worksheet) contains an example of this progression. Note that although the distributions look very similar, the upper bound of each distribution is different and progressively larger.

The Poisson distribution therefore models the number of occurrences of events over a continuous domain, where the intensity (probability) of the process is constant, and is often used in situations such as:

- In general frequency–severity models, where an aggregate quantity (often a loss) is calculated as a sum of a random number of individual occurrences. Many insurance applications use this distribution (number of earthquakes in the world per year, number of traffic accidents in a town per day). An example of a reinsurance model is provided later.

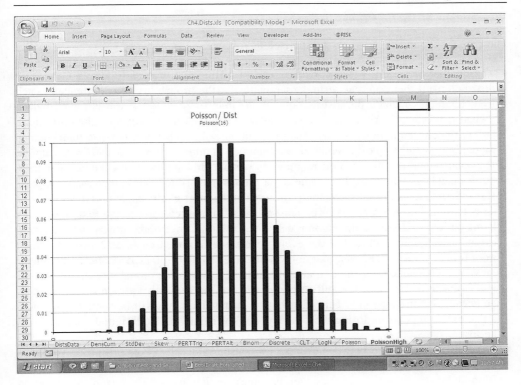

Figure 4.20

- The number of people arriving in a queue per minute.
- The number of new oil discoveries per year.
- The number of stock market crashes per decade.
- The number of spelling errors in a newspaper.
- The number of fish in a large body of water.

The file Ch4.Dists.xls (PoissonHigh worksheet) (Figure 4.20) shows a high intensity Poisson process, which looks approximately Normal (but is, of course, still discrete and bounded below at zero). When the time frame (or domain) for a Poisson process is extended (or equivalently that the intensity of the Poisson distribution is increased), then the resulting distribution is approximately Normal.

Further Aspects of the Science of Distributions

The topic of the science of distributions is a large one, and the above section has only covered the basic results as they are relevant to a large set of business and financial applications. This section briefly discusses some further extensions that are on occasion relevant in more specialised applications. In particular, we discuss distributions of the time-to-occurrence between random events (e.g. useful for maintenance or lifetime modelling) and some basic aspects of the distributions of parameter uncertainty.

Distributions of Waiting Time

The core results in this area are summarised as follows:

- The number of periods between occurrences of a Binomial process follows a Geometric distribution. It therefore has a single parameter, p, the probability of occurrence at each trial. Examples include the distribution for the number of times a coin is tossed before a head is produced, or the number of sequential bets that one needs to make on roulette before the chosen number occurs. The distribution can also be used in basic maintenance modelling, for example to represent the number of months before a car breaks down. However, since the distribution requires a constant probability of breakdown per trial, other models are often used, i.e. where the probability of breakdown increases with age. It is interesting and initially counter-intuitive that the most likely single outcome is that of an occurrence on the first trial. The reason is that we are referring to the first occurrence being at any individual time point, but once this has occurred, subsequent trials are excluded. The probability that the event occurs on the first trial is of course p, which may be very small. The distribution is sometimes thought of as describing beginner's luck and gambler's ruin; there is an approximately two-thirds probability that the event will occur at or before it is intuitively expected (so the gambler will perceive himself to be ahead), but the long tail of the distribution means that there will be some cases where a gambler is repeatedly losing their money, and over time the likely initial winnings will be lost.
- The time to occurrence between events of a constant intensity (Poisson) process follows an Exponential distribution. Just as the Poisson distribution is the limiting case of a Binomial distribution when the domain becomes continuous, the Exponential distribution corresponds to the continuous time version of the Geometric distribution.
- The time to occurrence for other continuous time processes is often assumed to follow a Weibull distribution, especially where it is desired to have a non-constant intensity of occurrence. The distribution is flexible enough to allow an implicit assumption of constant, increasing or decreasing intensity, according to the choice of its parameter α ($\alpha < 1, = 1$, or > 1 represent processes of increasing, constant and decreasing intensity respectively; a constant intensity process is the same as an Exponential distribution). Most cases in maintenance or lifetime modelling would use $\alpha < 1$ to represent that the older something is, the more likely it is to fail. The file Ch4.FailureSim.Geo.Weibull.xls (Figure 4.21) simulates in detail the first failure in a chain of possible events (using **MATCH** to find the first failure), according to whether the probability is constant or increasing. The results graphs show the distribution of times to first failure, indicating the general shapes associated with the Geometric and Weibull dsitributions.
- The time to first occurrence can be modelled using any distribution, with the intensity of occurrence (probability) that is implied being a derived quantity. The so-called intensity function of a distribution is the ratio $f(t)/(1 - F(t))$, where $f(t)$ is the density curve of the assumed distribution of time to occurrence and $F(t)$ is the cumulative distribution. For many distributions this expression has a simple closed-form formula; for others it may require a numerical evaluation. The intensity function simply states that the instantaneous occurrence (or failure) rate is the ratio of the relative frequency of occurrence when restricted to the subset of the population that has not yet already occurred (failed). The

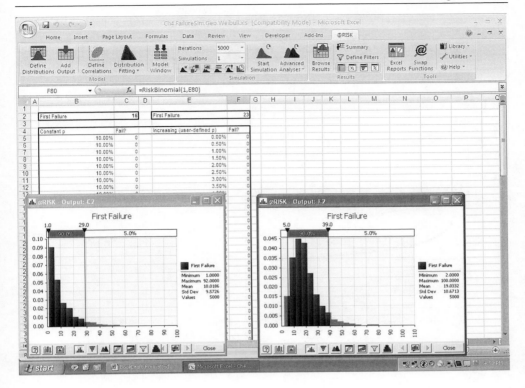

Figure 4.21

file Ch4.Intensity.Fns.xls (Figure 4.22) shows some examples of intensity functions for Exponential, Weibull and Gamma distributions.

- The number of failures before several occurrences of a Binomial process follows a Negative Binomial distribution. It may be used in models of quality control and production testing. The Gamma distribution is the continuous time equivalent of the Negative Binomial distribution, i.e. it represents the distribution of inter-arrival times for several events from a Poisson process. The parameter α of a Gamma distribution has a similar role to that parameter in a Weibull distribution, namely the implied intensity of the process will be increasing, constant or decreasing according to whether $\alpha < 1, = 1, $ or $ > 1$.

Distributions of Parameter Uncertainty

Parameter uncertainty relates to situations where one is trying to derive the parameters of a process (with an assumed distribution) based on an observed set of outcomes. For example, one may have tossed a coin 10 times and produced three heads, and would ask with what probability this coin actually produces a head (say whether it is 0.5 or 0.3). Whereas a traditional statistical approach may aim to estimate a single value for the probability and establish a confidence interval around that, the (Bayesian) approach taken in uncertainty

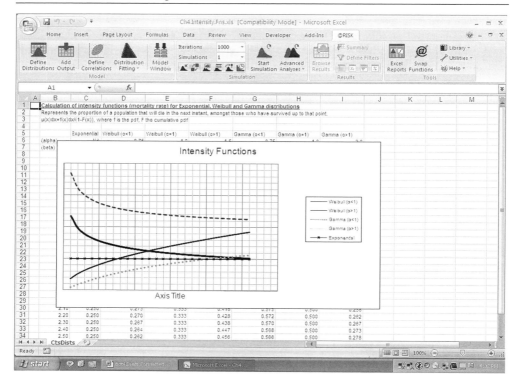

Figure 4.22

analysis is to consider the true probability as uncertain (i.e. to follow a distribution). The core points in this regard are:

- The Beta distribution represents the distribution of possible values of the probability of a Binomial process, when actual experimental observations are available, but the probability of success is unknown. For the coin-tossing example above, one could analyse this by considering for every possible value of the true (but unknown) probability (i.e. all values between 0 and 1) the likelihood that the observed result would occur. The likelihood of three heads out of 10 trials for a given probability p is proportional to $p^3(1-p)^7$. We could consider this expression as a function of p, resulting in the Beta distribution with two parameters, i.e. Beta$(\alpha, \gamma, p) = p^{\alpha-1}(1-p)^{\gamma-1}$. In the specific example, $\alpha = 4$, and $\gamma = 8$. (For simplicity of presentation here, we have excluded the required scaling factor so that the total probabilities over all outcomes add up to 100%.) The file Ch4.ParEstBeta.xls (Figure 4.23) shows the explicit calculation for a set of discrete probabilities and the comparison with the Beta distribution.
- The Gamma distribution represents the distributions of possible values of the intensity of a Poisson process, when actual experimental observations are available, but the intensity is unknown. This can be derived by an argument similar to that above in which the role of variables and parameters in the mathematical expressions are reversed.

Further information can be found in Bernardo and Smith (see Further Reading).

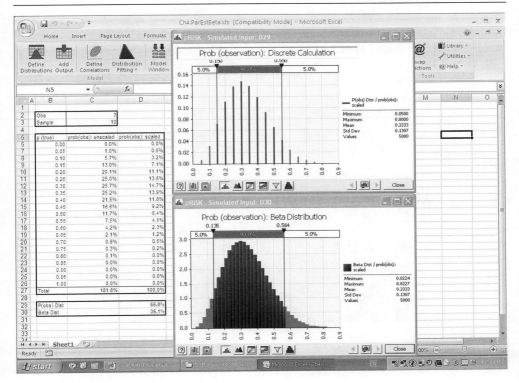

Figure 4.23

FURTHER EXAMPLE MODELS

This section describes a range of further risk models. Many of the structural aspects of these are relevant to situations other than the one directly described, often by a simple change of terminology or interpretation.

Example: Generalisations of Cost Budgeting

Earlier in the chapter we showed a basic cost model using the Triangular distribution. The model could be generalised in many ways, including the use of other distributions (such as PERT or Lognormal), the inclusion of event risks in the model (for example, to explicitly model some of the driving factors that may create a non-symmetry in the input distributions), and the use of correlation or other forms of dependency relationships between the variables. In addition, @RISK contains the possibility of defining the distribution parameters using percentiles (i.e. the alternate parameter formulation, mentioned earlier). This can be a superior method to calibrate the model, especially when making heuristic or expert judgements on the extreme points of a range.

The file Ch4.CostBudget.PERTAlt.Correl.xls (Figure 4.24) uses the alternate parameter form of the PERT distribution (with the original min–max values now assumed to correspond to the 5th and 95th percentiles), and where the sampling of the distributions of land, building, materials, and salaries and wages have been correlated with a coefficient of 30%.

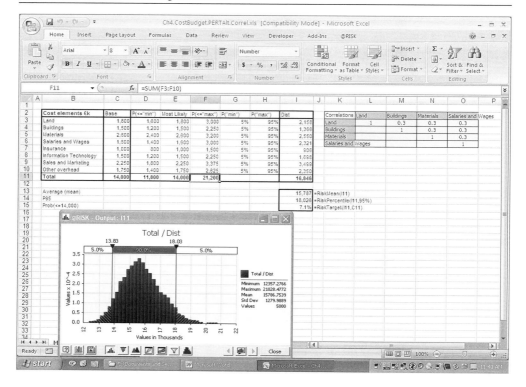

Figure 4.24

The effect of both the alternate parameter formulation and the positive correlations is to increase the spread of the distribution in both directions compared with a model without them.

Example: Discounted Cash Flow

Discounted cash flow calculations lend themselves naturally to risk analysis. When using the **NPV** function it should of course be remembered that the function only discounts the cash flow, whereas the net present value is technically the mean of the discounted cash flows (which can be seen from the graph of the simulation results, or by using the **RiskMean** function).

Where the discount rate is determined by consideration of the Capital Asset Pricing Model (CAPM, see Chapter 3), it will already reflect the risk in the cash flows (this is the purpose of β in the CAPM), and so the discount rate does not need to change during the simulation to reflect the risk of an individual scenario or iteration.

The file Ch4.CashFlow.xls (Figure 4.25) shows an example. The sum of the discounted cash flow (using the **NPV** function as an output of the simulation) is approximately Normally distributed, being the sum of several random variables. The sales figures are approximately Lognormally distributed, being the product of several random variables.

The @RISK functions **RiskMean** and **RiskTarget** have been used to show (post simulation) the mean discounted cash flow and the probability that it is less than zero. Since

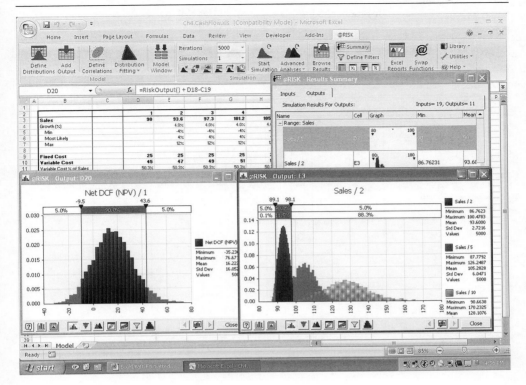

Figure 4.25

the mean is positive, one should as a general rule continue with the project, but in practice a particular decision-maker may decide not to proceed on the basis that the risk (or
probability) of a negative outcome is too large.

Occasionally, concepts such as cash flow at risk (CaR), and value at risk (VaR) are used.
The basic intention of these ideas is to calculate the position of some point on the distribution
of outcomes (e.g. a P1 point) to make a statement about the risk of the situation. Where
the output is close to a Normal distribution, then of course these values can be equivalently
expressed with reference to the mean and standard deviation; for example, the P1 point is
about 2.3 standard deviations below the mean for a Normal distribution.

Example: Financial Statement Modelling

A risk analysis on a financial statement model could be required for a number of reasons,
such as the generation of the possible values for sales, profits or valuation, or the distribution
of financing requirements (such as borrowing).

The file Ch4.BasicFS.xls (Figure 4.26) uses a basic financial statement model, and calculates the probability that the business will have a short-term financing requirement in 2009,
even though the static base model suggests that no such requirement exists.

It is assumed that the sales growth and cost factors are uncertain. Some of the distribution parameters have been defined using the alternative parameter form, so that the user
can specify the probability that sales growth will be zero or less (which in this case is

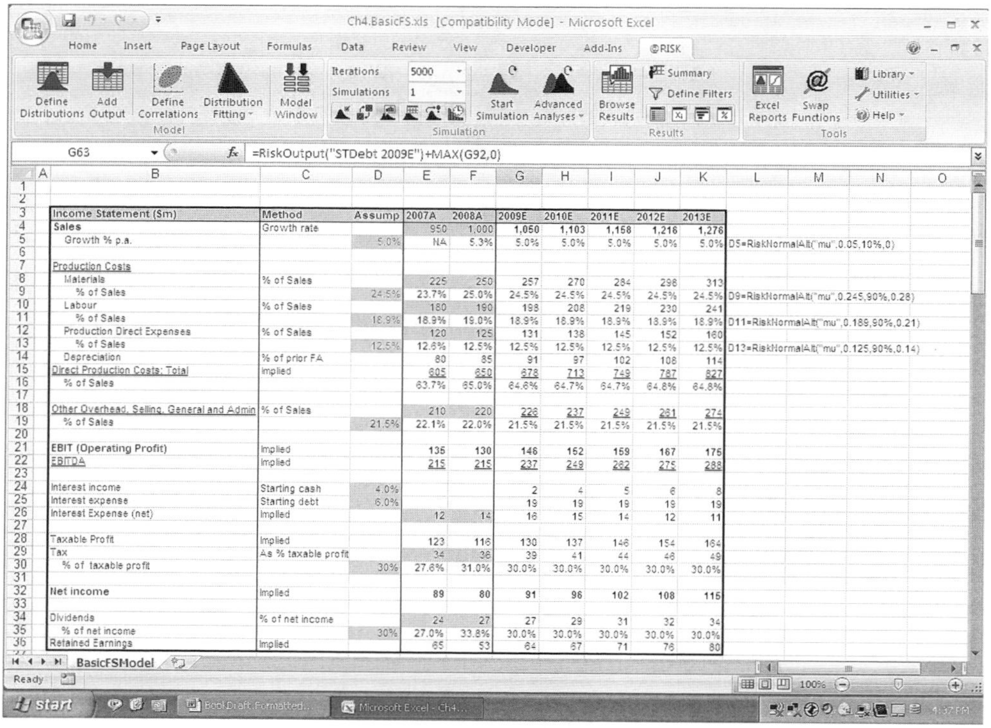

Income Statement ($m)	Method	Assump	2007A	2008A	2009E	2010E	2011E	2012E	2013E	
Sales	Growth rate		950	1,000	1,050	1,103	1,158	1,216	1,276	
Growth % p.a.		5.0%	NA	5.3%	5.0%	5.0%	5.0%	5.0%	5.0%	D5=RiskNormalAlt("mu",0.05,10%,0)
Production Costs										
Materials	% of Sales		225	250	257	270	284	298	313	
% of Sales		24.5%	23.7%	25.0%	24.5%	24.5%	24.5%	24.5%	24.5%	D9=RiskNormalAlt("mu",0.245,90%,0.28)
Labour	% of Sales		180	190	198	208	219	230	241	
% of Sales		18.9%	18.9%	19.0%	18.9%	18.9%	18.9%	18.9%	18.9%	D11=RiskNormalAlt("mu",0.189,90%,0.21)
Production Direct Expenses	% of Sales		120	125	131	138	145	152	160	
% of Sales		12.5%	12.6%	12.5%	12.5%	12.5%	12.5%	12.5%	12.5%	D13=RiskNormalAlt("mu",0.125,90%,0.14)
Depreciation	% of prior FA		80	85	91	97	102	108	114	
Direct Production Costs: Total	Implied		605	650	678	713	749	787	827	
% of Sales			63.7%	65.0%	64.6%	64.7%	64.7%	64.8%	64.8%	
Other Overhead, Selling, General and Admin	% of Sales		210	220	226	237	249	261	274	
% of Sales		21.5%	22.1%	22.0%	21.5%	21.5%	21.5%	21.5%	21.5%	
EBIT (Operating Profit)	Implied		135	130	146	152	159	167	175	
EBITDA	Implied		215	215	237	249	262	275	288	
Interest income	Starting cash	4.0%			2	4	5	6	8	
Interest expense	Starting debt	6.0%			19	19	19	19	19	
Interest Expense (net)	Implied		12	14	16	15	14	12	11	
Taxable Profit	Implied		123	116	130	137	146	154	164	
Tax	As % taxable profit		34	36	39	41	44	46	49	
% of taxable profit		30%	27.6%	31.0%	30.0%	30.0%	30.0%	30.0%	30.0%	
Net income	Implied		89	80	91	96	102	108	115	
Dividends	% of net income		24	27	27	29	31	32	34	
% of net income		30%	27.0%	33.8%	30.0%	30.0%	30.0%	30.0%	30.0%	
Retained Earnings	Implied		65	53	64	67	71	76	80	

Figure 4.26

assumed to be 10%). The **RiskMean** and **RiskTarget** functions have been used to show (post simulation) the probability (about 12%) that short-term financing is required in 2009, and that in 5% of cases an amount above about $18m will be required (see the Balance Sheet screenshot – Figure 4.27).

Example: Mean-Reverting Processes

Earlier we discussed basic models of asset value forecasting, where an asset value's growth rate in each period is random, but is independent of that in other periods. In other circumstances it may be desired for the changes in each period to depend either on the value of the asset or on the changes in the asset value in earlier periods. For example, in interest rate modelling, the effect of high rates is to cool the economy (thus allowing rates to be decreased), and the effect of low rates is the reverse. Such a process could therefore be mean-reverting in which rates tend to a long-term equilibrium. Other applications where mean-reverting behaviours can play a role include models of equity dividend growth rates, of dividend yields and of some commodities prices (such as oil, where it could be argued that a high price would lead to previously economically unrecoverable reserves becoming economically viable, thus encouraging further investment in new exploration activity, which will ultimately reduce the price).

The simplest modelling approach to capture mean-reversion is to link the average periodic change to the long-term equilibrium level (which may itself be uncertain), so that the base

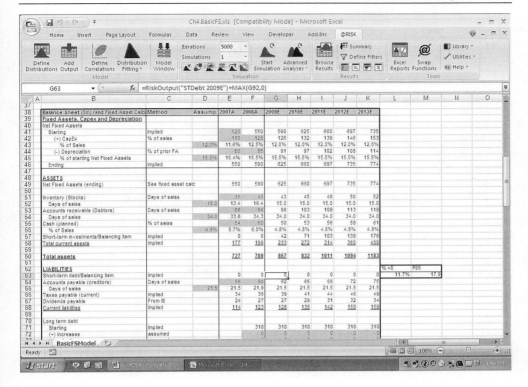

Figure 4.27

level of change (prior to including randomness) is positive when the asset value is below the long-term level and *vice versa*.

The file Ch4.MeanRev.xls (Figure 4.28) shows a 10-year model of an assumed mean-reverting process for interest rates. From the perspective of this text, the key modelling issue is the implementation of the drift term (i.e. the term which describes the base level of periodic change before considering randomness). The model is similar to the Cox–Ingersoll–Ross model (which is a continuous time mathematical description of the random walk, with the square-root term being used in the continuous time model to stop the interest rate ever becoming negative; in this simplistic discrete time model we use a simple **IF** statement to force this condition). For more information on such random walks and their theoretical and mathematical properties, the reader is referred to Wilmott (see Further Reading).

Example: Markov Chains

Markov chains are used to model time series of the various states that a system may take. For each state, there is a probability of moving from that state to one of the others at the next time step. For example, the weather could be considered to take one of three states (such as clear, dry but cloudy, rainy), or a machine could be considered to be either working or broken down on any particular day. Such chains can also be used to represent price processes, in which the parameters that define the distribution of price changes are dependent on the state

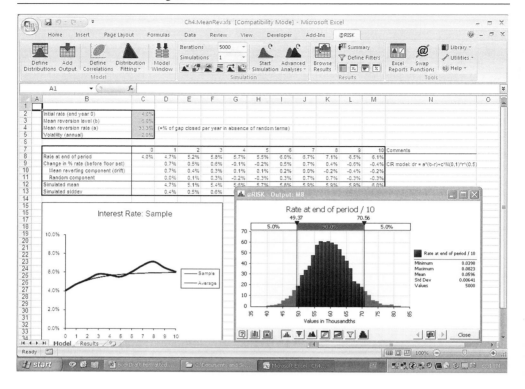

Figure 4.28

of the chain. In these cases jumping between the states creates extra volatility in addition to that captured in the assumed volatility parameter for the price process within each state.

The file Ch4.Markov.xls (Figure 4.29) shows such a model. The transition probabilities from each state are shown in the row elements, and a sample from a Discrete distribution is used to determine the next state in the chain (the **OFFSET** function returning an array argument to the Discrete distribution is used to look up the relevant probabilities). The model has two outputs: the distribution of time to first occurrence of each state (using **MATCH**), and the price process in which the periodic changes are state dependent (using the **INDEX** function to look up the required parameters for the distribution of price changes according to the state).

Example: Insurance Losses and Frequency-Severity Modelling

A typical insurance and reinsurance application is frequency–severity modelling, where an aggregate quantity (often a loss) is calculated as a sum of a random number of individual occurrences:

$$S = X_1 + \cdots + X_N$$

In these models N is a random variable (and a positive integer), and the X's are independent identically distributed variables. Such models can be used to represent situations such as

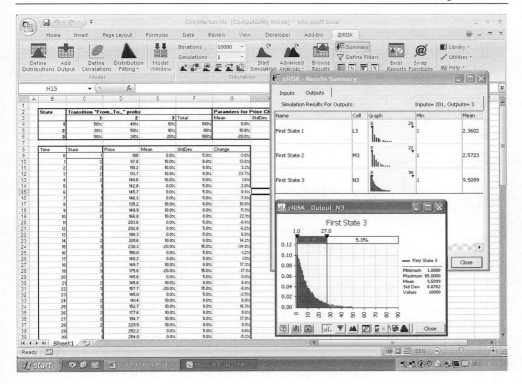

Figure 4.29

damage from accidents, fires, earthquakes, weather and other catastrophes, operational losses
(e.g. resulting from accounting problems, fraud, rogue trading, etc.), and are used in insurance pricing, the modelling of capital requirements, value-at-risk, and credit losses. In such
models the number of losses (the frequency distribution) is often chosen to be Poisson, capturing the potentially unlimited number of events that might occur (the Negative Binomial
or Binomial distributions are also sometimes used). The distributions of severity are often
assumed to be Pareto, although in this case are sometimes truncated from above to avoid
giving unreasonably high frequency of large losses. Other distributions that are commonly
used are the Lognormal, Exponential or the resampling method.

The file Ch4.ReinsuranceLayers.xls (Figure 4.30) shows an example where there are several possible events that may occur and where each has a different potential severity for
losses. In addition, each loss is allocated across several layers (for example, a different
insurance company is responsible for the losses within the layer but not for losses above
or below the threshold amounts). In fact, @RISK has a specific function (**RiskCompound**)
for the direct calculation of such distributions (this is not shown here, as the objective here
is a transparent presentation of the principles involved).

Example: Optimisation of Factory Capacity

Risk analysis problems very often contain an element of optimisation. After describing the
risk in a situation, one can always pose the question: What is the optimum behaviour given

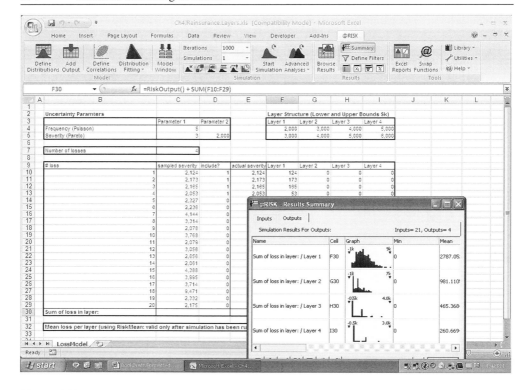

Figure 4.30

this risk? An example is the decision as to what size to build a factory, given an uncertain level of demand. Of course for the calculation to result in an optimum point, the model needs to reflect within its logic the trade-off that is inherent in the real-life situation (e.g. that a large facility will allow cases of large market demand to be fulfilled, but at the expense of excess capacity when demand is low, with the reverse applying if the facility is small). The simplest approach to undertaking such optimisations is to run several simulations, each one testing a different trial value for the variable to be optimised and then comparing the results.

The file Ch4.CapacityOptimise.xls (Figure 4.31) shows an example in which five simulations are run with different trial values for the size of the factory. The optimum capacity is defined as the one that maximizes the mean of the discounted cash flow (the optimum point could be determined with further accuracy by narrowing the range of trial values around this point and conducting further simulations). The process of running several simulations can be done manually (with the results recorded each time) or in an automated way using @RISK's **RiskSimtable** feature (as done here).

Example: Quality Control

The file Ch4.Quality.xls (Figure 4.32) shows an example of a failure rate model, for use in quality control and planning. Some property of the finished state (e.g. its width) of each of a set of components is assumed to be Normally distributed and is deemed to be unsatisfactory

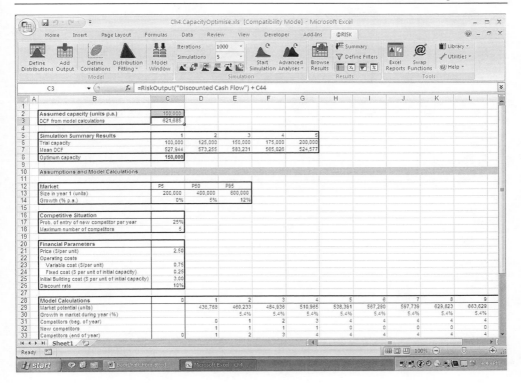

Figure 4.31

if the sample of that property lies outside defined tolerance bands. The aggregate product is deemed unsatisfactory if any individual component is unsatisfactory. The model calculates the component and aggregate failure (using @RISK's **RiskMean** function applied to the failure of individual components as well as to the aggregate product). @RISK also has some functions designed for six sigma analysis, but these are beyond the scope of this text.

Example: Economic Production Life

The file Ch4.ProdProfileLife.xls (Figure 4.33) shows a model of the economic production life of an oil well, given an uncertain profile of production volume, and an assumption on the production level required for economic viability. The distribution of production volume for each year is assumed to follow a Lognormal distribution (the volume of an oil well being the product of several uncertain factors, including the three spatial dimensions), and is derived using the alternate parameter form of the distribution (i.e. the distribution is specified in terms of its percentiles). The P50 point is calculated for each year from a starting value and assumed growth rates, with the P10 and P90 point derived from the P50. The minimum economic production volume is assumed to decrease over time to reflect that technology improvements may take place even as operating costs increase in an inflationary way. The simulation results show that the average production life simulation is less than the value shown when the model is populated using average values. This reflects those cases (that

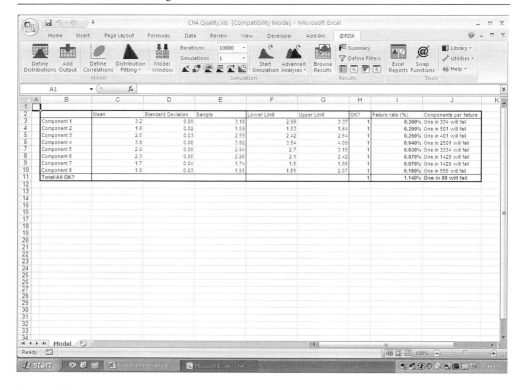

Figure 4.32

are picked up only by the risk analysis) where production in the early years turns out to be uneconomic.

Example: Uncertain Timing in Revenue Planning

In Chapter 1 we showed how **Lookup** functions can be used to make the (discrete) time axis of a model into a variable (so that sensitivity analysis can be performed with time as a dimension). We based those examples on debt financing and depreciation schedules. Such approaches can be used also for revenue forecasting (e.g. for a portfolio of customers or of drug development projects), where the start date of a project is assumed to follow a discrete distribution.

The file Ch4.RevForecast.xls (Figure 4.34) uses a revenue profile that is expected to apply for each customer once the customer has actually placed an order, and an order date (which is regarded as the uncertain variable for each customer). The order date is determined from a base line planning date, plus a distribution which represents the possible delay beyond the base date. In this example a Negative Binomial distribution for the delay is used (to represent the idea that for the order to be placed a certain number of commercial stages need to be successfully completed, each one of which has a probability of success). In practice, any distribution that the user thinks appropriate could be used including pragmatic ones (such as Discrete). Extensions to this model could include the addition of uncertainty

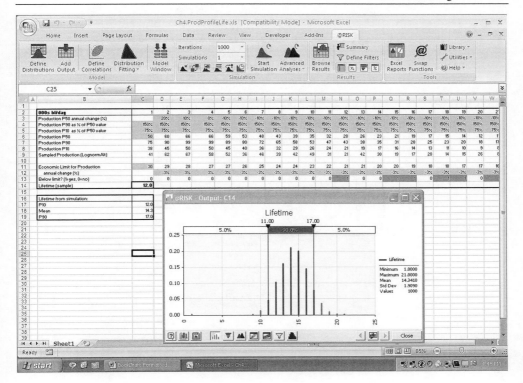

Figure 4.33

on the values for the revenue streams, as well as the use of a probability of order for each customer (e.g. using a Binomial distribution as in the earlier event risk models).

Example: Project Schedule Risk

An important aspect of risk analysis in project planning is to estimate the possible duration of a project, which is of course the length of the critical (i.e. the longest) path through the project. When undertaking risk modelling (by using distributions to represent task durations) the critical path may vary; indeed there could be many different paths that become the critical one for some iterations of the simulation. In many such cases Excel is not an appropriate platform to conduct the analysis, because the required formulae to identify the critical path become excessively complex, and other tools may be needed (such as the @RISK for Project tool from Palisade, which is an add-in to MS Project, but is beyond the scope of this text).

On the other hand, Excel can be used for such applications when the critical path can be easily identified and the total task duration represented in an Excel formula. Such projects include ones where there is a simple series of tasks where one always follows the same predecessor or where there are several such series but with no interaction between them (so that in the first case the project duration is the sum of the individual tasks, and in the second it is equal to the maximum of the sum of the individual series).

The file Ch4.ProjectSchedule.xls (Figure 4.35) shows an example in which there are four series of tasks. The series are conducted in parallel, whereas the tasks within each series

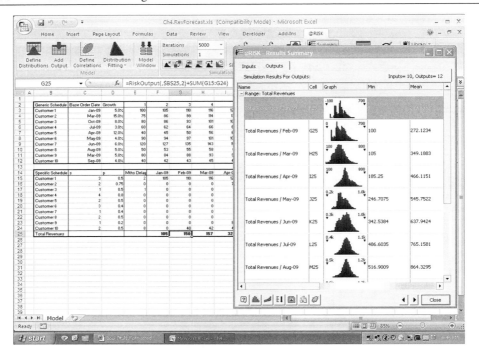

Figure 4.34

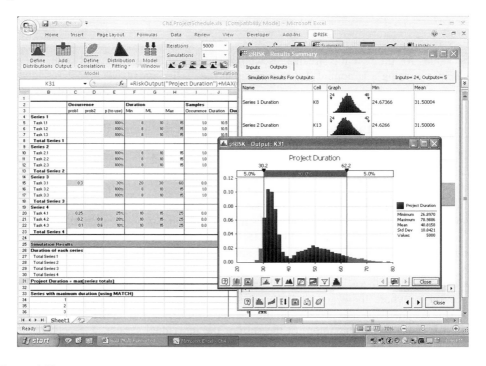

Figure 4.35

are conducted sequentially. The duration of each series is the sum of the durations of the individual tasks, whereas the project duration is the maximum of the durations of each of the series. The first series consists of a sequence of tasks whose lengths are independent of each other. The second series is similar, except that it is assumed that the tasks durations are correlated. The third series includes an event risk whose occurrence extends the length of the series but has no effect on the durations of the other tasks (e.g. representing the possibility that a project redesign needs to be conducted before continuing with the next tasks). The fourth series consists of a sequence of conditional event risks, i.e. a set of additional potential problems with the project, each of which has a probability of occurrence that is larger when the prior event in the sequence has occurred.

Note that in a project schedule context, relevant outputs may include the distribution of finish dates and the probability of finishing the project before some given target date, or the date by which the project would be finished with a given probability. The mean finish date of the project will generally not have the same relevance as the mean of a financial variable (because there is generally a highly non-linear relationship between a finish date and the ultimate impact of that finish date for the situation).

5
Introduction to Options and Real Options Modelling

This chapter treats the topic of options and real options modelling. We approach the subject as a natural extension of risk modelling (as covered in Chapter 4); a separate chapter is devoted to it mainly for the purpose of focus of presentation. The chapter starts with an introduction to the valuation of financial market derivatives, and then covers real options modelling. However, the approach taken to real options modelling does not depend on the financial market derivative framework. There is no specific requirement for readers who are interested only in real options modelling to first read the section on financial market derivatives. Some of the models are built in a pure Excel environment, and others use the @RISK or PrecisionTree add-ins from Palisade, as described in Chapter 4. For the reasons mentioned earlier, the models that use Palisade software have been built in Excel 2003 but are nevertheless presented in the screenshots in Excel 2007.

FINANCIAL MARKET DERIVATIVES: AN INTRODUCTION

A derivative is a financial instrument whose value depends on the value of something else, usually called an underlying. The simplest case is a European call option on a stock. This allows the holder to buy the stock (i.e. exercise the option) for a fixed price (the strike or exercise price) at a fixed date in the future (the maturity or expiry). Such an option will be exercised at maturity only when the value of the stock at maturity is above the strike price. Similarly, a put option allows the holder to sell the stock for a pre-agreed price. An American option is one that can be exercised at any time before expiry; for such an option the choice of whether to exercise before expiry can be potentially complex, as discussed later.

In recent decades powerful analytic methods and mathematical models have been developed to value financial market derivatives. Examples include the Black–Scholes equations, risk-neutral valuation and martingale-based techniques. In this section, we do not aim for a complete coverage of this large and potentially complex topic; rather the primary objective is to provide some insight into the core elements of the subject and the assumptions required, and to lay the foundation for interested readers to explore the area in more detail as appropriate. (For example, more in-depth information, which also cover a wider range of more complex and general financial market applications, can be found in Wilmott (see Further Reading).) In particular, in the simple examples used, we will assume that the stock is not one that pays a dividend.

Example: Valuation using Hedged Portfolio

In certain cases derivatives can be surprisingly easy to value. In particular, it is often possible to exploit links between the changes in value of the underlying and that of the derivative to create a portfolio of the option and the underlying which is risk-free (at any instant). The

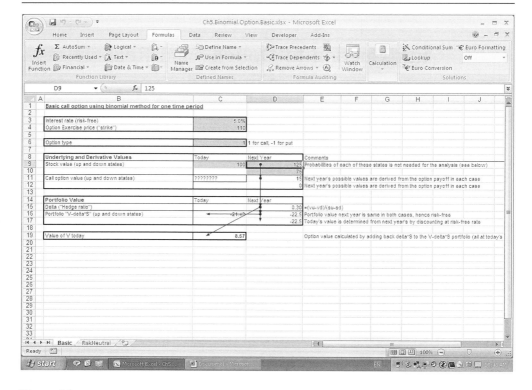

Figure 5.1

subsequent application of a no arbitrage assumption (i.e. that a risk-less portfolio would earn the risk-free rate) allows the portfolio to be valued, from which the option value can be derived.

The file Ch5.Binomial.Option.Basic.xlsx (Basic worksheet) (Figure 5.1) shows a simple example. It is a single time-period model and assumes that the stock price moves either up or down, with the following assumptions:

- The stock is currently priced at $100, and in one year's time its price could be either $75 or $125.
- We have an option to buy the stock in one year's time for $110; this option is the instrument that we are trying to value.
- Interest rates are 5% p.a.

The key steps involved are:

- Calculation of the option payoff at expiry for each of the two scenarios for the future stock price (i.e. $15 or $0 in this case).
- Calculation of a hedge ratio, i.e. the ratio of the differences in the option values to the differences in stock values in each state, which is $(15 - 0)/(125 - 75)$ or 0.3 in this case.
- Construction of a portfolio consisting of the option and a short position in the stock, where the amount of stock sold short is equal to the hedge ratio. One can then verify

that in each of the two future states the portfolio has the same value, and is therefore risk free.

- Calculation of the current value of the portfolio by discounting at the risk-free rate. The justification is that arbitrage opportunities cannot exist in efficient markets, and so risk-free instruments earn the risk-free rate. (This is different to the use of the Capital Asset Pricing Model (see Chapter 3), which states that such a portfolio would be expected to earn the risk-free rate.)
- Calculation of the current value of the option by adding back the current value of the short position in the stock to the current portfolio value (i.e. the hedge ratio multiplied by the current stock price).

Using this approach, the option value is determined to be $8.57.

Note that this argument has implicitly used some further assumptions, including:

- The future distribution of stock values is known (i.e. volatility is known).
- All instruments are traded.
- The stock may be sold short.
- There are no transaction costs.

Extensions of this framework can be developed in which the underlying asset is not traded, but where the option itself and another related option are both traded instruments, so that a risk-free portfolio of two options can be formed (by holding one short); Wilmott (see Further Reading) contains more details.

Example: Risk-Neutral Valuation

The process described in the above example did not use any assumption on the probability of each scenario for the future stock price. Of course, if such a probability were known then it would also apply to the probability of the option's value ending up in each future state. Similarly, if the probability for the states of the option's future value were known, it would apply to those for the stock. If such probabilities for future values were known, then of course the current values of the assets (both the stock and the option), could presumably be calculated as the weighted average future values (using these real-world probabilities), discounted at some discount factor. The discount factor would be different for the stock and the option, and generally also unknown for the purposes of calculation.

However, one could also try to find a different (artificial) probability value for the development path of the stock and option, in such a way that if those probabilities were used to calculate the average future values, then discounting could be done at the risk-free rate. Specifically, if one knew today's option value, V_0, the probability p required to make the average of the future values at payoff (V_u, V_d) equal to today's value, when discounting at the risk-free rate would be the one such that:

$$V_0 = (pV_u + (1 - p)V_d)/(1 + r)$$

Such a probability is known as the risk-neutral probability. It is different to the real world probability of such a movement, whose use to work out the average future value would provide a different average and also require a different discount rate to ensure that the current value equals the discounted average future value.

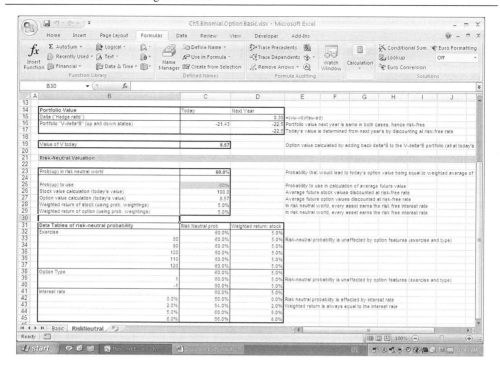

Figure 5.2

The file Ch5.Binomial.Option.Basic.xlsx (RiskNeutral worksheet) (Figure 5.2) shows an example of the calculation of this risk-neutral probability (the formula used in the model can be derived by simple mathematical manipulation of the above formula to isolate p).

The example demonstrates the following points:

- If the risk-neutral probability is used to calculate the average future returns, then the required discount rate that results in the discounted average future value, being equal to the current value, is the risk-free rate. This applies both to the valuation of the stock and the option; more generally, all derivatives (including the asset) have an expected return equal to the risk-free rate when the risk-neutral probabilities are used to calculate average future values.
- Conversely, a modelling assumption that an asset value's growth is expected to equal the risk-free rate is implicitly equivalent to the use of risk-neutral probabilities for the development path of values. Hence the value of a derivative can be established by assuming that an asset's value grows at the risk-free rate, working out the average of the future payoffs using risk-neutral probabilities, and discounting at the risk-free rate. (More generally, where the stock is a dividend paying 1, the assumed expected growth rate of the asset is known as the risk-neutral 1, where the average growth rate of the underlying is equal to the risk-free rate less the constant dividend yield, rather than just the risk-free rate.)

The **Data Tables** also demonstrate that the risk-neutral probabilities are unaffected by features that define the derivative (such as whether it is a call or put, or its exercise price), but do depend on the interest rates and the volatility of the stock (as well as the dividend yield in more general models); in this simple example the volatility is contained implicitly within the relationship between the current and possible future stock values.

Example: Options Valuation using Binomial Trees

The use of a binomial tree to value options in practice clearly requires the development of a more detailed tree to represent the wider range of future outcomes for the stock and options values. In addition, rather than the future stock values being directly specified, as in the simple example above, the range of values is established by an assumption on the stock's volatility (standard deviation of returns).

When working with the basic European options (on non-dividend paying stock, as for the examples above), the use of binomial trees therefore requires:

• The creation of a lattice of future stock values assuming a risk-free development (more generally a risk-neutral development must be assumed for dividend-paying stocks).
• The calculation of the option payoff at expiry for each possible value of the stock.
• The creation of a lattice of option values derived by backward calculation. Option values earlier in the lattice are calculated as the average of the future values in the lattice (using the risk-neutral probabilities), discounted at the risk-free rate.

Note that this process does not require the explicit formulation of the replicating portfolio.

The file Ch5.Binomial.Option.Euro.xlsx (EuroCallorPut worksheet) (Figure 5.3) shows a model for the calculation of a European call and put option (the screenshot shows the put option) The assumptions required for the size of the possible upward and downward movement in the stock at each stage and for the risk-neutral probability (u, d, and p) clearly need to be made in such a way that (as far as possible) the expected return and volatility in the resulting stock lattice correspond to the assumed values for the risk-free rate and stock's volatility. In addition, values that are measured in years (e.g. annual interest rate) will need to be appropriately adjusted for the time period between steps in the lattice. There are many possible ways to do this; however, the discussion of the advantages and disadvantages of each are beyond the scope of this text and further discussion and references can be found in Wilmott (see Further Reading). However, the model is set up to provide a choice between four commonly used methods, and a **Data Table** used in combination with the **INDEX** function to show the calculated value of the options for each method. As for the earlier example, the payoff for both a call and a put can be implemented within a general payoff formula using the 1 or -1 indicator for the option type.

In Chapter 6, we discuss the use of VBA code to generate such trees automatically so that, for example, the number of steps can be defined by the user (and increased until the calculated value has converged, so that the time discretisation error is reduced to insignificant levels).

Example: Option Valuation using Simulation

In an analogous way to the use of binomial trees, simulation techniques also allow the valuation of European options by assuming that the drift of the underlying asset is equal to the risk-free (risk-neutral) rate, calculating the option payoff for each future scenario, calculating the average value of these payoffs, and discounting it at the risk-free rate.

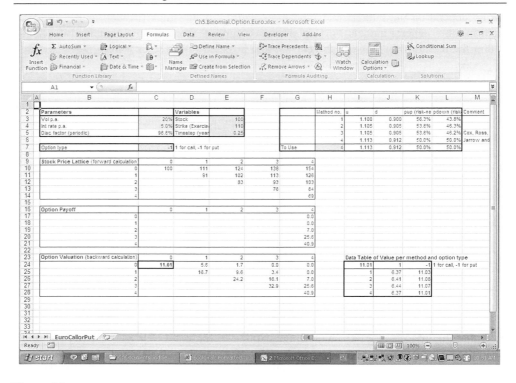

Figure 5.3

The file Ch5.Sim.Options.Multi.xls (simulation worksheet) (Figure 5.4) shows an example implemented by the use of @RISK. The **RiskMean** function is used to show the simulated option value. The model shows a time-series forecast of the value of a non-dividend paying stock, following a random walk increasing at the risk-free rate.

The Black–Scholes Equation and Formulae

Whereas the approaches above represent models in discrete time, the Black–Scholes equation is a model in which time is continuous. It can be thought of as a limiting case of the above models when the discrete time axis becomes very granular. There are many methods to derive the equation (including performing a Taylor-series expansion of the various terms in the binomial model or using mathematical tools from stochastic calculus). This is, however, beyond the scope of this text, and further information is available in Wilmott (see Further Reading).

The Black–Scholes model is in fact a partial differential equation which describes the value of a derivative at each point in time prior to the expiry of the option (and as such is valid for stock options in general, such as American options).

$$\frac{\partial V}{\partial t} + \frac{\sigma^2 S^2}{2} \frac{\partial^2 V}{\partial S^2} + (r - D)S \frac{\partial V}{\partial S} - rV = 0$$

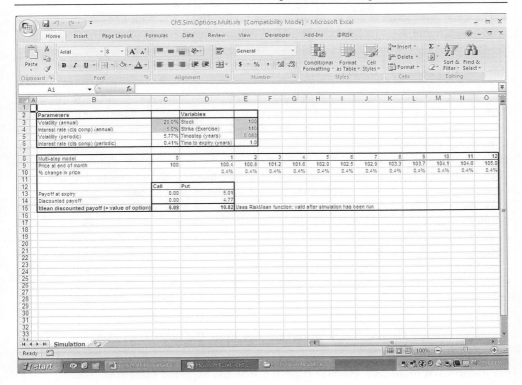

Figure 5.4

The equation describes the development of the option value in terms of S (the current price of the stock), σ (the volatility of the return of the stock), r (the risk-free interest rate), and D (the constant dividend yield). Finding a solution to the equation requires the provision of additional information, including τ (the time to expiry, or $T - t$, where t is the current time and T the time of expiry), and the payoff function at expiry, which for a European call or put simply requires knowledge of E (the exercise price).

As well as existing in their own right, simulation and tree-based methods can be thought of as numerical techniques to solve this equation. In simple cases (such as European options) it is possible through mathematical manipulations to solve the equation analytically, which results in a set of formulae known as the Black-Scholes formulae. Some analytic formulae that describe the solution were shown in Chapter 2 (see Figure 2 and the related formulae in the text for the implementation). A potential advantage of simulation and tree methods in solving the equation is that they can be used with essentially any types of payoff function.

As described earlier in relation to the basic binomial model, a number of assumptions are required for the Black–Scholes framework to be valid, including that:

- The underlying asset is traded, with no restrictions on short-sales and no transaction costs.
- There is a constant risk-free interest rate.
- There are no arbitrage possibilities on risk-free portfolios (i.e. risk free portfolios earn the risk free interest rate).

- The underlying asset follows a Brownian motion in time, and with known volatility.
- The underlying asset has a constant and continuous dividend yield.

American Options and Optimal Exercise

In practice, the use of simulation techniques for options valuation is often restricted to European options (i.e. those that are exercisable only on a single fixed date). Where an option can be exercised before expiry (e.g. an American option), the decision of whether to exercise or not at a particular point in time is non-trivial, as it needs to reflect all future possible outcomes, including the consequences and payoffs associated with exercise or not at that time and at future times (when not exercised now), with any future decision itself depending on further possible outcomes beyond that point, and so on.

Whereas tree-based methods at any point contain information on what may happen in the future from that point (and therefore allow the possibility to perform backward calculations to determine whether it makes sense to exercise the option), simulation techniques do not contain such information. To the extent that an accurate option value is required, the use of simulation techniques is therefore limited to European options, where the exercise decision is trivial (generally, attempts to use simulation techniques for American options would undervalue them, because any assumed exercise behaviour is likely to be suboptimal).

Example: Optimal Exercise of American Options using Binomial Trees

The process of optimal exercise when using tree-based methods involves checking whether the payoff from immediate exercise is greater than the expected value from holding it (i.e. which is itself calculated from the backward calculation using the risk-neutral probability average payoff). If so, then it would be optimal to exercise rather than holding the option, and so the value of the option at that point is equal to its exercise value, i.e. to the larger of the exercise value and the initially calculated value.

The file Ch5.Binomial.Option.US.xlsx (Figure 5.5) shows an example. The payoff from exercise at any time has been calculated and the option value replaced by the maximum of the payoff and the expected value from holding it. The exercise of the option is not explicitly calculated, but can be determined as having happened whenever the exercise value is equal to the option value in the grid. The example in the screenshot shows that an American put option on a non-dividend paying stock should be exercised early if the stock price drops sufficiently (for positive interest rates). Intuitively the general upward movement in the stock price (the risk-neutral prices in the lattice, increasing on average at the risk-free rate) means that the holder of a put should sometimes exploit a large downward movement in the stock to exercise the option rather than risk that the (risk-neutral) stock price may recover. This model could be adapted to allow the choice of the option type being either European or American by embedding the **MAX** statement within an **IF** statement which checks for the option type, and then applying the **MAX** statement only for American options.

REAL OPTIONS MODELLING

Real options analysis deals with the flexibilities that are inherent in many real-life decision situations. It is also related to other types of analysis, such as risk analysis, traditional net present value analysis and financial market options.

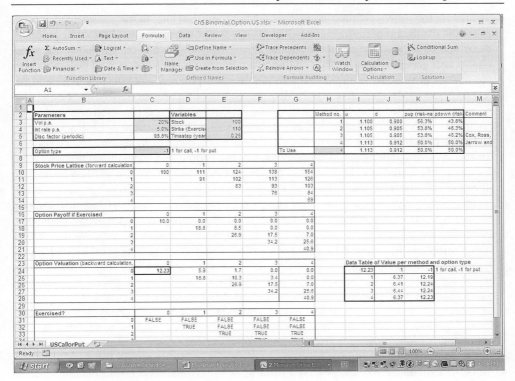

Figure 5.5

Uses and Relationships to Other Types of Analysis

Real options analysis can provide a more rigorous basis for decision-making than both static forecasts and basic risk analysis. Real options analysis requires two elements to be present (and explicitly modelled) in any situation:

- Risk or uncertainty in the basic outcome.
- Non-linearity: the flexibility to react in different ways according to the basic risky outcome, so that a new set of outcomes is achieved.

Where there is uncertainty in a situation, but little opportunity to react to the outcomes, then a risk analysis (as in Chapter 4) may provide a sufficient basis for decision-making.
Examples of the uses of real options analysis include:

- To value a business or project in which there is flexibility or uncertainty. Examples include establishing the value of a business (or any project, such as R&D) assuming that it may be either closed or expanded depending on whether future conditions are unfavourable or favourable, calculating the premium worth paying for capital equipment whose energy source can be switched between fuel sources as their costs vary, estimating the premium that is worth paying for a good management team (versus a normal one), or valuing a penalty clause in a service level agreement.

- To analyse the benefits of phasing a project, whose implementation may be adapted according to the likelihood of future success. The structuring of a project into phases will generally incur additional cost, whereas the results of any test or information yielded in the extra phases will generally also be only an imperfect guide to future success, and possibly delay the overall project. Nevertheless, where the range of potential outcomes is large and the test has reasonable predictive power, then the phasing of a project may be the best course of action. Examples include drug testing and development, oil exploration and geological testing, or the value created in property development by having some flexibility to finalise as late as possible the decision on the ultimate use of a piece of land.
- To facilitate discussions and communication where people may have different views as to the appropriate choice among a range of decision possibilities, and to explain instinctive decision-making behaviours. The real options approach generally forces the structure and assumptions underlying the decision situation to be made explicit, so that a discussion around the correct assumptions can help to build consensus, develop rational arguments, communicate and change behaviour. Such assumptions also include the consideration of the possibilities to respond to different possible outcomes (such as good or bad ones). Examples include strategic decisions i.e. where a project instinctively makes sense but an initial calculation of the overall benefit is negative (typically as shown by a net present value calculation). Typically cases include whether to buy another company at a premium, or to enter a new market at a loss in order to gain a strategic foothold. Real options analysis should be able to allow the development of the appropriate models, to identify sources of value creation, develop consensus around the correct course of action, and calculate the premium worth paying (or loss worth accepting) in such circumstances.
- To better explain natural and observed patterns of behaviour and decision-making, such as why in the face of uncertainty it is often better to postpone a decision, or why companies may be slow to leave a market as conditions deteriorate or slow to re-enter as they improve (e.g. staying in the market may retain at some cost certain assets that would be permanently lost if operations were closed and not recoverable if conditions improve, such as client relationships and skilled workers).

In many cases, no explicit valuation of the embedded flexibilities (options) is conducted; these are implicit in the calculation of the value of each possible course of action, and in the selected decision.

Links to Decision-Making under Uncertainty

Real options analysis can be considered as a natural extension of risk modelling, and is also clearly related to the topic of decision-making under uncertainty. This latter topic is often presented as concerning itself with the analysis of a decision before any uncertainty has been resolved. On the other hand, real options analysis concerns itself with situations where a decision is to be made after some aspect of the uncertainty has been resolved.

Links to Traditional Net Present Value Analysis

Traditional decision-analysis techniques in finance are based on the net present value (NPV) concept. While NPV is often calculated using a single point forecast, where uncertainty is modelled the NPV corresponds to the mean of the discounted cash flows. Such calculations typically involve no analysis of the response to the risky outcomes and the value created by doing so; this is the topic of real options analysis. In some circumstances such traditional analysis may underestimate the true value of a project, as the analysis does not reflect any explicit response to risk. However, it can be debated whether it is always the case that traditional NPV techniques understate the value of a project. For example, if a long-term forecasting model is calibrated so that the forecast growth assumptions are similar to the historic levels, then one can argue that already embedded within the historic levels are management's response to the real options that were historically present.

Links to Financial Market Derivatives: Similarities and Differences

The topic of real options analysis is sometimes approached from a financial market perspective—for example, by attempting to apply the Black—Scholes equation to value a real option. There are indeed a number of similarities between financial market derivatives and real options:

- The value is a function of a random variable (i.e. of the price of an underlying asset or uncertain process).
- The payoff function is usually a non-linear function of an uncertain variable (i.e. different decisions are taken in the future according to the outcome).
- Many of the factors that increase or decrease options values generally also increase or decrease real options values for analogous reasons (e.g. volatility, time to maturity, exercise price, etc.).

On the other hand, there are also a number of significant differences, including that for real options (and unlike for financial market derivatives) it is usually the case that:

- The object under consideration is usually not a traded asset. This difference is absolutely fundamental for the validity of the analytic models of financial market derivatives, which depends on the ability to form a risk-free portfolio of the derivative and an underlying asset (or another option).
- The contractual conditions for a real option are not precisely defined. In particular they generally do not have a fixed maturity or specified exercise conditions.
- Management or other participants may be able to influence the outcomes, e.g. by negotiation to change the implicit nature of the contracts or sources of risk.
- There are likely to be higher transaction costs or taxes for real options.
- In real options situations the explicit calculation of the value of the flexibility embedded in a decision is often not required for the analysis, which may be focused more on the choice of the best decision alternative. On the other hand, the focus of the analysis of financial market derivatives is almost always explicitly on their valuation.
- Although most real options are American in nature (with no specific life), the issue of optimal exercise may be less important for real options. For many real options situations (unlike in financial markets) the accurate valuation is less important than having a general idea of the correct decision. Simulation techniques (which would tend to undervalue options as they may implicitly implement suboptimal exercise) may therefore have wider validity in real options situations that in financial market situations, where lattice methods, such as trees and finite difference methods are often more effective. More information can be found in Wilmott (see Further Reading).

The consequence of these differences is that there are a number of disadvantages in rigidly applying the results from financial market derivatives to real options models:

- It can be argued that such an approach is theoretically incorrect, because the fundamental assumptions required in the financial market context do not apply to more general situations.
- The use of such an approach tends to result in an overemphasis on quantitative analysis, rather than in an analysis that helps to generate a clearer and more in-depth understanding of the situation. This latter objective is often the more relevant one in real options situations.
- It gives the modeller few practical tools to create models that apply to their own situation or can be adapted as new knowledge or insight arises. The toolkit required to conduct a wide set of real options analysis needs to be flexible and pragmatic, because the range of modelling situations that may arise is much wider and less precisely defined than for financial market derivatives. For example, when attempting to apply formulae such as the Black–Scholes equation to real options valuation it is often difficult not only to know which variables in the real life situation correspond to those required for the Black–Scholes formula but also to see how to apply the resulting option value to the decision-making situation.

The approach taken in this text is to consider each real options modelling situation in its own right and to de-emphasise the use of the theory of financial market derivatives. We nevertheless refer to some of this theory where analogies or further insight are to be gained.

Discount Rates for Real Options

As mentioned above, in real options (and unlike in financial market derivatives), a tradeable risk-free portfolio containing the option is usually not possible to create. An arbitrage argument cannot therefore be used to support the use of discounting at the risk-free rate. One may therefore be tempted instead to apply the Capital Asset Pricing Model (CAPM) in which the discount rate reflects the risk (see Chapter 3). However, it could also be argued that the discount rate in the presence of flexibility should be different to the one that may be initially derived when using this approach. The ability to react flexibly to different outcomes generally reduces the risk and so, perhaps, a lower discount rate should be used than if the flexibility were not considered. In other words, the correct choice of discount rate may be unclear and require an element of judgement.

Sometimes risk-free discounting is applied to real options models, for example in those related to drug development or oil exploration. The decision to use a risk-free rate in such contexts cannot be justified simply by the identification of the presence of flexibility. Rather, justification can be found through the CAPM, i.e. that although these projects are risky (large standard deviation of outcomes), their outcomes are also uncorrelated with the overall market.

Examples using Simulation

The following is a set of simple examples using simulation techniques, implemented using @RISK. The models are in many ways similar to the risk models in Chapter 4, but with the addition that the response to the risky outcome is built explicitly within them, i.e. usually through the use of conditional statements (such as **MIN**, **MAX**, **IF**, etc.).

Example: Basic Valuation

The file Ch5.BusValueBasic.xls (Figure 5.6) shows perhaps the simplest possible example of a real option, and is useful from this reference perspective. It concerns the valuation of a project that may be closed at no cost if conditions deteriorate. The project is assumed to operate for a single year. Its base forecast is that it will have revenues of $100 m, costs of $80 m and to make a profit of $20 m so that the value would presumably be $20 m (it is implicit that there are no non-cash expenses, and no timing differences between revenues expenses and cash flow). The same valuation would also apply if the revenues and costs were uncertain, as the average profit would also be $20 m (assuming that the base represent mean values, which as we saw in Chapter 4 may not always be the case in practice). On the other hand, if it were assumed that the business could be closed down (in advance of any losses and at no cost) whenever a loss would arise, then the avoidance of such losses creates extra value. The average value of the business in this case is $21.1 m (shown after a simulation using the **RiskMean** function). This extra value of $1.1 m is the real option associated with this flexibility. Of course, a real option may exist but have no value, such as if different modelling assumptions had been used in which the business were always profitable.

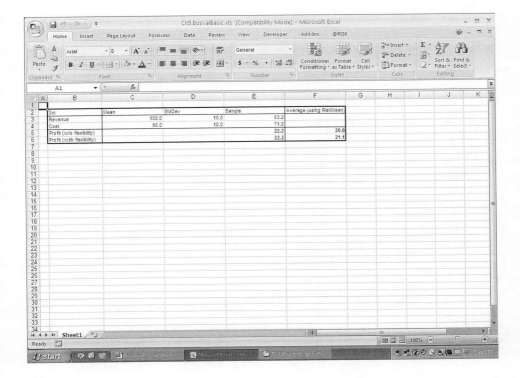

Figure 5.6

Example: Penalties in a Service Level Agreement

In service level agreements, it may be the case that penalties are to be paid if target performance levels are not met. To the extent that the service level is uncertain, a real options model can be built, in order to calculate the distributions of penalty payments as well as its mean value (which would represent the value associated with the penalty clause).

The file Ch5.PenaltyClause.xls (Figure 5.7) assumes that the performance follows a Normal distribution, and that the penalty function is a linear one below some threshold level (i.e. $1000 is paid for every percentage point of performance shortfall). The performance target is assumed to be 95%, with an average performance of 96% and a standard deviation of 2%. The simulation results show that the average penalty is about $395 (shown using @RISK's **RiskMean** function).

Such a model can also be used as an optimisation tool in which different investment scenarios are run, the impact on the average penalty calculated, and the optimum investment selected. For example, if it were known that an investment of $200 could achieve a reduced standard deviation of performance of 1%, then by changing these input assumptions and running the simulation, the average penalty would fall to about $80 (i.e. a saving of over $300, and so such an investment generally would be worthwhile). It would also be easy to experiment with different types of penalty function, e.g. for which the penalty is not linear with the performance shortfall, but increases more steeply, such as using the square of the shortfall, or an exponentially rising curve, and so on.

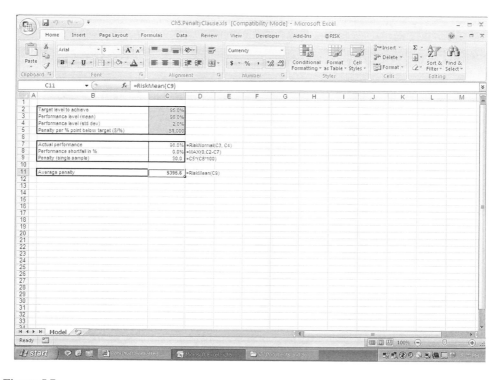

Figure 5.7

Example: Switching Option for a Dual Fuel Machine

There are many situations in which production facilities can be equipped to be flexible. These include certain automotive assembly lines (which may be configured to be able to produce a variety of vehicles), and multi-fuel industrial furnaces. Small-scale examples also exist, such as multi-fuel cookers for residential use, and dual fuel cars (using petrochemical versus ethanol-based fuels). These flexibilities would normally be associated with extra costs (either up-front or when in operation) and a key question may be whether the benefits of having this flexibility compensate for the extra cost.

The file Ch5.DualFuel.xls (Figure 5.8) models a decision as to whether to buy a stand-alone gas cooker, a stand-alone electric cooker, or one that regularly can be switched to the cheaper of the two sources. For simplicity it is assumed that the cookers each have a life of 10 years and that the respective energy prices are set at the beginning of each year, at which point the owner of a dual-fuel cooker would switch to the cheaper fuel source. The model uses a random walk for gas and electricity prices and calculates the total discounted expenditure on fuel for each case (for simplicity a constant discount rate of 6% is used for each case); the fuel cost for the dual fuel cooker in each year is the minimum of the costs associated with the other fuel types. (The numbers used are generic and not intended to actually represent true price levels.) The model calculates the total average expenditure by adding the initial capital cost to the average discounted fuel expenditure. The purchase of

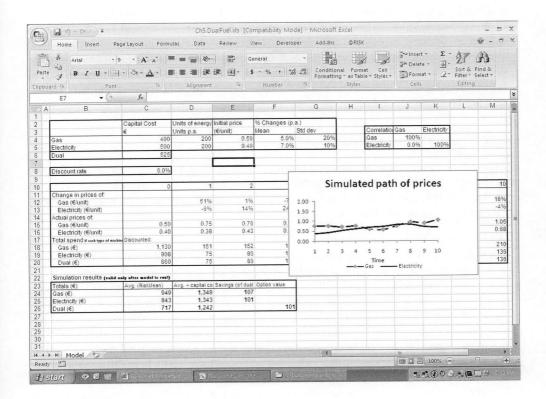

Figure 5.8

the dual fuel machine represents the cheapest overall choice (by about $100, which may be considered to be the real options value associated with the flexibility to switch between fuel sources.) Generally, the purchase of the dual fuel machine would make sense providing it cost less than about $625. The model has been set up so that a correlation coefficient between the changes in gas and electricity prices can be used. The reader may choose to verify that if the assumed correlation coefficient is set to 30%, then there is a reduction in the value of the switching option to about $75, as the positive correlation reduces the frequency and impact of such switching possibilities.

Examples using Trees

The tree-based models in this section use the PrecisionTree add-in from Palisade Corporation. As mentioned at the beginning of Chapter 4, a trial version of the software may be obtained from the Palisade website. The basic functionality of the software is intuitive and easy to use, and readers who wish to simply review the models of this chapter will not need to learn to operate the software. Those readers who nevertheless wish to learn to do so can use the tutorial on Palisade's website.

Tree-based modelling approaches can have several advantages in certain circumstances:

- A model using a tree shows the assumed structure of a decision, including all the factors that have been considered (and implicitly those that have not), and does so in a visual and intuitive way. This can aid discussion of a decision situation as well as the creation of the appropriate model and the process of building consensus around the results.
- Trees can be used to capture the embedded decisions that are present in some model situations. Where each decision path is followed by future uncertain outcomes that are different to those on the other paths, the model must ensure that the decision path selected for the calculation of the output value is the appropriate one. This issue of optimal exercise was partly discussed earlier.

Use of Trees to Capture Optimal Exercise

In each of the earlier simulation-based examples it was clear what the appropriate flexible response was. In other words, the embedded decisions were easy to make and were reflected in the logic of the model (through the use of **IF**, **MIN**, **MAX** statements). However, general situations may not be so clear cut. For example:

- Where a business is expected to be profitable in several years' time, it might not be best to close the business if it were unprofitable in the first year, but rather to keep it open with the hope of making a profit in later years.
- In the above dual fuel example, if there were costs associated with switching fuel sources, it may not always be optimal to switch to the cheaper fuel. For example, where the potential switch would be to the fuel which is currently cheaper but whose cost is expected to grow more quickly, there would then be an increased likelihood of this fuel becoming the more expensive source, thus requiring a switch back to the original fuel. This effect is more likely to be relevant where switching costs are large and where the remaining life of the machine is small (e.g. in the extreme case that the switching cost is larger than the average savings that could be achieved over the remaining life, then it would be better not to switch).

In general, the calculation of the optimal decision to follow at any point involves consideration of all future possibilities after this point, whereby some of these possibilities themselves may involve decisions that need to reflect the future possibilities and decisions after those points. Tree-based approaches use a discrete set of possibilities to reflect all these future decisions and outcomes, from which the optimal decision at any point can be derived through backward calculation (i.e. the last decision in the model can be optimally taken by considering any chance outcomes after that event, and once this is known the optimum path for the next earliest decision can be calculated). Once the full decision structure is known, the output of the model can be calculated, as this involves reflecting the result of only those decisions that are on the optimal path. In other words, the applicable path through the model for calculation of the output is known only after the construction of all possible paths through the model (the forward model) and then by working backwards from the end of the tree (the backward model) to calculate the optimum path.

Example: Basic Decision with Flexibility

Perhaps the simplest possible example of a tree-based real options (RO) model is one which involves a decision–chance–decision structure. Such a structure can also be used to illustrate the difference between RO analysis and pure decision-making under uncertainty (which has a decision–chance structure).

The file Ch5.PT.RO.Course.xls (Figure 5.9) shows a decision on whether to attend a training course according to some estimation of its usefulness. The amount of work (or

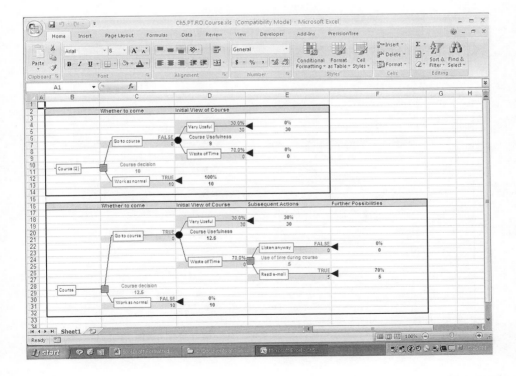

Figure 5.9

benefit) that would be achieved by not attending the course is compared with the likely usefulness of the course. Two models are compared. The first represents a pure decision under uncertainty, in which the decision to attend is followed by the uncertain outcome of its usefulness. With the assumptions used, the decision-maker would not attend the course (based on calculation of the average outcome). The second model explicitly takes into account that the training facilities are equipped with e-mail, so that the participant may read his or her e-mail in the case that the course is not useful, and hence achieve some additional benefit. This flexibility is enough to create some extra value and to switch the decision. The extra value of the decision (i.e. 12.5 for the optimal branch in the second model versus 10 for the optimal branch in the first model) can be considered as a real options value.

Example: Project Phasing

Traditional net present value calculations are often performed using a static assumption as to what is most likely to happen in the future. Where a business situation involves additional decisions that may be taken after the start of a project and in accordance with the development of the project's success (e.g. where a decision may be taken to expand, or abandon a project as future conditions deem appropriate), then very often such a static approach will incorrectly value (undervalue) the project.

The file Ch5.PT.NPV.Phasing.xls (Figure 5.10) shows an example of a regular cash flow calculation (the basic Excel model in the top part of the file) in which the net present value is negative. Although the project is divided into phases, the possibility to expand or abandon

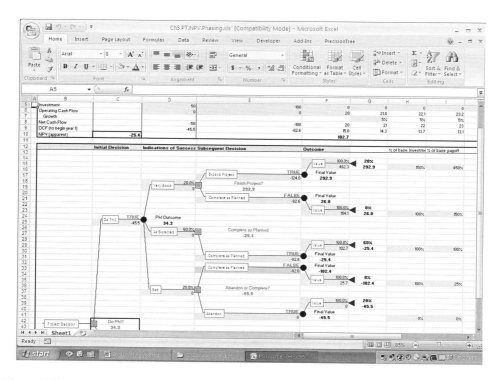

Figure 5.10

the project is not reflected in the logic of the basic Excel model. The second model uses a tree structure which reflects these possibilities (and also requires additional assumptions on the probabilities of each case arising as well as the associated investments and payoffs). The ability to expand or abandon the project creates extra value and results in the situation having a positive net present value.

Example: Bayesian Analysis and Imperfect Information

In the above example, the phasing of a project created value by allowing the project to be changed in some way as a result of information on the likelihood of project success. The implicit assumption was that the information was a perfect guide to the future state of the project (i.e. both that an indication of failure would always be followed by a failed project if it were continued, and that an indication of success would always be followed by a successful project).

In practice, indications of the future state of a project are likely to be imperfect. A project may fail even though it was indicated as a likely success or it may succeed even if it was indicated as a likely failure.

The reflection of imperfect information in a model therefore requires:

- That the tree structure reflects a wider range of decisions and outcomes (i.e. one may choose to continue a project even where failure is indicated or to abandon it even where success is indicated).
- That the probabilities used in the tree are appropriately calibrated to reflect the quality of the information.

The techniques of Bayesian analysis can be used to calibrate tree probabilities. At its core, such analysis is nothing more than basic manipulations in probability theory, although the topic can be developed using more advanced mathematics; further information can be found in Bernardo and Smith (see Further Reading).

The file Ch5.PT.Bayes.Football.xls (Figure 5.11) provides a simple example of Bayesian analysis. The aim is to determine the quality of the test "did someone play football today?" as an indicator of the weather. The assumption is that historic data exists on the frequency in which football is or is not played in each state of the weather. In this sense Bayesian analysis is sometimes thought of as reversing a probability tree. In the example, the historic information is provided and the probabilities that apply to the reversed tree can be directly calculated:

- The historic information directly provides the aggregate frequency that football is played by addition of the end points of the historic tree for both states of the weather. This can be used to calculate the probabilities for the first branches in the reversed tree.
- The historic information directly provides the frequency with which each end point is reached (e.g. football is played and weather was good); the end points in the reversed tree are the same as in the historic tree, but are just presented in a different order.
- The (conditional) probabilities that must hold for consistency (e.g. probability of good weather given that football was played) are then derivable from the ratio of these.

The analysis can also be done in the form of a matrix in which the frequency of all possible states is calculated with the conditional probabilities derivable from the column sums (see file for the formulae).

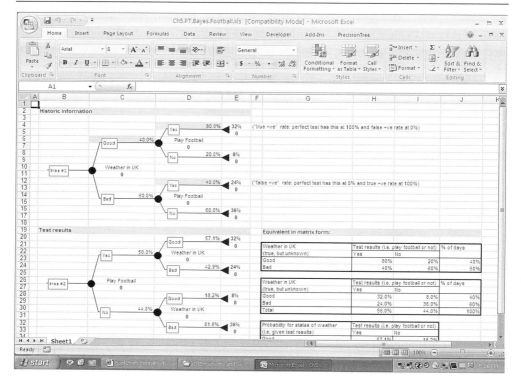

Figure 5.11

Example: Project Phasing with Perfect and Imperfect Information

One practical example of the use of imperfect information is to calculate the value of phasing a project. Such a model also allows one to determine the maximum amount worthwhile to invest in a test to gain this additional information, or to decide between two tests that have different accuracies but also different costs (e.g. whether to conduct an expensive high-quality test or a cheaper and less accurate test). Other typical applications are in the areas of drug development and oil exploration.

The file Ch5.PT.ImperfectInfo.Drug.xls (Figure 5.12) shows an example where one wishes to decide whether to abandon a project, invest in it straight away or conduct further imperfect testing. The phased approach will incur extra testing costs, but presumably allow savings in the case that the information provided allows early termination of projects that are likely to be unsuccessful. In addition, for the situation to be interesting and realistic, the cost of pursuing the phased approach (if it were conducted to completion) has to be more than the cost of immediately conducting the entirety of the project, and the remaining cost of completing the project after conducting the test has to be no greater than that of completing the project in a single phase. The example uses the more compact matrix form of Bayesian analysis to calculate the conditional probabilities of success and failure, given the historic or assumed data.

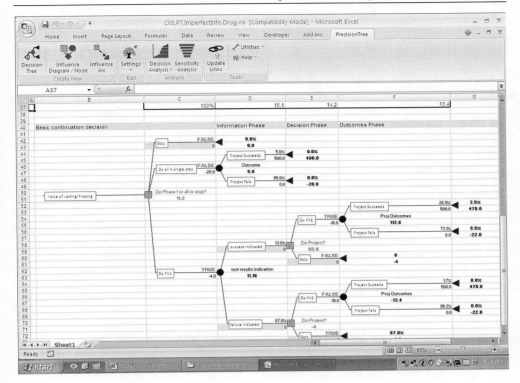

Figure 5.12

With the particular assumptions used, although, in theory, it makes sense to complete the project (average net value of $5 m) rather than abandon it, the phased approach generates more value still, with this branch being worth $11.2 m. The difference between these values may be thought of as the value of the embedded real option, and corresponds to the maximum additional expenditure that would be worth spending on the test. A **Data Table** is used to show how the value of the real option varies as the quality of the test varies. The quality of the test is represented by two factors: the true-positive rate and the false-negative rate; when these are not simultaneously equal to 100% and 0%, the test is imperfect.

6

VBA for Financial Modelling

INTRODUCTION

This chapter discusses the use of Visual Basic for Applications (VBA) in a range of practical financial modelling situations. Despite the fact that often even a small amount of pertinent knowledge in this area can be used to great effect, many otherwise competent modellers never learn VBA. There are a variety of reasons for this:

- Good modelling practice would suggest avoiding the use of VBA where possible, as its use may complicate a model from the perspective of a third party.
- Many books (and training courses) on the subject are presented from a programming perspective, rather than a financial applications one. The lack of apparent direct relevance of much of their content and examples does not motivate further exploration of the subject.
- It can appear unintuitive at the beginning, especially to those modellers who do not have a programming background; even for those who do, its object-oriented aspect can initially appear complex.
- There are often many ways to achieve the same basic functional effect in VBA than in pure Excel. More time can be spent in considering the appropriate approach to use in a particular case, and this can reinforce the impression of complexity.

In this chapter we assume that the reader is a beginner in VBA. We start with a presentation of some core building blocks and key operations, and then discuss a range of specific financial modelling applications using VBA to:

- Facilitate communication with a user by asking the user to provide the values of some model inputs.
- Automate the process of resetting some or all of a model's inputs after some other information is provided (e.g. by taking data from another source, and then using **GoalSeek** or **Solver** to determine the required value of some of the other model inputs).
- Create models whose equivalent in pure Excel would either have a cumbersome structure or essentially be impossible to create. Examples include where the input values of a variable impact the model's structure, such as if the user can set the number of steps to use in a binomial tree options valuation.
- Create functions that do not exist in Excel.
- Build simulation models, where a recalculation of essentially the same model using different input values needs to be performed many times.

This chapter aims to cover the fundamental aspects that a well-rounded financial modeller at the advanced level would need to know or be aware of. We do not aim for a complete coverage of VBA; rather the topics have been carefully chosen so that a wide range of practical financial modelling applications can be implemented. Whereas more emphasis is given than in many other texts to the techniques required in the specific practical applications, certain topics are emphasised less (such as object-oriented methods and the use of recorded macros). Indeed some topics are not covered at all (such as user forms and class modules). In this way, we hope to have created a text that is accessible for the beginner while still being of high value when applied to real-life modelling situations. Readers who wish to develop their knowledge of VBA beyond that covered here can use the `Help` menu within VBA, or refer to other texts, such as Walkenbach (see Further Reading).

This chapter starts by covering key aspects of VBA with the aim of creating the capability to write some basic code and to become familiar with the most important features. The later sections of the chapter cover specific applications, such as the use of **Solver** with VBA, the creation of simulation models and of user-defined functions. Regarding terminology, although VBA is contained within Excel, we use the term Excel in this chapter to refer to the traditional (non-VBA) part of Excel (i.e. consisting of the workbook and worksheet grid and so on). This is to make a clear distinction between when we are referring to VBA versus the non-VBA parts of Excel.

When running code in the example files it will be necessary to enable the macros in them. This can be done either on an individual basis (in response to the security warnings that are likely to appear each case), or by temporarily enabling all macros under **Office/Excel Options/Trust Center** then **Trust Center Settings/Macro Settings** (under **Tools/Macros/Security** in Excel 2003), providing of course that other potentially dangerous files are not worked with at the same time. Alternatively, the folder containing the files may be set as a trusted location under **Trust Center Settings/Trusted Locations/Add new location/Browse** (where appropriate the option **Subfolders of This Location are Also Trusted** may need to be selected).

The Bare Essentials

This section contains a quick-start guide to enable readers to rapidly become familiar with some core VBA operations and write and use some simple code. It attempts to present only those concepts which are essential to getting started. Some technical features and other characteristics that would be necessary for a strictly complete presentation have been omitted, in order to keep the presentation as simple as possible and focused on the key knowledge required at this stage.

Creating Code using the Visual Basic Editor

Code can be generated by recording macros (see later), although this is not how it is mostly created in practice. In this text we emphasise the creation of code by direct typing in the `Code` window of the Visual Basic Editor (VBE). The key steps in doing so are:

- Accessing the VBE from Excel using **Alt+F11**. An alternative way to access the VBE is on the **Developer** tab under **Visual Basic** or **View Code** (if the **Developer** tab is not displayed, check the relevant box under **Office/Excel Options/Popular/Top Options**). In Excel 2003, one can use **Tools/Macro/Visual Basic Editor**.
- In the `Project` window (or `Project Explorer`) selecting the workbook (or project) where one desires to place the code (typically the one which is being worked with at that point). Other projects are likely to be displayed in the window depending on the other workbooks open at the time, whether any add-ins are active, and whether the user has

a **Personal Macro Workbook** (see later). The list of projects is therefore likely to be different from user-to-user and for different working sessions of a given user.

- Inserting a new code module using `Insert/Module` from the menu.
- Ensuring the `Code` window is visible (using `View/Code` if it is not). The new code module will be blank, or possibly contain a few short instructions, such as `Option Explicit`, depending on how the defaults have been set up (under `Tools/References`).
- Writing code. This is achieved by simply typing into the `Code` window of the inserted module. (Note also that double-clicking on any object in the `Project` window will ensure that the contents of this module are displayed in the `Code` window, but it is important to ensure that the code is placed in the correct place, typically in the inserted module.) The creation of code is, of course, the principal content of this chapter, and some basic examples are provided in the next section.

For the scope of this text, code consists of two types of possible procedures (or macros):

- Subroutines, which consist of a sequence of tasks or processes that is to be performed. A subroutine can be created by typing of the words `Sub` followed by a name (such as `Sub FirstCode()`); the words `End Sub` appear automatically. The empty brackets after the name indicate that the subroutine has no parameters associated with it. Many subroutines are task sequences which do not require arguments, although more complex subroutines may do so.
- User-defined functions, which return a value (or an array of values). A function can be created by typing `Function` followed by a name and argument list in brackets; the `End Function` words will appear automatically. As in Excel, functions generally have arguments (Excel's **RAND** function is an exception).

The name of the procedures (subroutine or functions) can be chosen to be essentially anything (subject to a few restrictions, such as not containing any spaces, not using reserved words and so on; see later for more details).

The following points are also worthy of note here:

- The `ThisWorkbook` and `Sheet` object modules are not used to place general purpose code, but are used for event procedures. For example, the `ThisWorkbook` object within the `Object` list box is used when code is included in the `ThisWorkbook` module that executes whenever the workbook is opened (see later for an example). The `Properties` window displays properties for the selected object, and is not required further for the purposes of this text. The `Class Module` and `UserForm` module possibilities that one sees when using the `Insert` menu are also beyond the scope of this text.
- Where several procedures are to be written, these can either be included within the same module or in a new module. If several procedures have been created in a module, the drop-down list in the `Procedure` box can be used to rapidly move between them. The issue of the general structuring of code is discussed later.
- Where it is required to continue a line of code on another line, this can be done by use of SPACE followed by UNDERSCORE at the end of the line to be continued.
- Comment lines are simply notes in the code that have no effect when the code is run. A comment line starts with an apostrophe, may reside on a code line (after the code) and may be continued on the next line using SPACE followed by UNDERSCORE. The use of comments is discussed in more detail later.

- Indentation can be used to make the code visually more attractive. The **Tab** key can be used to indent code, and **Shift+Tab** to un-indent. The **Tools/Options/Editor** menu in VBE can be used to alter the tab width (when using several levels of indenting the default tab width is often too wide).
- When in the `Code` window, the typing of a full stop after an object will result in a drop-down menu appearing, and which presents the available list of menu items relating to that object. For example by typing `Range("A1").` one sees the menu items that are relevant to a range, such as `Range("A1").Activate` (Figure 6.1) to make A1 the active cell, `Range("A1").ClearContents` to clear the contents of cell A1, and `Range("A1").Value` to refer to its value (the value is also the default property of a range, so `Range("A1")` would be interpreted as referring to the value).
- The code will be saved whenever the workbook is saved as an. xlsm file (a. xlsx file may not contain code, unlike a. xls file which may or may not contain code). This does not apply to add-ins however (see later).

Running and Using Code

To use the code it is necessary to distinguish between subroutine and function procedures.

- Subroutines can be run in a number of ways:
  — When in VBE with the cursor within the code of the subroutine to be run, press **F5** (or use the menu `Run/Run Sub`).

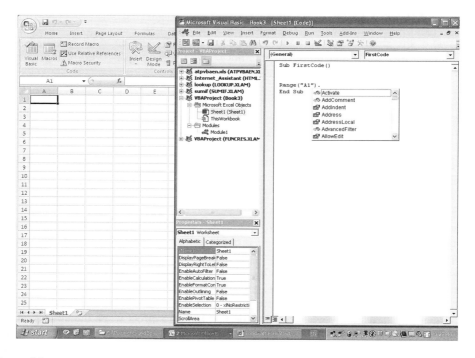

Figure 6.1

— When in Excel, one can use **Alt+F8** to invoke the **Macro** dialog, select the appropriate macro from the list and select **Run**. Alternatively one can access this macro list under **Developer/Macros** or **View/Macros/View Macros** (or **Tools/Macro/Macros** when in Excel 2003).

— A button can be created on an Excel worksheet and a macro assigned to it (so that clicking on the button will run the macro). This can be achieved using **Developer/Controls/Insert**, clicking the **Button** control under **Form Controls**, drawing the button on the worksheet, and selecting the macro from the list that appears in the **Assign Macro** dialog. The button can be renamed, resized, and repositioned as desired (e.g. by right-clicking to edit). It is important to label it clearly to ensure that macros are not run by accident. (In Excel 2003, this can be achieved by right-clicking on any menu icon, selecting **Forms**, and following the same procedure.)

— Macros can also be run using shapes, with icons on the **Quick Access Toolbar** in Excel, by calling a subroutine from another procedure, and by the use of user forms. These topics are discussed later in the chapter (except for user forms, which are not covered in this text).

• User-defined functions are accessed like other Excel functions, that is either by using Excel's **Formula/Insert Function** (where they will be listed under the user-defined category) or by direct typing in Excel (providing functions have the default scope of `Public`; see later in the chapter). Functions may also be used within subroutines (see later).

If the code does not run (producing a run-time error with execution halted) or runs (but produces an incorrect result) then some checking or debugging of the code will be necessary. A variety of techniques to do so is discussed in more detail later. At this stage, the following key points are worth mentioning:

• Often it is sufficient to step through the code line-by-line by pressing **F8** (or `Debug/Step Into` on toolbar) in order to see at what point the error is occurring.

• When stepping through, the step that is about to be conducted is highlighted in yellow, and the value of a variable at that point can be seen by letting the cursor hover over the variable in the code.

• It can often be useful to use a split screen; that is to simultaneously view the `Code` window and any relevant parts of the Excel workbook that relates to the code. A vertically split screen can be created simply by resizing each of Excel and the VBE to take half the screen and then to arrange them to be side-by-side. It is also created satisfactorily in most cases using **Developer/View Code** when in Excel (one may also need to select the appropriate module when doing so in order to see the relevant code displayed).

• The VBA `Help` menu can be accessed from the toolbar or using **F1**.

• The `View` menu can also be used to display the `Immediate` window, `Watches` window and `Locals` window. These are useful for and checking and debugging more complex code, and are discussed later.

• The debugging of functions is often slightly more complicated than that for subroutines (and so is discussed in detail later).

Examples of simple code which demonstrate these points and perform basic operations are presented below.

Simple Examples

The file Ch6.SimpleExs.xlsm contains the code for the following simple examples. The reader may choose to use the techniques above (e.g. to run the subroutines line-by-line using **F8** with split screen) to follow the examples in detail. The examples include:

- Writing numbers into a cell in Excel.
- Using values from Excel cells in the code.
- Clearing the contents of a range, and of an entire column.
- Using an InputBox to take values from the user and a MsgBox to display the results of calculations performed on the inputs.
- A simple function.

Example: Writing Numbers into Excel

The code:

```
Sub PlaceNos()
Range("A1").Value = 10
Range("A2").Value = 4
End Sub
```

places the numbers 10 and 4 in cells A1 and A2 of the active worksheet in the workbook. The screenshot shows the use of the step-through method using a split-screen, in which the first instruction has been executed (Figure 6.2).

Example: Using Values from Excel in the Code

In the above example, values were placed from code into an Excel worksheet. The process can work in the opposite sense in which variables that are used in the code take their values from an Excel worksheet. The following code relates to Module 2 of the same file and takes values typed into two cells in the worksheet and uses these values to calculate a further quantity, which is then written into the worksheet:

```
Sub MultiplyTwoCells()
x = Range("A1").Value
y = Range("A2").Value
z = x * y
Range("A3").Value = z
End Sub
```

In other words, variables x and y are set to be equal to the values in the cells A1 and A2, and a third variable z is set equal to their product, whose value is placed in cell A3.

Note that this result could also be achieved by writing the code in different ways, such as:

```
Sub MultiplyTwoCells2()
Range("A3").Value = Range("A1").Value * Range("A2").Value
End Sub
```

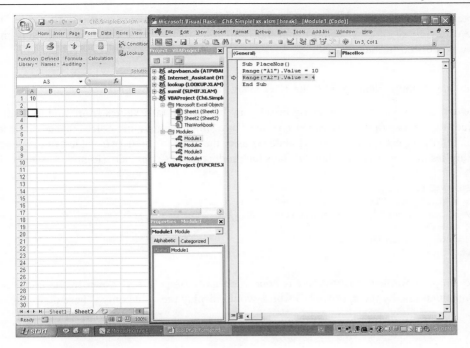

Figure 6.2

or

```
Sub MultiplyTwoCells3()
Range("A3") = Range("A1") * Range("A2")
End Sub
```

Example: Clearing Contents

A frequent application of a subroutine (or macro) is to clear the contents of a cell or range. This could be required in the simple example above in order to rerun the code (and to be able to see that the code has actually worked), and in more general cases where a results range of a calculation should be cleared before new results are generated. The code (contained in Module 2) that could be used in this simple case is:

```
Sub ClearContentsThreeCells()
Range("A1:A3").ClearContents
End Sub
```

Similarly, the contents of the entire column A could be cleared with code such as:

```
Sub ClearContentsColA()
Range("A:A").ClearContents
End Sub
```

Note that (as in Excel) there is the option in VBA to use `Clear` or `ClearContents`. The use of `ClearContents` would retain the formatting of the cells, which is something that may be desired in many cases.

Example: Communicating with the User using InputBox and MsgBox

The `InputBox` and `MsgBox` dialog boxes may be used to take values from, and to display values to, the user (a `MsgBox` can also be used as a simple debugging tool, as discussed later). The following code (shown in Module 3) asks the user to input two values in sequence, multiplies these values, and then displays the product of these numbers (Figures 6.3 and 6.4):

```
Sub MultiplyInputValues()
x = InputBox("Type first value", "Value 1")
y = InputBox("Type second value", "Value 2")
Z = x * y
MsgBox "The product is " & Z
End Sub
```

The simplest form of the `MsgBox` is code such as `MsgBox Z` (as shown in the code as a commented line by the apostrophe) which would display the value only. These dialog boxes

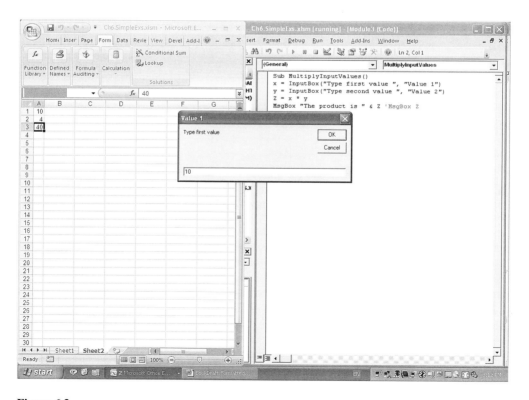

Figure 6.3

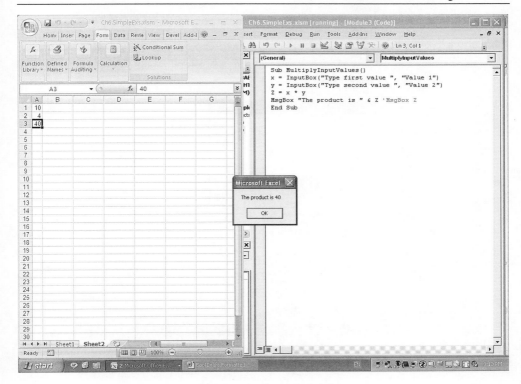

Figure 6.4

may be set up in more complicated ways, but for the purposes of this text this functionality is sufficient (more information can be found under `Help` (**F1**)).

Example: A Basic User-Defined Function

On occasion, a modeller may desire to create a function that is not one of the pre-defined Excel functions. Of course, as is the case when using other VBA procedures, user-defined functions have the disadvantage that the model may be less transparent to other users who are not familiar with them. Their use can nevertheless be a powerful tool in the right circumstances, as discussed later. At this point we provide a simple example for illustrative purposes.

The code for a simple function that multiplies two numbers could look something like (Figure 6.5):

```
Function MultiplyUs(x, y)
MultiplyUs = x * y
End Function
```

Note that the code must contain a return statement (before `End Function`) which explicitly assigns the value of the calculation to the function's value.

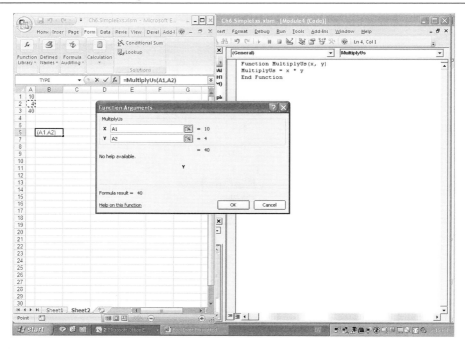

Figure 6.5

BUILDING BLOCKS

Working with Ranges

One of the core aspects of writing code is working with Excel ranges. It is also an area where many users new to VBA experience the most difficulty; this is partly due to the large number of possibilities that there are to refer to and manipulate ranges and the data within them. This section discusses some of the key possibilities and good practices in this area.

The file Ch6.RangeExs.xlsm shows the code that is used to illustrate the points.

Full Referencing and the Use of With... End With

One principle of best practice coding is to ensure that the ranges used are referenced through full addressing. For example, in a statement such as Range("A1") it is not directly clear in which worksheet nor which workbook the desired range is to be found. In fact, the range used when such code is run would be the one that is in the currently active worksheet (and workbook). The use of full referencing would make explicit which workbook and worksheet is desired to be referred to, and so will generally ensure that the code is more transparent and reduce the risk of error.

For example, the code (see Module 1 (Figure 6.6) of Ch6.RangeExs.xlsm) could be written as:

```
Sub MultiplyTwoCells()
x = ThisWorkbook.Worksheets("Sheet1").Range("A1").Value
```

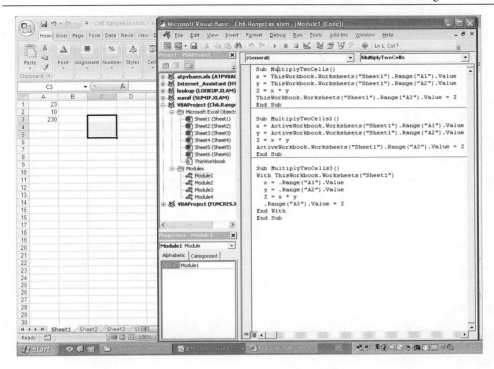

Figure 6.6

```
y = ThisWorkbook.Worksheets("Sheet1").Range("A2").Value
z = x * y
ThisWorkbook.Worksheets("Sheet1").Range("A3").Value = z
End Sub
```

Note that the above code would work with the ranges in the workbook in which the code module resides (which in general could be different to the workbook that is currently active when the code is run); if it were desired to refer to the workbook which is active at the time that the code is run (even if the code does not reside in it), then this could be achieved by using ActiveWorkbook in place of ThisWorkbook in the above.

The With... End With construct can be used to overcome the long lines of repetitive code that often arise when using full referencing. The construct allows for repeated referral to the same range or object, and hence reduces not only the time required to create the code but also the volume of code. The first example above would become:

```
Sub MultiplyTwoCells3()
With ThisWorkbook.Worksheets("Sheet1")
x = .Range("A1").Value
y = .Range("A2").Value
z = x * y
.Range("A3").Value = z
End With
End Sub
```

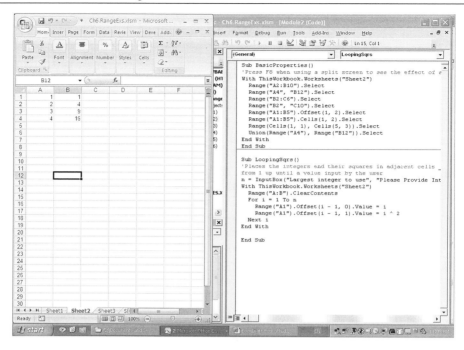

Figure 6.7

The Range, Cells and Offset Properties

The `Range`, `Offset`, and `Cells` properties provide a variety of ways to refer to ranges (see code in Module 2 (Figure 6.7) of Ch6.RangeExs.xlsm):

- The use of the `Range` property results in a `Range` object that represents a cell or a range of cells. The format is `Range(Cell1, Cell2)` where `Cell1` and `Cell2` are ranges, of which `Cell2` is optional. Thus each of the following lines of code would refer to the range consisting of cells B2 to C10 in Sheet1 of the active workbook:

```
Worksheets("Sheet1").Range("B2:C10")
Worksheets("Sheet1").Range("B2","C10")
```

- The `Offset` property is superficially similar to Excel's **OFFSET** function (in that it allows the reference point of an operation to remain unchanged while working in other cells or ranges). However, it is a property of a range (not a function), and can be used to represent a range that is offset from another specified range. For example:
- `Range("A1:B5").Offset(1,2)` refers to the range that is one row and two columns from cell A1, i.e. to the range consisting of cells C2 to D6.
- The `Cells` property of a range (which should not be confused with Excel's **CELL** function described in Chapter 1) can also be used to identify cells in a relative sense to the range of which it is a property. For example:

- `Range("A1:B5").Cells(1,2)` refers to the cell in the first row and second column of the range, i.e. to cell B1 `Range(Cells(1, 1), Cells(5, 3))` refers to the cells A1 to C5.

A few further points are worthy of note:

- The `Union` method can be used to unite several ranges. So the following would refer only to cells B2 and C10:

```
Union(Range("B2"), Range("C10"))
```

- `Cells` can also be used in the context of the cell number in the worksheet (from left-to-right and then top-to-bottom) so that A1 and B1 correspond to `Cells(1)`, `Cells(2)` and so on. However, since Excel 2003 had 256 columns, `Cells(257)` would correspond to cell A2 in Excel 2003 but to cell `IW1` in Excel 2007, so that there is a risk of lack of compatibility and errors when this form is used. The expression `Range(A3:B10).Cells(5)` refers to cell A5 (i.e. the fifth element of the range when read from left-to-right and top-to-bottom).
- `Offset` and `Cells` could of course also be used together, with `Cells` being interpreted as being relative to the prior range. Thus `Range("A1").Offset(2, 0).Cells(1, 3)` refers to the cell which is in the first row and third column relative to the range offset from cell A1 by two rows (to A3), that is to cell C3.
- A frequently required technique is to work through individual elements of a range and write a different value in each cell. This can be achieved by use of `Offset` within a `For ... Next` loop (such loops are essentially self-explanatory, but are discussed in more detail later), such as:

```
Sub LoopingSqrs()
'Places the integers and their squares in adjacent cells _
from 1 up until a value input by the user
n = InputBox("Largest integer to use", "Please Provide Integer")
With ThisWorkbook.Worksheets("Sheet2")
  Range("A:B").ClearContents
  For i = 1 To n
    Range("A1").Offset(i - 1, 0).Value = i
    Range("A1").Offset(i - 1, 1).Value = i ^ 2
  Next i
End With
End Sub
```

Selecting Ranges

Many of the examples used so far have shown that (unlike when working in pure Excel) it is not always necessary to select an Excel range in order to change the values or other properties of the cells in that range. However, the selection of ranges in Excel is often required, and this and related techniques are the focus of this section (see code in Module 3 (Figure 6.8) of the file Ch6.RangeExs.xlsm).

The above example used the `Select` method as applied to a range, such as `Range("A2:B10").Select`. Where a range is selected either using this method or directly in an Excel

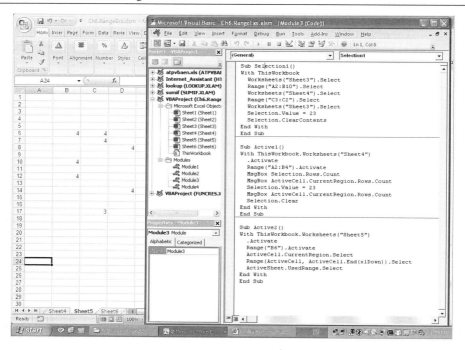

Figure 6.8

worksheet (by using the mouse), the resulting selected range can be referred to in the code using `Selection`. For example:

```
Range("A2:B10").Select
Selection.Value=23
Selection.ClearContents
```

will place the value 23 in each cell of the selected range and clear the contents of the range respectively.

A few further points are worthy of note when using the `Select` method:

- It may also be applied to other types of objects, such as `Worksheets`. In such a context it can be important to remember that `Selection` refers to the current selection on the active worksheet, so that when a worksheet is made active the use of `Selection` will refer to the range that was selected the last time that the worksheet was active in the working session (see `Sub Selection1` for an example).
- It is to be distinguished from the `Activate` method, which activates the object (for example a range, workbook, worksheet or range). When activating a range it should be remembered that only the first cell in the range will be the active cell, but the entire range will be selected. The difference can be seen by running the code, such as the following:

```
Sub Active1()
With ThisWorkbook.Worksheets("Sheet4")
```

```
   .Activate
   Range("A2:B4").Activate
   MsgBox Selection.Rows.Count
   MsgBox ActiveCell.CurrentRegion.Rows.Count
   Selection.Value = 23
   MsgBox ActiveCell.CurrentRegion.Rows.Count
   Selection.Clear
 End With
 End Sub
```

When working with the `ActiveCell`, it should be noted that:

- The `CurrentRegion` property of a range can be used to define the two-dimensional range that is bounded by empty cells but where every row or column in the range has some non-empty cell (or includes the `ActiveCell` if empty). For example, `Active-Cell.CurrentRegion.Select` would select this region. `CurrentRegion` does not exist by itself, only as a property of another range.
- The `ActiveCell` may be used as part of a range definition, and also combined with the `End` property of a range, such as `Range(ActiveCell, ActiveCell.End(xlDown))`. This would be equivalent to using **CTRL+SHIFT+DOWN** in Excel; similarly `End (xlUp)`, `End(xltoLeft)`, `End(xlToRight)` can be used.
- The `UsedRange` property of a worksheet defines the two-dimensional range which consists of the current regions associated with all non-empty cells.
- Some range definitions that one may initially expect to be available do not exist in VBA (e.g. one might perhaps expect to find `CurrentRange`, `ActiveRegion` or `Active Range`).

Named Ranges and the Set Statement

In Chapter 2, we discussed the advantages and disadvantages of using named ranges when working in Excel. Whereas for many Excel models it may not always be worthwhile using them, their use in code is indispensable in order to create robust and flexible code. For example, if a name had been given to the cell C5 (such as `InputData`), then `Range ("InputData")` will provide a robust reference to the appropriate data, whereas the use of `Range("C5")` would not be robust if a row or column were inserted or deleted before cell C5. Of course, the failure to use the correct cell reference would generally result in incorrect calculations without any form of error message or warning appearing when the code is run. If named ranges were not used then any changes made to the Excel workbook would also require significant rework of the code, which would be time-consuming and prone to errors.

Similar comments apply to the use of worksheet names in the code; the changing of a worksheet name by the user in Excel may result in the code not working correctly. However, in most situations it is less important to create flexibility in the use of worksheet names than it is to create flexible cell references: first, any such error will very likely produce a run-time error, so the existence of the mistake will be clear (unlike if the value from the wrong cell is taken); second, worksheet names are generally less frequently changed than the structure of an Excel worksheet. Much code is written under the implicit assumption that worksheet names will not be changed. For model auditing and restructuring, this issue is nevertheless potentially important.

Two generic possibilities exist for the process used to define named ranges:

- Directly in the Excel workbook (before the code is run) using the tools of Chapter 2 (such as the **Name Manager**). A range defined in this way would be referred to in the code using inverted commas, i.e. Range ("DataRange"). There would of course be no direct way of seeing within the code what range of cells was being referred to by this name, but this could be seen from the **Name Manager** in Excel or by use of the Immediatewindow in VBA (see later).
- Within the code (as it runs). This is something that is very frequently required; in particular the size or location of a range may be known only once the code is run. A range named in this way (such as DataRange) would be referred to in the code using Range (DataRange), that is without inverted commas.

The process of defining names within the code will often require the use of the Set statement. This is used to define (or assign) a variable as an object, in other words to create an object variable (the failure to do so is a common error, resulting in a VBA error message, such as Object variable not set (Error 91)). The Set statement can be used in various contexts, including:

- Defining names within the code (see below).
- To create a short name for a range or other object that is frequently required. For example the variable wsf may be assigned to represent worksheet functions, where these are frequently used in the code (see later).
- When using code to add a new worksheet to a workbook (see later).

The simplest form of the Set statement to define a named range would be code such as:

```
Set DataRange=Range("A1:A100")
```

More generally, one could use the Set statement when the size of the range is to be defined only when the code is run. For example, a data set may be in the range A1:A100 of a worksheet, but one wishes to give the user the possibility to perform some calculation on a subset of those points. The following (see Module 4 (Figure 6.9) of the file Ch6.RangeExs.xlsm) shows an example where an InputBox takes from the user the number of the first and last row in the data set to be used to define the range, and the Set statement is then used to assign the range:

```
Sub SetDemo1()
Worksheets("Sheet6").Activate
RowN1 = InputBox("Row Number (<= 100)", "Number of First Row")
RowN2 = InputBox("Row Number (<= First Row)", "Number of Second Row")
StartCell = "A" & RowN1
EndCell = "A" & RowN2
Set DataRange = Range(StartCell, EndCell)
MsgBox "Number of points is " & DataRange.Count
End Sub
```

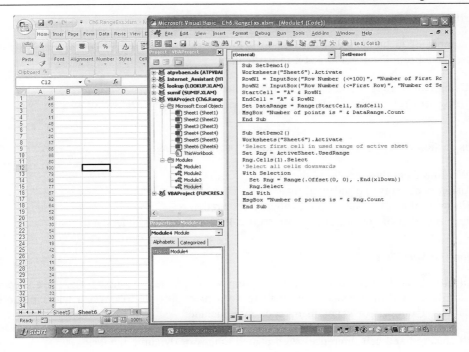

Figure 6.9

(The data provided using the `InputBox` could of course instead been taken from the values of other cells in the worksheet.)

The `Set` statement can also be used to define ranges using some of the techniques discussed earlier. The following code selects the first cell in the used range and then selects all cells from that cell downwards to the end of the range:

```
Sub SetDemo2()
Worksheets("Sheet6").Activate
'Select first cell in used range of active sheet
Set Rng = ActiveSheet.UsedRange
Rng.Cells(1).Select
'Select all cells downwards
With Selection
  Set Rng = Range(.Offset(0, 0), .End(xlDown))
  Rng.Select
End With
MsgBox "Number of points is" & Rng.Count
End Sub
```

Such code could be useful if the position of the data set within the worksheet is unclear (but of course will generally work as intended only if this data resides in a single column).

Writing Robust Code

A number of techniques can be used to help to write robust and flexible code. Some of these have been discussed already, in particular:

- Using named ranges and flexible ranges where possible.
- Using full referencing, but keeping code visually compact by use of the With... End With construct.

This section covers a number of other key aspects including:

- Working from the specific to the general.
- Using comments and indented text.
- Ensuring that all variables are explicitly declared.
- Ensuring that the names are chosen so that they are easy to understand.

From the Specific to the General

Typically it can be helpful to start by creating some simple code that works in a specific circumstance and then generalising it to make it more flexible to cover a wider range of situations. Examples of generalising code may include:

- Replacing fixed cell references with named ranges or dynamic ranges.
- Ensuring that the code still works if the input data set is changed in some way.
- Building in error-checking or error-handling procedures (see later).

Each time a generalisation is added, further testing of the code should be done, and the functionality and limitations of the code recorded (e.g. by using comments).

Comments and Indented Text

The use of comments within the code to document the purposes of key lines of code is important, especially as code becomes more complex. Comment lines are simply notes that have no effect when the code is run. A comment starts with an apostrophe and may reside on a code line (after the code) and may be continued on the next line using SPACE followed by UNDERSCORE (see earlier code examples). Some points to consider when creating comments and deciding on their content include:

- Comments should describe the aim and functionality of the procedures and key lines (especially the more complex ones).
- Comments can be used to state what is out of the scope or where the code has other limitations that the user needs to be aware of. For example, code may have been written that would work only if the data were arranged in contiguous cells in a column, or if certain inputs need to be set by the user within the code, rather than taken from the worksheet, etc. No code can be perfectly flexible and robust; the use of comments about code limitations also signals to a user that the developer has adequately tested the code.
- As a general rule, it is better to over-comment rather than under-comment; if the code writer views the code after a break of a few days and is not quickly able to see what the code does, then it is probably not commented clearly or has insufficient detail.

- Code that is desired to be retained for later reference can be commented out (by adding an apostrophe before it) and copied or commented back in (by deleting the apostrophe) when needed. This can be particularly useful for checking and debugging code, where `MsgBox` and `Debug.Print` statements can be commented in and out as needed.
- Where it is desired to ensure that a user receives adequate warning about some key aspects of the code, these can be placed in comments, although a more powerful method can be to make such text appear as the workbook opens, using event code (see later).

The use of indented text to make the code visually more attractive is also an important tool, and a few points are worthy of note here:

- The **Tab** key can be used to indent code, and **Shift+Tab** to un-indent.
- The **Tools/Options/Editor** menu in VBE can be used to alter the tab width (when using several levels of indenting the default tab width is often too wide).

Data Types and Variable Declaration

The data type of a variable describes its nature (and specifically represents the type of storage space that will be used for it when the code runs). While it is not necessary for the code writer to specify the data types of the variables used, doing so generally will have several advantages, including:

- The code will run more quickly.
- The code will generally be more robust. If variables are not declared, any errors (e.g. mistyped variable names) may not be obvious, so the code is more likely to contain hidden errors, and be more difficult to debug.
- It will help to avoid name-conflict errors.

The default data type (i.e. where unspecified) is `Variant`, in which case the storage space associated with the variable is allocated when the code runs. Where it is desired to specify the data types, the following are most frequently required:

- `Integer`. These range from $-32,768$ to $+32,767$.
- `Long`. These are integers that range between -2^{31} to $2^{31}-1$. The total range allowed for the `Integer` type (i.e. 65536 or 2 16) is also equivalent to the maximum number of allowed rows in Excel 2003. This may be too limiting for some purposes (e.g. the number of times to recalculate a simulation model), so `Long` is very often preferable.
- `Object`. These are objects in the `Excel Object Model`, such as `Range`, and also includes `Collections`, such as `Names`, and `Comments` (see later for more on objects).
- `Single`. These are values in the approximate range 10^{-45} to 10^{-38} (both positive and negative).
- `Double`. These are values in the approximate range 10^{-324} to 10^{308} (both positive and negative).
- `String`. These are variable-length strings. `String*` can be used length for fixed-length strings.

Other data types include `Boolean` (which can be either `True` or `False`), `Byte` (unsigned, eight-bit numbers in the range 0 to 255), `Currency`, `Date` (which allows dates from AD 100, unlike pure Excel which allows dates from AD 1900), and `Type` (which is a user-defined type, and is beyond the scope of this text).

The following points are worthy of note:

- The `Dim` statement (e.g. `Dim NDataPts As Long`) is used to declare a variable, that is to specify its existence and data type.
- When declaring variables of the same type, one must use a separate `As` clause for each variable (e.g. `Dimi AsLong, j As Long` is acceptable, but `Dimi, j As Long` is not).
- The declarations are placed in the code according to the scope of a variable (see later). Often for many initial applications, variables will have procedure-level scope (and so should be declared at the beginning of the procedure).
- Type-declaration characters exist for legacy reasons, e.g. `Single` is represented by `!`, `Double` by `#`, `Integer` by `%`, `Long` by `&`, and `String` by `$`, etc. It is useful to be aware of them when reviewing code, but arguably preferable to avoid their use when developing new code.
- The code writer can be forced to declare all variables by placing the `Option Explicit` statement at the top of the code module. This can either be typed directly on the code window or made an automatic part of all code windows by checking the `Require Variable Declaration` box under `Tools/Options/Editor` tab of the VBE menu.

Working with Arrays

Multiple values or data of the same type may be stored in VBA arrays. For example, the calculated value of a cell during various recalculations of a simulation could be stored in this way. If the values of several outputs need to be stored then a multi-dimensional array can be used (the maximum allowed number of dimensions is 60). Some key aspects of using arrays include:

- The declaration of an array is similar to the declaration of other variables, but also includes its size and dimensions. For example if a two-dimensional array were to be used to store the values of two outputs during a simulation with 1000 recalculations, one may declare the array with a statement such as:
`Dim ResultsArray(1 to 1000, 1 to 1000) As Double`
- The elements of an array must all be of the same data type, so that a multi-dimensional array could not in general be used to store the elements of a database (where, for example, some columns would contain values and others would contain text). Such a situation could be dealt with by having a separate one-dimensional array for each database column or by creating a user-defined data type (this is beyond the scope of this text, but may crudely be thought of as being rather like a one-dimensional array, but where each element has multiple information attached to it).
- The VBA default is for the first element of an array to have the index number zero. This can be desirable in some cases (for example, where the elements of the array are used to represent the values of an asset in a time-series, it may provide clarity if the current value were represented by `AssetValue(0)`, with `AssetValue(1)` denoting the value in one

period and so on). Where it is desired to ensure that arrays always start with a particular index number, this can be achieved either by explicitly stating this when declaring the array or by placing statements such as Option Base 0 orOption Base 1 at the beginning of any code (before the subroutines).

- In many cases the required size may not be known until the code is run (for example, where the number of recalculations for a simulation is taken from a cell in Excel or by use of an InputBox). In such cases, the ReDim statement can be used to redefine the dimensions of an array once it is known (doing so will erase the values currently held in the array; if these values need to be kept, then the statement ReDim Preserve can be used). So in practice the relevant part of the code may take a form such as:

```
Option Base 1
Sub SimExample()
Dim ResultsArray() As Double
Dim NSize As Integer
'NSize is the number of recalculations, as defined in a named range
NSize = Worksheets("Model").Range("NRecalcs").Value
ReDim ResultsArray(NSize) 'Redimensionalise the results array
   ... Rest of Code ...
End Sub
```

Choice of Names

For very short pieces of code (such as 3–5 lines), the functionality of the code and role of each variable within it is usually fairly clear. In such cases arguably little attention needs to be given to the choice of names. For larger pieces of code (including several short pieces in a modular structure), a good choice of the names can help to make the code more transparent and less error prone. The following are some guidelines when choosing names of ranges, variables and procedures:

- Names should be clear and reasonably descriptive. For example, one may use i_loopcountfor an integer variable that serves to count a loop. Some code writers systematically employ naming rules such as that any variables beginning with the letters i j or k are Integer (or Long), and that any variable beginning with the letters v, x, y, z are Double, and so on. This can be achieved by using the DefType statement (which only affects the module in which the code resides). For example, the declaration statement becomes: DefInt i-k, DefLng i-k, DefDbl v-z and so on (see VBA Help or **F1** for more information).
- Names should be kept as short as possible subject to their role being clear (even short code which contains long variable names can be tiresome to read and therefore less transparent).
- There are some constraints on the choice of names, but they usually pose little difficulty. These include that there must be no blank spaces, and no & symbol within the name (underscores are acceptable and indeed frequently used). Reserved words (e.g. "return") may not be used. Names are not case sensitive. Care must be taken so that names do not unintentionally refer to cell references (especially in the wider column structure of Excel 2007) or that names are not confusing when viewed in the context of Excel cell references (DCF, NPV, ALL, DEL are also column references in Excel 2007 and Q1, Q2, etc., are also cell references, etc.).

FURTHER TOPICS

Object Orientation: An Introduction

This section provides an introduction to object-orientation in VBA. Although aspects of the topic have been touched upon already (for example, we discussed Excel ranges as objects), we have not emphasised it. For many modellers it is not a topic that immediately appears to be of direct relevance. However, object-oriented methods can be powerful tools to work with ranges, manipulate data sets, manage named ranges, control formatting and error checking, and to create customised user interfaces. A deeper knowledge of this area is therefore required in order to achieve the maximum functionality and efficiency when using VBA and to develop a wider set of modelling applications.

Objects are essentially parts of Excel that can be seen, including for example cells, ranges, rows, columns, workbooks, worksheets, charts and so on. The natural language equivalent of objects is the nouns. Objects may have one or more properties (and which are analogous to adjectives in natural language), and may be manipulated by methods (which are the equivalent of verbs in natural language). For example, a range object could have properties such as `Count`, `Format`, `Rows`, `Value` or `Width`. Some properties of objects may result in an another object, for example `Range("A2:B5").Rows` would represent the rows in the range, so `Range("A2:B5").Rows.Count` would return the value 4. Methods associated with a range object include `Activate`, `ClearContents`, `ClearFormats`, `Copy`, `PasteSpecial`. (More information can be found within the VBA `Help` menu (**F1**) using search terms such as `range object members`, `workbook object members` or `application object members`, and so on.)

Objects may exist in a hierarchy, and the notion of collections of objects is important. Examples of collections include: `Workbooks` (the set of all open workbooks), `Worksheets` (the set of worksheets in the active workbook), and `Charts` (the set of chart sheets within the active workbook). Collections of objects can have properties and be manipulated. Such an approach can allow certain operations to be conducted easily that might otherwise appear to be complex or time consuming. For example:

- The `Worksheets` collection can be used to add a worksheet to the active workbook and to name this new worksheet. This is used later in this chapter to store simulation results in the added worksheet. The relevant line of code could be: `Worksheets.Add.Name = "Results"`
- The individual items in collections can be accessed using code such as `Workbooks.Item (3)` or simply `Workbooks(3)`. Such a technique may also be used to access individual elements of a range (for example, `Range("DataSet")(i)` corresponds to `Range ("DataSet").Cells(i, 1).Value`).
- The `For Each ... Next` construction is particularly useful to work through the items in a collection as some operation is performed on them. Several examples of this are provided in the following.

Example: Use of For Each ... Next with Collections

The file Ch6.Obj.ForEach.xlsm (Figure 6.10) shows examples of the use of the `For Each ... Next` construction to loop through all items in a collection and perform some operation on the individual items. The following are examples:

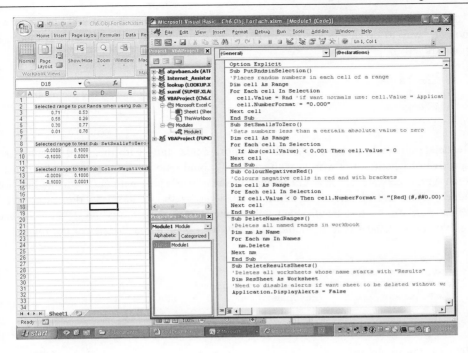

Figure 6.10

- To put random numbers in the selected range:

```
Dim cell As Range
For Each cell In Selection
   cell.Value = Rnd
   cell.NumberFormat = "0.000"
Next cell
```

- To set to zero any values in the selected range that are less than a predefined tolerance:

```
Dim cell As Range
For Each cell In Selection
   If Abs(cell.Value) < 0.001 Then cell.Value = 0
Next cell
```

- To set the colour of any cell in the selected range that has a negative value to red and format the value with brackets and two decimal places (the upgraded **Conditional Formatting** features in Excel 2007 mean that such procedures are of less use than in previous versions of Excel):

```
Dim cell As Range
For Each cell In Selection
   If cell.Value < 0 Then cell.NumberFormat = "[Red](#,##0.00)"
Next cell
```

- To delete all named ranges in a workbook (this was useful in Excel 2003 as there was no easy way to do this otherwise; in Excel 2007 the **Name Manager** allows this to be done directly):

```
Dim nm As Name
For Each nm In Names
   nm.Delete
Next nm
```

- To delete all worksheets in a workbook whose name starts with the word Results (irrespective of whether it is written with small or capital letters). This can be useful if many such worksheets are in a model (perhaps if a new worksheet with such a name has been added at the end of each of a set of simulations, as shown later). In this case Excel's DisplayAlerts must be disabled unless one wishes to confirm the deletion of each individual worksheet (and it should generally be re-enabled at the end of the routine):

```
Dim ResSheet As Worksheet
Application.DisplayAlerts = False
For Each ResSheet In ActiveWorkbook.Worksheets
If VBA.UCase(VBA.Left(ResSheet.Name, 7)) = "RESULTS" Then ResSheet.Delete
Next
Application.DisplayAlerts = True
```

- To reset the minimum range of the data bars in a selected range (in Excel 2007 only). Excel's default is that the smallest data bar is 10% of the cell width, so that if the relative size of the smallest point is less than this, the corresponding bar will appear too big. The PercentMin property of the Databar object can be used to reset this (to say 1%) as follows:

```
Sub DataBarResetMin()
Dim dbar As Databar
For Each dbar In Selection.FormatConditions
 dbar.PercentMin = 1
Next dbar
End Sub
```

Example: Workbook Events

Event code describes procedures that execute when a specific event in Excel occurs. Examples include code that executes when a workbook is opened or when a change is made to a specific range in a worksheet, or when the data source of a chart is changed. Further examples are provided in Walkenbach (see Further Reading).

In each case the code to be executed must be placed in the appropriate module in the Project window. For example, code that is to execute when a workbook is opened must be placed in the ThisWorkbook object module (i.e. the ThisWorkbook object module must be selected in the Project window, the Workbook option selected from the drop-down list in the Object box, and the Open procedure from the procedure list box). This will create a subroutine called Workbook_Open (Figure 6.11), into which the relevant code can be written (such a subroutine has a scope called Private ; see later). Similarly, code relating

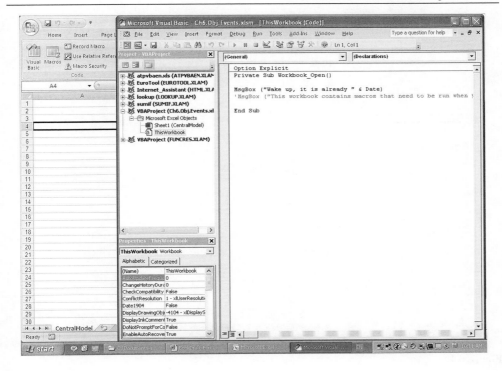

Figure 6.11

to changes in a worksheet must be placed in the relevant Sheet object module (rather than in the code modules that we have inserted up to this point when creating code).

The file Ch6.Obj.Events.xlsm (Figure 6.12) shows an example of code to be executed when a workbook is opened. In practice, such a message may be used to describe some important limitation of the model, or how to use it, or other key information that the user needs to be aware of before using the model.

Controlling Execution and Related Topics

There are a number of possibilities in VBA to control the execution of the code. These include:

For ... Next Loop

In an earlier example we used the most basic form of the For ... Next loop, where the implied step is positive 1. The step size may be changed, for example using code such as:

```
For i = 1 To 15 Step 2
... Code to be executed
Next i
```

which would loop through the values for i of 1, 3, 5, 7, 9, 11, 15.

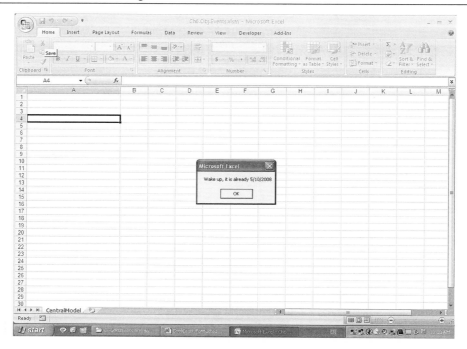

Figure 6.12

Similarly a descending loop can be created (using the values 15, 14, 13,..., 1):

```
For i = 15 To 1 Step -1
... Code to be executed
Next i
```

Note that the `i` after the `Next` statement is optional, but where there are multiple loops (and especially embedded loops) the code is easier to read and so is less error prone if the loop is closed in this way.

For Each ... Next

`For Each...Next`. This structure was referred to earlier when working through the items in a collection using object-oriented methods. The items are worked through in their numerical order, in an analogous way to that in a `For ... Next` loop that uses a positive step of 1.

If... Then

The simplest (single-line) form of the `If ... Then` statement results in an operation being conducted if a condition is met, otherwise no operation takes place. More generally the construction can be used in the form:

```
If condition1 Then
... first possible set of instructions
```

```
ElseIf condition2 Then
... second possible set of instructions
ElseIf condition-n Then
... nth possible set of instructions
Else
... final possible set of instructions
End If
```

Where there are only two cases to be considered, the `ElseIf` statements will not be needed, and the statement takes the form `If... Then... Else... End If`. Where there are more than two cases, the `ElseIf` statements can also be avoided by use of further `If ... Then ... Else` conditions within the first set of possible instructions, creating embedded conditional statements.

Other possibilities to control aspects of code execution exist. They are not covered in detail here as they are not required for the example models used in this text. More information can be found in Walkenbach (see Further Reading) or in the VBA `Help`. Examples include:

- `Select Case TestExpression`. This statement executes one of a set of statements depending on the result of a test. This can be a more transparent alternative to the `If ... Then` statement in some situations.
- The `GoTo` statement may also be used to determine branching that is to apply as the result of the evaluation of an `If ... Then` condition or with an `On Error` statement to branch to an error-handling procedure (see later).
- The `Do... While` and `Do... Until` statements providing looping structures where the loop executes only according to some condition that is tested at the beginning of the loop.

Displaying Alerts

In some cases messages that display warnings in Excel must be disabled for the code execution to continue as desired. For example (as demonstrated earlier), one may wish to use the code to delete a worksheet without having to suspend the execution of the code in order to confirm the deletion (the requirement for such confirmation being Excel's default to avoid accidental deletion). The default warnings can be switched off by using:

```
Application.DisplayAlerts = False
```

Of course in general it is beneficial to have such warnings active, and once they have been disabled in a section of code for a specific reason, they typically will need to be switched on again at the end of that section of code using:

```
Application.DisplayAlerts = True
```

Screen Updating

Where contents (or other aspects) of Excel cells are changed during the execution of a procedure, the changes will be visible when the code is running (when in split-screen mode, for example). While having this visibility is useful in some cases (especially when debugging code) it will also slow down code execution. Where the run time of code is desired to be reduced, the use of `Application.ScreenUpdating = False` will switch off the updating of the screen and will generally speed up the procedure (although by itself it is generally not enough to make order-of-magnitude differences to run time).

Measuring Run Time

In principle the time required to run code can be measured by using the VBA `Timer` function, which is directly expressed in seconds. (Since it is based on elapsed time since midnight it could be misleading were to code to be run around midnight.) The `Time` function could also be used (this provides the current system time in days and generally needs to be converted by the appropriate multiplication to express the value in seconds). The code would look something like:

```
Starttime = Timer
'Calculation area of simulation model
... .
Endtime = Timer
RunTime = (Endtime - Starttime)
```

(Note that if a step-through approach is used to check that such code is working, it will not return values that are representative of what would happen if the code were to be run, as the elapsed time will of course include that taken to step through the code.) Also, if other applications are running at the same time or the computer is involved in other processing activities in the background (e.g. virus checking), then these will affect the run time.

Working with Functions

Worksheet and VBA Functions

VBA has a number of in-built functions that can be used in the code. For example, `Sqr()` returns the square-root of its argument (equivalent to Excel's `SQRT()`), `Log()` gives the natural logarithm (equivalent to Excel's **LN**), and `Rnd` returns a uniformly distributed random number between 0 and 1 (equivalent to Excel's **RAND**). The key points about these functions for the purposes here are:

- A list of the available VBA functions can be seen by typing `VBA.` in the `Code` window, from which it will be seen that the number of arithmetic operations is very limited when compared with Excel.
- A function that is not in VBA but is an Excel function (such as **SUM** and **MAX**) can be implemented within VBA by typing `WorkSheetFunction.Sum()` and so on. A list of all available worksheet functions can by seen by typing `WorksheetFunction` in the code window (or by searching for `list of worksheet functions` in VBA `Help`).
- Where VBA and Excel functions for the same calculation both exist (including `Sqr`, `Rnd`, `Log`) , the VBA functions must be used.
- Where worksheet functions are required in several lines of code, the size of the code can be reduced by use of the `Set` statement to create a worksheet function object variable:
- `Set wsf=Application.WorksheetFunction` and then using expressions such as `wsf.Sum()` to implement the functions.

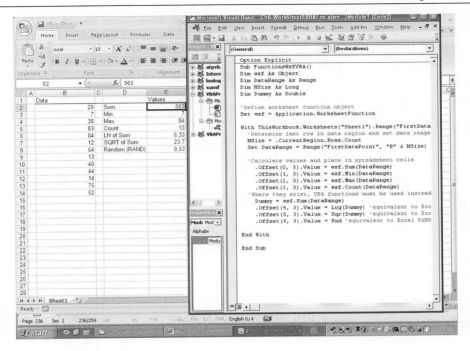

Figure 6.13

The file Ch6.Worksheet&VBAFns.xlsm (Figure 6.13) shows an example, including a mixture of worksheet and VBA functions that are used to perform calculations in VBA and to place the results into the worksheet. The data range of the worksheet is defined through the code so that it expands if new data points are added (assuming that the data is always in column B and is contiguous; the cell currently shown as B2 is named as FirstDataPoint in Excel).

In addition, there are of course some cases where it is desired to use code to insert a function into a worksheet, and this can be achieved using code such as:

```
Worksheets("Sheet1").Range("B1:B100").Formula = "=RAND()"
```

Model Recalculation and Volatile Functions

When in Excel the pressing of **F9** causes a recalculation of all open workbooks; its VBA equivalent is Application.Calculate (or simply Calculate). However, during such a recalculation it is not in general necessary for a function's value to be recalculated unless one or more of its arguments has changed. Therefore for the sake of computational efficiency Excel functions generally do not recalculate when **F9** or Application.Calculate is invoked.

An example of a function that does not follow this default rule is the **RAND** function; this recalculates whenever **F9** or Application.Calculate is used, and is an example of a Volatile function. By default, functions are not Volatile.

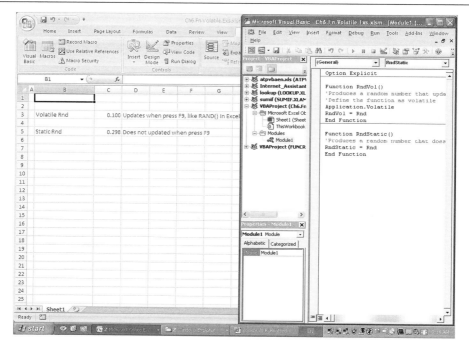

Figure 6.14

To create a user-defined function that is `Volatile`, the statement `Application.Volatile` (or `Application.Volatile True`) can be placed at the beginning of the function procedure. As discussed later, this can also be used to support the debugging of function code, even when it is ultimately desired to create a function that is not `Volatile`.

The file Ch6.Fn.VolExs.xlsm (Figure 6.14) shows a simple example of two functions, where one is defined as `Volatile` and the other is not.

Note also that occasionally one may wish to recalculate only a specific workbook or a specific worksheet rather than all open workbooks (something not possible when using Excel's recalculation settings). This can be achieved by using the `EnableCalculation` property, such as:

```
Worksheets("Sheet1").EnableCalculation = False.
```

Checking and Debugging Code

Core Techniques

A number of basic tools to check that code is working have already been discussed, including:

- Checking that the code is robust over a wide range of input values.
- Stepping through the code line-by-line using a split screen to watch directly the effect in Excel, noting also that the value of a variable after that line of code has run can be seen by placing the cursor to hover over that variable.

- Using `Help` (**F1**). When help on a specific item within the code is desired, the pressing of **F1** when that text is selected (or when the cursor is within that text) will result in the `Help` menu being accessed directly at the relevant part.

Some further tools that can be helpful for more complex code include:

- Using break-points combined with a step-through approach. Break-points can be used where it is believed that the code works correctly up to a particular point. Rather than stepping through the code to reach that point, it can be set as break-point and the code run to that point (using **F5**). Thereafter (once execution is broken), a step-through approach can be used (using **F8**). A break-point can be set by clicking into the left margin of the `Code` window next to the code line (or pressing **F9** when the cursor is in a code line). Alternatively, one can use the menu **Debug/Run To Cursor** (or **CTRL+F8**), which will run the code to the line prior to where the cursor is currently placed.
- Using the `Watches` window (available under the `View` menu) to monitor the values of specific variables (set the variables of interest using `Debug/Add Watch`). Similarly, the `Locals` window (also under `View`) can be used to show the values of all variables in a subroutine during a run, allowing the values of many variables to be checked simultaneously.
- Using the `Immediate` window (under `View` or using **CTRL+G**), either directly or in conjunction with the code. The `Immediate` window provides immediate results for statements typed in. Preceding the name of an expression in the window with ? or `Debug.Print` will evaluate that expression in the window (for example ? `Range("C3").Value` or? `Range("NCalcs").Address`). These expressions can also be placed within the code, in which case the evaluation of the expression is shown in the `Immediate` window. Similarly, a procedure can be executed immediately by entering the procedure name in this window.
- Using `MsgBox` to report the value of a variable at a particular point in the code. Several such statements can be used at various points, and they may be commented out or back in as required. The disadvantage of this approach is that code execution is halted until the user provides a response and so this can be cumbersome if used in many places.

Debugging Functions

The techniques to check and debug functions are slightly more cumbersome than for subroutines. While functions without arguments can be stepped through rather like subroutines, functions with arguments will not allow their code to be stepped through nor break-points to be set. However, the debugging of functions can be facilitated by the use of the following methods:

- Using the function from a subroutine, so that step-through using **F8** is allowed, such as:

```
Sub DebugbyCallingFunction()
Dummy=FntoDebug(12, 5)
End Sub
Function FntoDebug(x, y)
'... lots of code ...
FntoDebug = calculated value from the code
End Function
```

- Forcing the function to recalculate, so that the reporting tools above can be used at certain places in the code (e.g. `Debug.Print` and `MsgBox`). Some techniques to achieve this include:
  - — To change an input value of the function or to edit the function in the **Formula Bar** (followed by entering it using **RETURN**).
  - — Temporarily adding a dummy argument to the function code (i.e. one which in fact plays no role in the code that evaluates the function) and to populate this dummy argument with **RAND** when using the function from Excel; the function will then recalculate whenever **F9** is pressed. Similarly, one could temporarily set one of the function arguments to be equal to **RAND**, or something scaled from a random number. This would of course require the argument reference to be reset afterward, and so is perhaps slightly less robust if one were to forget to go this.
  - — Define the function as `Volatile` (see earlier) so that **F9** can be used without changing the function in any other way. Generally it is not ultimately desired for functions to be `Volatile`, so that once checking is complete, this can be removed.

In addition, some other tools can help on occasion:

- Using the `Immediate` window to execute the function.
- Verify that the values calculated by the function are correct by first building the same calculation steps in Excel for a specific case of the function's arguments. This is usually worthwhile only in complex cases.
- Using **DataTables** to evaluate the function for a wide range of input combinations in order to check the robustness of the function and to detect further potential errors or limitations (see Chapter 2). They can be deleted once the function is working correctly.

Dealing with Errors: An Introduction

Error codes in VBA have a number attached to them. The full list of VBA error codes can be seen by searching for `trappable errors` within VBA `Help`. For each error there can be many causes; a selection of the most frequent includes:

- `Invalid procedure call or argument (Error 5)` : Possible causes include that an argument exceeds the range of permitted values.
- `Subscript out of range (Error 9)` : Arises frequently when an array has not been dimensioned using the `Dim` or `ReDim` statements to specify explicitly the number of elements in the array.
- `Type mismatch (Error 13)` : Causes may include that a variable or property is not of the correct type.
- `Object variable not set (Error 91)` : Often caused by omission of the `Set` statement to create an object variable.
- `Object doesn't support this property or method (Error 438)` : A method or property was specified that does not exist for the object.
- The error code `1004` occurs when an error results from Excel rather than VBA, but has its effect within the code.

In general, errors of the above nature will correspond to unintentional errors that will cause code execution to stop and which must be corrected by the appropriate adjustments. On the other hand, there can be cases where errors are acceptable or there is no desire for the code to stop executing. An example discussed earlier was the disabling of Excel's warning message, so that worksheets of a particular name could be deleted (see earlier use of `DisplayAlerts`). In particular, the `On Error` statement provides instructions as to what to do in case of an error (so that code execution is not stopped):

- The `On Error Resume Next` statement can be used so that code will continue execution, where the occurrence of an error is not regarded as important.
- The `On Error` statement can be combined with a `GoTo` statement to jump to another part of the code (designated by a label) within the same subroutine. In this case, the `Exit Sub` statement may also be required in the code to ensure that the running of the code associated with the label occurs only where relevant. For example:

```
...  earlier part of code ...
On Error GoTo ErrorLabel
...  code to be executed even if no error
Exit Sub
ErrorLabel:
MsgBox "There was an error somewhere"
```

- The `On Error GoTo 0` (or `On Error Resume 0`) statement can be used (at the end of such a block of code) to restore VBA's normal error handling for the subsequent code. The relevant code block could look like:

```
...  earlier part of code ...
On Error Resume Next
...  code to be executed even if error detected
... On Error Resume 0
...  any code here is subject to VBA's normal error handling ...
```

EXAMPLES: RECORDING MACROS AND RELATED TOPICS

Introduction

Subroutines can be created by recording macros. However, the code that results from the recording process is usually large and contains unnecessary items, and is also likely to not fully reflect the generality of what one is trying to achieve. In addition, many types of code (such as those involving functions, looping, or conditional statements) can in any case not be created by recording. In practice, the recording of macros is used mostly as a reference tool in order to explore ways to achieve some functionality, from which a smaller subset of specifically relevant instructions are derived, and is then used as a reference point to write the required more general code.

A macro may be recorded using the **View/Macros/Record Macro** or **Developer/Record Macro** (under **Tools/Macros** in Excel 2003). Before doing so it is useful to practise and to note the exact sequences that will be followed. The recording process would otherwise also include any unnecessary processes (such as the selection of the wrong worksheet tabs or menu items) that were undertaken during the search for the required sequences. In addition, it may also be necessary to select whether to record in absolute or relative cell reference mode (absolute mode will record code using absolute cell references, and relative mode will record relative to an active cell); in some cases where the code is to be re-edited afterwards, this may not be so important, as the cell references in the code are likely to be edited or changed to named ranges, etc. If desired, the recorded macro can be given a name, a short-cut key, and a description. Of course, as soon as the desired steps have been carried out, the recording must be stopped using **Stop Recording**.

The Personal Macro Workbook

When recording a macro, one of the options under **Store macro in** is the **Personal Macro Workbook**. The selection of this option creates a file (of the type Personal.xlsb in Excel 2007 or Personal.xls in Excel 2003) in the **XLStart** folder. This file is loaded automatically whenever Excel starts, so that any code in it is available (though it is not visible as an Excel workbook). Note that such a workbook must be created the first time by recording and saving a macro to it; thereafter code can be added in the normal way without recording a macro.

The **Personal Macro Workbook** is an appropriate place to store macros that will be required to be used from other workbooks (macros intended only for use in a specific workbook may as well be stored within that workbook).

Example: Copying and Pasting Data

The file Ch6.RecordCopy.xlsm (Figure 6.15) shows a simple example of a macro (called CopyTrialRec) created by recording the sequence of steps in selecting the range of data in cells B2:B17 and then pasting these values to the adjacent column.

```
Sub CopyTrialRec()
' CopyTrialRec Macro
    Range("B2:B17").Select
    Selection.Copy
    Range("C2").Select
    Selection.PasteSpecial Paste:=xlPasteValues, _
       Operation:=xlNone, SkipBlanks:=False, Transpose:=False
End Sub
```

Once such a macro has been created, in practice one may wish to copy the relevant parts of the code and adapt or generalise it in some way. The file shows several possible ways in which this could be done according to what specifically is required to achieve.

For example, if the range of data to be copied had been given an Excel range name (perhaps a dynamic one as described earlier and in Chapter 2), then the code block could be altered to:

```
With Range("DataRange")
   .Select
   Selection.Copy
   .Offset(0, 1).Select
   Selection.PasteSpecial Paste:=xlPasteValues
End With
```

Alternatively, if it were first desired to select the range of cells in Excel and then perform the copy and paste procedure, one could modify the code to:

```
With Selection
   .Copy
```

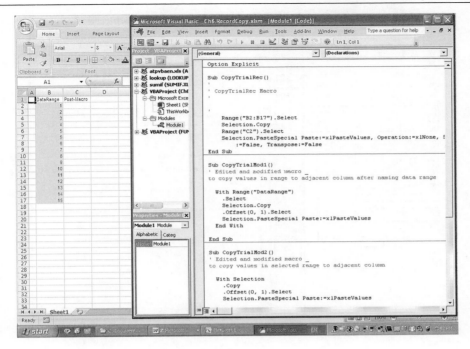

Figure 6.15

```
        .Offset(0, 1).Select
        Selection.PasteSpecial Paste:=xlPasteValues
    End With
```

Similarly, if it were desired to copy and paste the values but where only the top cell of the range to be copied (assumed contiguous) is required to be selected, then one could write:

```
With Selection
    Range(.Offset(0, 0), .End(xlDown)).Select
    Selection.Copy
    .Offset(0, 1).Select
    Selection.PasteSpecial Paste:=xlPasteValues
    End With
```

The recording of macros could of course be extended to the recording of other operations, such as the sorting of a data set, and so on.

Using GoalSeek and Solver

Example: GoalSeek for Calculation of Implied Volatility

The use of Excel's **GoalSeek** can be automated through a macro that can easily be created by recording it.

The file Ch6.Record.GS.xlsm (Figure 6.16) shows the code that is recorded when the Range.GoalSeek method is used to find the value of the volatility that would result in the

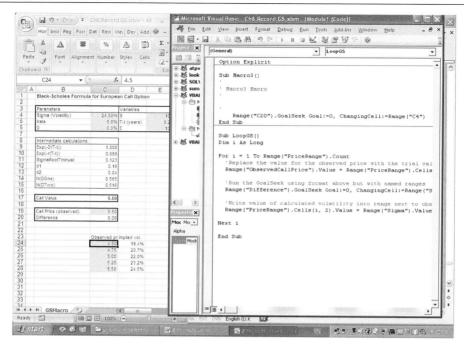

Figure 6.16

option value to be equal to the observed market price of five (the option value is calculated in the worksheet using the Black–Scholes formula as described in Chapter 2). The recorded code shows:

```
Range("C20").GoalSeek Goal:=0, ChangingCell:=Range("C4")
```

The recorded code was then adapted by:

- Using named ranges instead of cell references.
- Embedding the **GoalSeek** within a loop, so that the implied volatility is calculated for a range of observed market prices.

This resulting code is:

```
For i = 1 To Range("PriceRange").Count
  Range("ObservedCallPrice").Value = Range("PriceRange").Cells(i, 1).Value
  Range("Difference").GoalSeek Goal:=0, ChangingCell:=Range("Sigma")
  Range("PriceRange").Cells(i, 2).Value = Range("Sigma").Value
Next i
```

Example: Using Solver to Generate the Optimal Portfolio

The use of **Solver** within VBA is an ideal application to create code by recording, as the required specifications can otherwise be cumbersome.

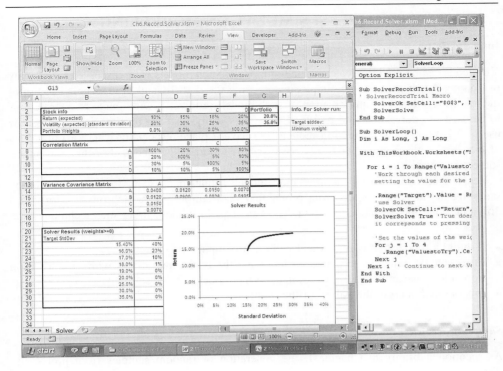

Figure 6.17

When using add-ins (such as **Solver**) from VBE, one first needs to make a reference within VBE to the add-in. This can be achieved using `Tools/References` and checking the relevant box for the add-in under consideration (if the add-in box is not visible it should be verified that the add-in has been loaded in Excel as described in Chapter 1).

The file Ch6.Record.Solver.xlsm (Figure 6.17) shows an example of the automated use of **Solver** to find the mix of assets that maximises the return for a given level of risk. The example is essentially an automated version of the corresponding model in Chapter 1. The set of assets and their expected return and standard deviations of returns are input parameters, and **Solver** is applied in which the weights of each asset are constrained to be positive.

The recording of the use of **Solver** in this case results in:

```
SolverOk SetCell:="$G$3", MaxMinVal:=1, ValueOf:="0", ByChange:="$D$5:$F$5"
    SolverSolve
```

The code was then copied and modified into a new macro, including named ranges and a loop which sequentially sets the cell containing the target value to the values in the ValuesToTry range, runs **Solver**, and records the weights for each asset in results area.

Note that the automation of this process requires the addition of the `True` statement after `SolverSolve` (which did not appear in the recorded code). In this way the optimal portfolio for each desired level of risk is determined. In this example the `i` loop could have been replaced by the `For Each` construct (see earlier) to loop through the values in the ValuesToTry range.

EXAMPLES: SIMULATION MODELLING

Introduction

VBA code can be used to create simulation models. Such models were discussed extensively in Chapter 4, where they were implemented using the @RISK add-in to Excel. The use of the add-in enabled the rapid creation of such models, allowed a wide range of distributions to be used and correlated, and provided automated analysis of the results. Nevertheless, the use of VBA to create simulation models can have a place, especially where a limited set of distributions is required and only basic results reporting is needed. For this reason, the subject is covered here.

Recall that the essence of a simulation model is that many scenarios are generated by sampling the uncertain inputs from probability distributions, with each one resulting in a different value for the model's output. The key steps in implementing such techniques are:

- To build a model that is robust and valid as the inputs are changed.
- To repeatedly generate scenarios by replacing the base input values with samples from probability distributions, and to recalculate the model with these inputs.
- To store and analyse the values of the outputs.

Sampling Revisited

As mentioned briefly in Chapter 1, the generation of random samples from probability distributions can be achieved by first generating samples from a uniform distribution between 0 and 1 and then inverting the cumulative distribution at that probability value. For example, the sampling of a uniform distribution on [0, 1] would result in a random number in the range 0 to 0.1 being drawn in 10% of cases; the inverted Normal distribution for each of these values would produce a sample in the range $-\infty$ to -1.28 in those 10% of cases. A few further points are worthy of note in this respect:

- If the sampling is done in Excel, then formulations such as **NORMSINV(RAND())** can be used to generate samples from a Normal distribution. The samples would apply for a distribution with mean of 0 and standard deviation of 1. These can be scaled for any desired mean and standard deviation by multiplying the sample by the standard deviation and adding the desired mean. However, the more general approach (which is arguably preferable in this case) would be to use the **NORMINV** function, which explicitly requires the mean and standard deviation as input parameters. Whereas for a Normal distribution, its shape (standard deviation, skew, kurtosis, etc.) is independent of the mean, such a statement cannot be made for most other distributions, so that this scaling approach could not be so readily used in general.
- If sampling is done in VBA, the Rnd function would be used as the argument to the inverse distribution function (the inverse distributions are not VBA functions but are accessible as worksheet functions, as covered earlier).
- The sampling from other distributions can be achieved whenever the required inverse cumulative functions are available (as worksheet functions). This includes the Lognormal, Beta, Chi-squared, F-, Gamma, and T-distributions by using **LOGINV**, **BETAINV**, **CHIINV**, **FINV**, **GAMMAINV** and **TINV**.

- A Binomial distribution can be sampled by using an **IF** statement to check whether a sample from a uniform distribution is less than or greater than a specified probability and returning 1 or 0 respectively.

Possibilities for Model Structure

When designing simulation models, there are a number of possibilities that can be considered for the overall structure of the model's calculations and the repeated generation of random numbers:

- The "Excel max" approach. This involves building the model in Excel, generating the random numbers using **RAND**, and inverting the probability distributions in Excel. The `Application.Calculate` statement would be placed within a code loop to recalculate the Excel workbook many times. An advantage of this approach is that it generally provides the most transparent model, and it allows the use of **F9** in Excel to directly demonstrate the randomness in the situation to others. Clients of a model who are familiar with Excel but less so with VBA are likely to find this approach preferable; such clients would only need to be told that an additional automated procedure is also available if needed to repeatedly recalculate the model and store the results.
- The "Excel min" approach. This involves building the entire model and its logic in VBA. The main advantage is that the run time of such a model will generally be shorter. This approach can be advantageous where a pure simulation model is built from scratch, and where the relationships between the model's variables, as well as the required formulae in the model, are quite straightforward. However, where there are many formulae in a model, of which some are larger and complex, then the code can become quite cumbersome and less transparent. While appropriate in some circumstances, this approach is not pursued further in this text, as we focus here on situations where it is desired to retain Excel as the core modelling interface.
- The "mixed" approach. This involves building the model in Excel, but using VBA to generate the random sampling using `Rnd` and inverting the probability distributions in VBA. The random samples are fed into the appropriate places within the Excel model, all within the loop. There is no explicit requirement to use `Application.Calculate` within the loop (providing that the workbook is set on the default automatic recalculation mode). An advantage of this approach is that when sampling in VBA one can force the repetition of the random numbers used, so that the calculations can be repeated exactly if desired. This involves using `Rnd` with a negative argument (such as `Rnd(-1)`) to repeat the sequence followed by `Randomize` with a positive argument (such as `Randomize(1)`, where a different value for the argument could be used to give a different (but repeatable) sequence.)

Similarly, when considering how to store and analyse the results, one could generically either:

- Directly write the calculated value of the output for each sample of the iteration into a cell in an Excel worksheet (perhaps a separate worksheet specifically used to store results).
- Store the calculated values in an array in VBA and use this array to either analyse the results directly or to write the array's values into a results worksheet for analysis.

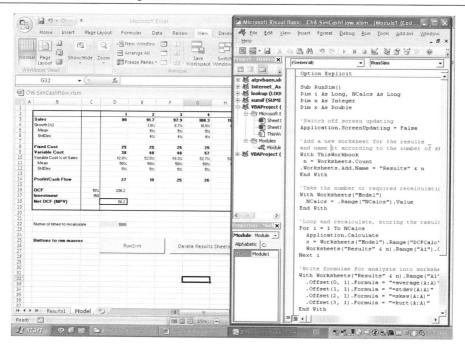

Figure 6.18

In the example below we use the first approach, as this is the most transparent. The user may wish to experiment with other approaches, and find the one most suitable in their own applications.

Example: Cash Flow

The file Ch6.SimCashFlow.xlsm (Figure 6.18) is similar to the cash flow model used in Chapter 4, in which the growth rate for sales and the variable cost percentage are treated as following a Normal distribution. The output of the model is the discounted cash flow, and this cell has been named in Excel (using the **Name Manager**). A button has been created to run the code (see earlier). The code contains a loop which runs for the number of recalculations that is specified by a named range in the worksheet. At the beginning of the run, a new results worksheet is added and named, into which certain formulae are written at the end of the simulation for analysis purposes. The code also switches off screen updating (although it may be kept switched on for the purpose of testing the code initially). Finally a subroutine is also included in the module which allows for the deletion of all results worksheets. Note also that number of recalculations is declared as a variable which is Long, rather than as an Integer, in order to allow the flexibility to perform many recalculations in case this is ever desired.

```
Sub RunSim()
Dim i As Long, NCalcs As Long
Dim n As Integer
Dim x As Double
```

```
'Switch off screen updating
Application.ScreenUpdating = False


'Add a new worksheet for the results _
and name it according to the number of sheets in the workbook
With ThisWorkbook
  n = Worksheets.Count
.Worksheets.Add.Name = "Results" & n
End With


'Take the number or required recalculations from the named range
With Worksheets("Model")
  NCalcs = .Range("NCalcs").Value
End With


'Loop and recalculate, storing the results in the new worksheet
For i = 1 To NCalcs
  Application.Calculate
  x = Worksheets("Model").Range("DCFCalc").Value
  Worksheets("Results" & n).Range("A1").Offset(i - 1, 0).Value = x
Next i


'Write formulae for analysis into worksheet in column B
With Worksheets("Results" & n).Range("A1")
  .Offset(0, 1).Formula = "=average(A:A)"
  .Offset(1, 1).Formula = "=stdev(A:A)"
  .Offset(2, 1).Formula = "=skew(A:A)"
  .Offset(3, 1).Formula = "=kurt(A:A)"
End With
End Sub
```

EXAMPLES: USER-DEFINED FUNCTIONS

In the right circumstances the creation of user-defined functions can be a powerful tool.
The key to such a circumstance is when a fairly complex or repetitive calculation involving
several variables is required on multiple occasions.

In some cases one may be tempted to create a user-defined function when it is in fact not
necessary, such as where a calculation is required only once (so that it can usually be built as
a standard worksheet calculation, even where it is complex), where a calculation is required
several times but uses only one or two variables (so that a **DataTable** can sometimes provide
a satisfactory alternative), or where a multi-variable calculation is sufficiently simple that it
can be performed in a single cell in Excel (perhaps as a compound or embedded formula).
Of course, as for the general use of VBA, such functions should be created only where it
is genuinely necessary.

In this section we describe the key aspects of user-defined functions and provide some
specific examples.

Creating Functions

As mentioned earlier, the basis process to create a function is to write some code, stating that a `Function` is being created and ensuring that the function contains a return

statement (before End Function) which explicitly assigns the value(s) of the calculation to the functions value.

A few further points are worthy of note:

- Functions can be accessed using Excel's **Formula/Insert Function**, where they will be listed under the category of user-defined functions or can be typed directly in Excel (and will appear in the **AutoComplete** list in Excel 2007). As discussed later, functions in other workbooks can be accessed by preceding the function name by the name of the workbook in which it resides or by creating a reference to the workbook. These comments in fact apply to functions which have the default scope of Public ; a function declared as Private will not be accessible in this way. Reasons to declare a function as Private include so that it can be used within the code without users being able to access it through the Excel menu (see later for more details).
- Functions may also return arrays of values, in which case they must be entered in Excel using **CTRL+SHIFT+ENTER**, just as for Excel array functions.
- A description may be added to a function by activating the workbook containing it, displaying the **Macro** dialog box in Excel (using **View/Macros/View Macros** or **Developer/Macros**), typing the function name into the box, clicking the **Options** button, and entering the description. Functions may be assigned to categories other than the user-defined functions if desired, but doing so may often arguably result in less transparency, and so is not covered further here.

Examples

The following are some examples of user-defined functions which calculate:

- The value of a European call or put option using the Black–Scholes formula.
- The value of a European or American call or put option using a binomial tree.
- The rank correlation of two sets of data.
- The correlation matrix associated with several data sets (as an array function).
- The standard deviation, skew and kurtosis of a data set when both the values and the probabilities of each value are given.
- The sum of the reciprocals of the squares of the integers from one up to a specific number, as an example of a mathematical calculation.

Example: Black–Scholes Formula for a European Option

In Chapter 2, we showed that it is straightforward to calculate the value of a European call or put option using the Black–Scholes closed-form formula in Excel. However, where several (or many) options need to be valued over a range of input values, the approach using pure Excel would typically create a very large worksheet, so that the creation of a function may be preferable.

The file Ch6.Fn.BlackScholes.xlsm (Figure 6.19) shows the implementation of the formula as a user-defined function. As is frequently done in such applications (and mentioned in Chapter 2), this implementation uses the mirror feature of the formula, which means that by denoting a call with the indicator type of 1, and a put with -1, a single formula can be used, providing that the relevant variables (S, E, d_1, d_2) are replaced with their mirror values at the appropriate point in the calculation.

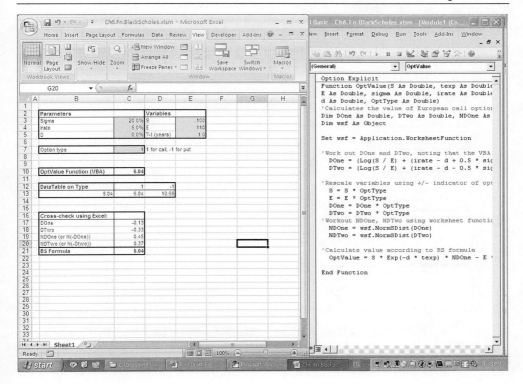

Figure 6.19

Example: Option Valuation using a Binomial Tree

In Chapter 5, we calculated the value of a European or American option using a binomial tree in Excel (see Figure 5.5). Clearly the Excel approach is not flexible if it were desired to attempt to achieve more accuracy by using a finer grid (i.e. number of branches in the tree). A way to achieve this is to use VBA to replicate the tree calculations in code, where the number of branches can be set by the user.

The file Ch6.Fn.Binomial.Option.US.xlsm (Figure 6.20) shows a user-created function which essentially mimics the calculations for the various branches of the tree (which are stored in arrays, whose first elements are zero, to correspond to current values). The backward calculation of option values uses a descending loop. In practice, the writing, testing and debugging of the code would most easily be achieved by reference to values in a specific example (such as the fixed tree of Chapter 5). The file can also be used to test the rate at which the results of the various grid calibration methods converge to stable values (see the **DataTables**).

Example: Rank Order Correlation

As covered in Chapter 1, the rank order correlation between two data sets of equal size can be calculated in Excel by first ranking each point within its own data set (using **RANK**) and then calculating the correlation coefficient between them (using **CORREL** or **PEARSON**). A user-defined function can be created to do this, which would have the advantage that the

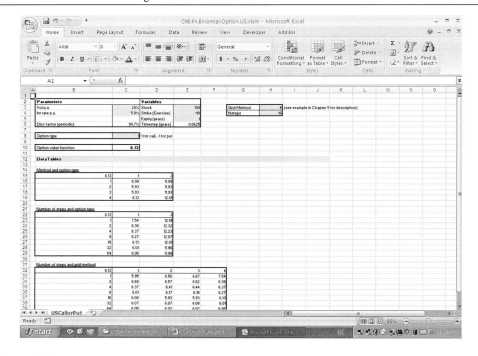

Figure 6.20

intermediate step required to create a new Excel range containing the rank of the data is not required to be conducted.

The file Ch6.Fn.RankCorrel.xlsm (Figure 6.21) shows an implementation of this, and also verifies that the results are the same as if the detailed steps of the calculation were done in Excel.

Example: Correlation Matrices

In Chapter 1, we showed that a **Lookup** function (such as **OFFSET**) can be combined with **CORREL** to create a single formula that can be copied to every position in a correlation matrix. One may also consider writing an array function to do this.

The file Ch6.Fn.CorrelMat.xlsm (Figure 6.22) shows an example. As for other array functions, the range in Excel where the matrix is to be placed needs to be highlighted (using the correct size for the data set), and the function entered using **CTRL+SHIFT+ENTER**.

Example: Standard Deviation and Higher Moments of a Data Set

When calculating the standard deviation of a data set, the **STDEV** function takes the raw data as its inputs (i.e. each data point represents an individual sample and implicitly has the same probability of occurrence). If a data set were provided where each value has some frequency or probability attached to it, then no such function is available. Similar comments apply to the Excel functions for the higher moments (i.e. the **SKEW** and **KURT** functions for the coefficients of skew and excess kurtosis).

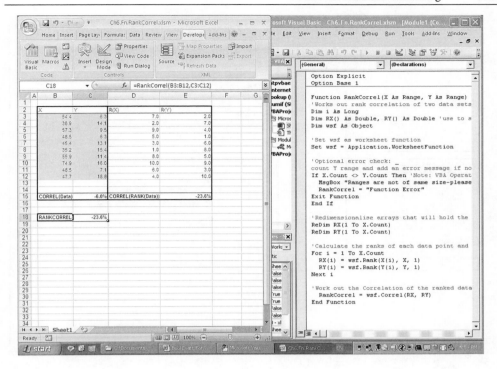

Figure 6.21

The file Ch6.Fn.Moments.xlsm (Figure 6.23) shows a function that calculates the mean, standard deviation, skew and kurtosis of set of values with associated probabilities. The array function has four outputs, and so is entered Excel using **CTRL+SHIFT+ENTER** after inserting the function in the first cell of a selected range of the appropriate size. (Recall from Chapter 4 that: the mean is defined as the weighted average of the values; the standard deviation as the square root of the weighted average of the square of the deviation from the mean; the skew as the weighted average of the cube of the deviation from the mean, divided by the cube of the standard deviation; and the kurtosis as the weighted average of the fourth power of the deviation from the mean, divided by the fourth power of the standard deviation. The moments calculated in this way are those that apply when it is assumed that the set of data represents the entire population rather than a sample, i.e. the calculation of the standard deviation corresponds to Excel's **STDEVP** function and so on. Also, the kurtosis calculation is the raw (not excess) kurtosis.)

Example: Summing Inverse Squares

A well-known result in mathematics states that the sum:

$$S(n) = \sum_{i=1}^{n} \frac{1}{i^2}$$

converges to $\pi^2/6$ as n becomes large.

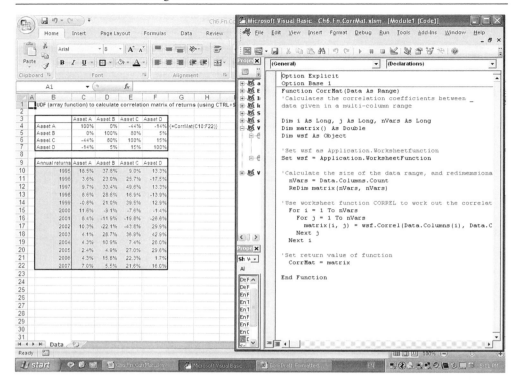

Figure 6.22

The file Ch6.Fn.SumInvSqr.xlsm (Figure 6.24) performs this calculation, and a **DataTable** has been applied to the result to test the rate of convergence as n increases. The graph of the difference (or error) between the sum and the converged value is shown on logarithmic axes, from which it can be seen that a doubling of n approximately halves the difference.

STRUCTURE AND ORGANISATION: FURTHER TOPICS

Running Subroutines using Shapes and Other Icons

Earlier we discussed a variety of methods to run code, both from the VBE window and from Excel. Here we briefly mention some additional ways, including:

- Using an icon on Excel's **Quick Access Toolbar**. Under **Office/Excel Options/Customize** select **Macros** from the **Choose commands from** drop-down, select the macro from the list and click **Add**. Since this will both change the general Excel interface and create an icon that will have an effect only when the workbook that contains the macro is active, it is probably worthwhile doing only for procedures that are to be used in a variety of workbooks, such as some of those in the **Personal Macro Workbook** (see earlier).
- Using shapes. A macro can be assigned to a shape in Excel (or to another object, such as a **SmartArt** object), so that clicking on the shape will run the macro. This can be achieved by first creating the shape (under the **Insert** menu), right-clicking on it, selecting **Assign**

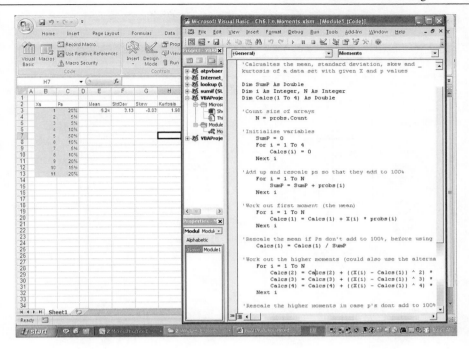

Figure 6.23

Macro and then double-clicking on the macro name. Of course, it should be made clear in some way to the user that clicking on the shape will run a macro (e.g. by labelling the shape) otherwise there is a chance that the macro will be run unintentionally.

- User forms (beyond the scope of this text).
- Executing procedures from other procedures (see below).

Executing Procedures from Other Procedures: An Overview

When code becomes large it is useful to structure it into separate procedures, with each having a limited and clear functionality. This will require that subroutines and functions in the same module, workbook, or other workbooks are used.

When using several procedures, one will need to take care that the scope of the procedures is appropriate. The scope of a procedure refers to its availability for use by another procedure. Subroutines and functions can have one of two scopes:

- `Public`. When used in general code modules, such procedures are available within the project (workbook), as well as to any other project that references it. `Public` is the default scope for procedures (except for event procedures, which are `Private` by default), so most procedures do not need an explicit definition as `Public`.
- `Private`. The declaration of a procedure as `Private` (e.g. using `Private Sub Nameof-Sub()`) would mean that it is available only to other procedures in the same module of the workbook, and not to the whole workbook or to other modules within it. A subroutine

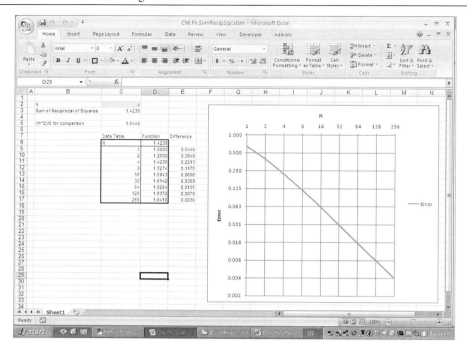

Figure 6.24

declared as `Private` will not display in Excel's **Macro** dialog box (other procedures that will not show in this dialog are those that require arguments, and those contained in add-ins). Similarly, a function declared as `Private` (e.g. using `Private MyFunction(arg1, arg2)`) will not be accessible from Excel and only available within its own code module. The `Option Private Module` statement can be used at the beginning of a module to make all procedures in a module `Private`.

Subroutines and functions that are `Public` can be executed from the Excel workbook in which they are contained using the methods earlier in this text (e.g. use of the **Macro** dialog or the **Formula/Insert Function** menu). This already has been covered extensively and so is not discussed further here.

When executing procedures from other procedures in the same workbook, the following possibilities exist:

- Subroutines that are `Public` can be executed (as can `Private` subroutines in the same module) by:
  — Using the `Run` method, typing the name in inverted commas followed by the parameter list (not enclosed in brackets), e.g. `Run "SubName", arg1, arg2`.
  — Using the `Call` statement, typing any required arguments in brackets, e.g. `Call SubName(arg1, arg2)`. The `Call` statement can be omitted if the argument list is not enclosed in brackets, e.g. `SubName arg1, arg2`. The use of the `Call` statement is arguably preferable as it is a more explicit statement that control is being transferred to another procedure.

- Functions that are `Public` (or `Private` in the same module) can also be accessed in the above ways, although generally one is interested in knowing the return value of a function, so that alternatives or variants of these methods are used:
  - Using a variable to represent the value returned by the function (e.g. `ValueToUse=` `MyFunction(arg1, arg2)`).
  - Using the `Run` method, enclosing the procedure name and arguments in brackets (e.g. `ValueToUse=Run("MyFunction", arg1, arg2)`).

When executing `Public` procedures in another workbook (whether from Excel or from VBA code), a reference needs to be created to this procedure either by:

- Preceding the name of the procedure with the name of the workbook in which it resides and using the `Run` method or the return value method (e.g. `Run "Book2.xlsm!Sub Name"` or `x=Book2.xlsm!MyFunction(arg1,arg2)`).
- Creating a reference to the second workbook, using `Tools/References` in the VBE. In this case the procedure can be accessed without preceding it with the workbook name, and the referenced workbook does not need to be open.

When procedures with arguments are called from other procedures, it is important to remember that the default method for passing arguments in VBA is by reference (`ByRef`). This means that the memory address of the argument is passed. If the second procedure changes the value of its arguments within the procedure then this new value will apply to the value of the variable in the original procedure when control is passed back. The solution

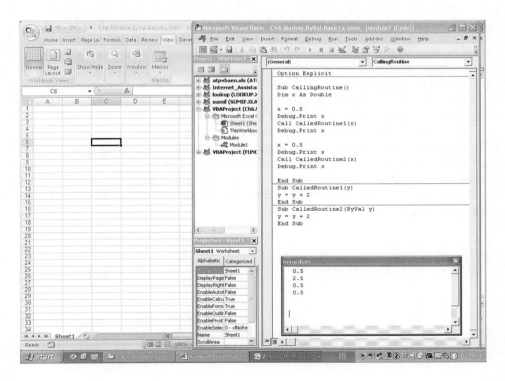

Figure 6.25

to this is to place the `ByVal` specification in the called procedure before the argument to be called.

The file Ch6.Module.ByVal.BasicEx.xlsm (Figure 6.25) shows an example. By ensuring that the `Immediate` window is visible (under the `View` menu; see earlier), and stepping through the code one observes how the calling of the `CalledRoutine1` results in the value of the variable x being changed from 0.5 to 2.5, whereas this does not happen for `CalledRoutine2`.

Creating and Using Add-ins

This section gives only a brief overview of the creation and use of add-ins. More information can be found in Walkenbach (see Further Reading).

Add-ins can be used to store code that is frequently used or is required to be accessed from a number of workbooks. The main advantage of doing so is that the filename qualifier is not needed, as when accessing `Public` procedures in other workbooks. An add-in can also be protected with a password so that it can be distributed without it being viewed, copied or modified, which may be desired in some circumstances. As mentioned earlier, another possibility to store frequently used code is to use the **Personal Macro Workbook**, but code within it would in general need to be copied to a new workbook before distributing it to others.

Some further points are worthy of note:

- An add-in can be created simply by saving the original. xlsx workbook with the. xlam file extension from the drop-down list in Excel's **Save As** dialog (in Excel 2003, a file would be saved with the. xla extension). The original workbook can be deleted once it is no longer needed. Subsequent changes to the add-in can be made and saved directly within VBE.
- Since neither an add-in nor its subroutines would appear in the **Macro** dialog, another method will be required to execute such procedures (such as the addition of a new command to the **Quick Access Toolbar** as discussed earlier); where a function is saved as an add-in it can be accessed using Excel's function menu.
- As mentioned earlier, when using add-ins (such as **Solver**) from VBE, one first needs to make a reference within VBE to the add-in. This can be achieved using `Tools/References` and checking the relevant box for the add-in under consideration (if the add-in box is not visible it should be verified that the add-in has been loaded in Excel as described in Chapter 1).

Further Reading

The following is a short list of materials that provide further background and breadth to some topics that we covered in this text but which could not be explored in full.

Bernardo, J.M. and Smith, A.F.M. *Bayesian Theory*. John Wiley & Sons Ltd.
  ISBN 0471924164.

Brealey, R.A. and Myers, S.C. *Principles of Corporate Finance*. McGraw Hill.
  ISBN 0-07-007386-4.

Dimson, E., Marsh, P. and Staunton, M. *Triumph of the Optimists: 101 Years of Global Investment Returns*. Princeton University Press.
  ISBN 0-691-09194-3.

Dixit, A.K. and Pindyck, R.S. *Investment Under Uncertainty*. Princeton University Press.
  ISBN 0-691-03410-9.

Neftci, S.N. *An Introduction to the Mathematics of Financial Derivatives*. Academic Press.
  ISBN 0-12-515392-9.

Walkenbach, J. *Excel 2007 Power Programming with VBA*. John Wiley & Sons Inc.
  ISBN 978-0-470-04401-8.

Wilmott, P. *Paul Wilmott on Quantitative Finance*. John Wiley & Sons Ltd.
  ISBN 0-471-87438-8.

Index

B

balance sheets (BS)
  balancing items, 107, 108, 109–10, 113,
    117–18
  concepts, 60–3, 99–101, 107–10, 170–1
  deferred tax, 106, 117–18
  depreciation, 61, 101, 104, 106, 116, 117–18
  dividends, 106, 107, 108–9
  equity, 107, 109–10
  error-checks, 112–13
  examples, 107
  fixed assets, 107
  forecast methods, 107–10
  interest earned, 60, 72, 105
  inventory, 107–8, 114–16
  long-term debt, 107, 108–9, 112
  multiple worksheet models, 62–3
  payables, 107–8, 112
  planned cash, 107–8
  receivables, 107–8, 112, 116–17
  retained earnings, 106, 107, 109
  risk modelling, 170–1
  short-term investments/debt, 107, 108, 112
  tax, 107, 108
  trial BS, 110, 119
balancing items, BS, 107, 108, 109–10, 113,
    117–18
bankruptcies, 109, 122
Bayesian probability, 165–6, 199–200
best practices, modelling, 49–50, 60–2, 70,
    97–8, 100–1
beta, 19, 123, 148, 149, 166–9, 240–3
biases, decision-making issues, 134
binomial distributions
  see also Poisson...
  American options, 188–9, 244–6
  beta distributions, 166–7
  concepts, 147–8, 150–3, 158–9, 161–3,
    164–7, 173, 176–8, 182–3, 184–8,
    240–3, 244–6
  examples, 151–2, 158–9, 182–3, 244–6
  negative binomial distributions, 165, 173,
    176–8
  options valuations, 185–8, 244–6
Black–Scholes options pricing formula (BS)
  concepts, 41–2, 68–70, 131, 181, 186–8,
    191–2, 244–6
  named ranges, 68–70
  real options modelling, 191–2
bonds, 6–9, 27, 123–31
  convertibles, 128–9
  risk-free rates, 123–4
Boolean, 222–3
borders, 76–7
bounded distributions, 149–50
break-points, lists, 3

Brownian motion, 188
Browse, 204
BS *see* balance sheets; Black–Scholes options
    pricing formula
budgets, 55–9, 73–5, 116–20, 143–4, 167–8
building of models
  comments, 49, 74–8, 99–101
  concepts, 50, 74–85, 97–8, 136
  formatting considerations, 61–2, 74–8, 86,
    97–8, 101
  risk modelling, 136
Button, 207
ByRef, 251–2
Byte, 222–3
ByVal, 252

C

Calculate, 231–2, 241–3
Calculation Options, 69, 71, 89
Calculations, 69, 89
Call, 250–2
call options, 68–70, 131, 181–5
  see also options
capital asset pricing model (CAPM)
  concept, 19, 122–31, 168–9, 183, 192
  definition, 122–3
capital employed (CE), 115–16, 126–31
  see also economic profit
capital expenditure (capex), 38, 40, 101, 104–5,
    111, 121–31
capital expenditure (capex)/sales ratio, 128
capital investment/sales ratio, 114–16
CAPM *see* capital asset pricing model
cash
  asset line, 105
  BS, 107–8
  waterfalls, 117–18
cash flow at risk (CaR), 169
cash flow statements (CFS)
  concepts, 62–3, 99–101, 102–3, 105, 106,
    110–12
  direct/indirect presentation methods, 111
  error-checking role, 111–13
  examples, 111–12
  financing cash flow section, 110–12
  forecast methods, 110–11
  interest expenses/income, 105, 110–11
  investing cash flow section, 110–12
  multiple worksheet models, 62–3
  operating cash flow section, 110–12
  tax, 110–11
cash flow valuations
  adjustments, 121
  concepts, 120–31, 242–3
  discount rates, 120–31, 158, 168–9, 192–3
  enterprise value, 128–31

Index compiled by Terry Halliday